HURDLE

THE BOOK ON

BUSINESS PLANNING

A step-by-step guide to
creating a thorough, concrete
and concise business plan.

Tim Berry

Publisher: Palo Alto Software, Inc.

488 E. 11th Ave. , Suite 220

Eugene, OR 97401

USA

Fax: (541) 683-6250

Email: info@paloalto.com

Website: www.paloalto.com

Library of Congress Control Number: 2006930174

ISBN: 978-0-9712185-2-9

PA-1183

Book layout and editing: Teri Epperly, Steve Lange, Sara Prentice Manela

About the Author

Tim Berry has also written *On Target: The Book on Marketing Plans* (in 1999, co-authored with Doug Wilson), *CPA's Guide to Business Planning* (published first in 1998 by Harcourt Brace, republished by Aspen Publishers, and now in its fifth edition, published by Palo Alto Software), as well as several other books on business planning with spreadsheets that were published in the 1980s by Dow-Jones-Irwin, Microtext/McGraw-Hill, and Hayden Books. His business-planning software has been published by Palo Alto Software and M & T Publishing. He has been a professional business planner since 1974, as an employee of Business International and vice president of Creative Strategies, as a consultant to Apple Computer, as a member of the founding board of directors of Borland International, and as president and founder of Palo Alto Software. He has given seminars on business planning in 13 countries on four continents, in two languages.

Berry holds a Stanford University MBA degree, an MA *with honors* from the University of Oregon, and a BA *magna cum laude* from the University of Notre Dame.

Acknowledgements

I want to thank Paul Berry for not just cover design, but for inspiration as well. I was recently introduced to the phrase "Entrepreneur in Heat." If you have to ask what that means, then you've never been involved with somebody starting a business. The shortcut is simply "EIH." Paul has been EIH a lot lately.

Teri Epperly and Steve Lange have done a wonderful job with this book, designing the layout, managing the graphics, and patiently waiting on me through the ups and downs of my developing software, writing this and one other book, and managing a company all at the same time.

To Vie Radek, Cristin, Megan, and most of all Vange, thanks for putting up with me while this was coming together.

Sample Business Plans

This book includes two complete sample business plans. One sample is a computer store that is actually a composite of several computer reseller businesses the author consulted with during the early 1990s. The other was a consulting company that was accepted for financing by a major venture capital firm, although it was never actually formed. Both were originally published as part of *Business Plan Pro®* published by Palo Alto Software, Inc.

Hurdle Book Online

The electronic version of this book is available at Tim Berry's personal website www.timberry.com.

This page intentionally blank.

Contents

PART 1: FUNDAMENTALS

As you start the planning process, begin with a general view of the whole project. Review your goals and consider your options.

PART 2: TELL YOUR STORY

A standard business plan includes company background information, history, and basic descriptions.

PART 3: GATHERING INFORMATION

A good plan will include useful information about your market, your customers, and the business you're in.

PART 4: FORECASTING

Forecasting is more art than science, a combination of good research, logic, simple math, and educated guessing. It's hard to forecast but it's harder to run a business without forecasting.

PART 5: FINANCIAL ANALYSIS

The financials aren't as hard as you think, particularly if you have the patience to follow the steps. A good plan includes sales, cash flow, profits, and related financials.

PART 6: STRATEGY AND TACTICS

Strategy is focus. You also need tactics to implement the strategy, and tactics require concrete milestones and well-defined management responsibilities.

PART 7: FOLLOWING UP

The plan is really only the first step. Now you need to act on it. Publish your plan where you and your team can use it. Your polished plan is your primary tool in acquiring funding.

Appendices

SAMPLE PLANS:

Acme Consulting
American Management Technologies, Inc.

GLOSSARY

INDEX

CHAPTER 1:

IT'S ABOUT RESULTS

What's a business plan worth to you? How do you evaluate a plan? What makes a plan good or bad? This chapter looks at some of the basic premises, dispels some myths, and offers a new, practical, business-oriented way to look at the value of a plan.

As you start the planning process, begin with a general view of the entire project. Review your goals and consider your options.

A Business Plan is Worth the Results it Causes

About 25 years ago, I was having lunch with Professor James March, a business school professor whose class I'd enjoyed a few years earlier as a grad student. I was then in my late 30s, making my living mostly through business plan consulting. I'd had some successes. One of my plans was for a company that went from zero to more than $100 million of sales in four years. Apple Computer's Latin American group increased sales from $2 million to $27 million during the four years I'd done its annual plan. I'd had some failures too, but we won't mention those.

"So what is the value of a business plan?" Professor March asked at one point.

"Thousands of dollars," I answered. "Tens of thousands, in some cases."

"Wrong," he answered, to my shock. "Very wrong."

The value of a plan is the decisions it influences, he explained, and ultimately, how much money is in the bank as a result.

He was very right, although I was fairly smug about my successes and didn't like his response. And the underlying lesson, as valid today as it was then, is vital to this book.

I've absorbed the idea into my work on business planning. Plans should be measured by results. No matter how well researched, beautifully written, or excellently presented, what really makes a difference is how it impacts the results of the business.

What Makes a Good Plan?

The illustration on the next page shows a business plan as part of a process. You can think about the good or bad of a plan as the plan itself, measuring its value by its contents. There are some qualities in a plan that make it more likely to create results, and these are important. However, it is even better to see the plan as part of the whole process of achieving results, because even a great plan is wasted if nobody follows it.

PLANNING IS A PROCESS, NOT JUST A PLAN

A business plan will be hard to implement unless it is simple, specific, realistic and complete. Even if it is all these things, a good plan will need someone to follow up and check on it.

The plan depends on the human elements around it, particularly the process of commitment and involvement, and the tracking and follow-up that comes afterward. I'm going to deal with those elements in later chapters of this book. They are vital. But for now, let's look at the qualities that make the plan itself better or worse.

Successful implementation starts with a good plan. There are elements that will make a plan more likely to be successfully implemented. Some of the clues to implementation include:

1. Is the plan simple? Is it easy to understand and to act on? Does it communicate its contents easily and practically?

2. Is the plan specific? Are its objectives concrete and measurable? Does it include specific actions and activities, each with specific start and completion dates, specific persons responsible and specific budgets?

3. Is the plan realistic? Are the sales goals, expense budgets, and milestone dates realistic? Nothing stifles implementation like unrealistic goals.

4. Is the plan complete? Does it include all the necessary elements? Requirements of a business plan vary, depending on the context. There is no guarantee, however, that the plan will work if it doesn't cover the main bases.

Uses of Business Plans

Preparing a business plan is an organized, logical way to look at all of the important aspects of a business. First, decide what you will use the plan for, such as to:

- Define and fix objectives, and programs to achieve those objectives.
- Create regular business reviews and course corrections.
- Develop and establish a new business.
- Support a loan application.
- Define agreements between partners.
- Set a value on a business for sale or for legal purposes.
- Evaluate a new product line, promotion, or expansion.

No Time to Plan? A Common Misconception

"Not enough time for a plan," business people say. "I can't plan. I'm too busy getting things done."

Too many businesses make business plans only when they have to. Unless a bank or investors want to look at a business plan, there isn't likely to be a plan written. The busier you are, the more you need to plan. If you are always putting out fires, you should build fire breaks or a sprinkler system. You can lose the whole forest for paying too much attention to the individual trees.

A good planning process should save time, day by day, month to month. It helps keeps businesses focused on what's most important. Maintaining priorities is efficient.

Review your plan vs. actual results regularly to save time by avoiding mistakes, maintaining progress towards goals, identifying problem areas, and watching the business for areas which need attention.

Keys to Building Better Plans

- Use a business plan to set concrete goals, responsibilities, and deadlines to guide your business.
- A good business plan assigns tasks to people or departments and sets milestones and deadlines for tracking implementation.
- A practical business plan includes ten parts implementation for every one part strategy.
- As part of the implementation of a business plan, it should provide a forum for regular review and course corrections.
- Good business plans are practical.

Business Plan "Don'ts"

- Don't use a business plan simply to show how much you know about your business.
- Nobody reads a long-winded business plan: not bankers, not bosses, not venture capitalists. Years ago, people were favorably impressed by long plans. Today, nobody is interested in a business plan more than 50 pages long.

The Planning Process

As you develop that plan you need to get over the business hurdle, always remember that there is potentially much more value to planning than just the plan itself. Aside from the importance of overcoming the hurdle, it's the process around the plan that makes this such a valuable tool for business management.

The planning process includes bringing teams together to develop the plan, making firm commitments within the team, publishing a plan to cement those commitments, then tracking results and following up with plan vs. actual analysis and course corrections.

Professional planners realize that a good business plan is never done, and a good business plan is rarely if ever right. What makes a plan valuable isn't as much the prediction of the future as the guideposts and milestones that keep objectives in mind as the future reveals itself and events are managed.

Control Your Destiny

The business planning process is about controlling your own destiny in a business sense. Set your long-term business goals and use a plan to break the journey from present to future into manageable concrete steps. Don't let the real world of phone calls and daily routines determine your future. Certainly, in the real world, there will be business problems and changes in economic environment, customers paying slower than expected, costs going up on one product, down on another. In business school they called the real world the RW, pronounced "are-dub." Use your business plan to make measured responses to the vagaries of the RW, instead of scattered reactions.

A good planning process helps a plan stand up to the real world. As each month closes, the plan absorbs plan vs. actual results. Each manager keeps track of milestones and budgets, and at the end of each month the actual results are compared to the plan. Managers look at the variance. They make adjustments. They review the performance of their peers. Changes are made in the plan — organized, rational changes — to accommodate changes in actual conditions. Managers are proud of their performance, and good performances are shared with all.

Summary

Business plans don't sell new business ideas to venture capitalists. Venture capitalists invest in people and ideas, not plans. A business plan, though necessary, is only a way to present information.

Please remember that your plan is yours. The content and outline are not dictated by your software. You can easily omit the company chapter, for example, in an internal plan, or the marketing or personnel chapters, for that matter. The choices are yours.

CHAPTER 2:

PICK YOUR PLAN

❖—◆▣◆—❖

Make the contents of your plan match your purpose. Don't accept a standard outline just because it's there. There is a "classic" business plan that covers all the normal bases, and then there are strategic plans, operational plans, annual plans … all of them business plans that match their specific business purpose.

You can find dozens of books on the subject, about as many websites, two or three serious software products, and courses in hundreds of business schools, adult education and continuing education schools, and community colleges. Although there are many variations on the theme, a lot of it is standard.

What is a Business Plan?

A business plan is any plan that enables a business to look ahead, allocate resources, focus on key points, and prepare for problems and opportunities. Business existed long before computers, spreadsheets, and detailed projections. So did business plans.

Unfortunately, people think of business plans first for starting a new business or applying for business loans. They are also vital for running a business, whether or not the business needs new loans or new investments. Businesses need plans to optimize growth and development according to plans and priorities.

What is a Start-up Plan?

A simple start-up plan is a bare-bones plan that includes a summary, mission statement, keys to success, market analysis, and break-even analysis. This kind of plan is good for deciding whether or not to proceed with a full-blown plan, to tell if there is a business worth pursuing. However, it is not enough to run a business with. I'll talk more about this in *Chapter 3: Initial Assessment*.

The "Standard" Business Plan

A standard business plan, one that follows the advice of business experts and is prepared for formal presentation to outsiders such as a bank, investors, or corporate managers, includes an expected and customary set of elements. It should start with an executive summary. It should describe the company, its background and history, what it sells, its market, its strategy, its management team, and its financial projections.

Your plan depends on your specific situation. For example, if you're developing a plan for internal use only, not for sending out to banks or investors, you may not need to include all the background details that you and everyone in your company already knows. Description of the management team is very important for investors, while financial history is most important for banks. Make your plan match its business purpose.

What's Most Important in a Plan?

It depends on the case, but usually what's most important is the cash flow analysis and specific implementation details.

Cash flow is important because it is both vital to a company and hard to follow. Cash is usually misidentified as profits. They are, however, very different. Profits don't guarantee cash in the bank. Lots of profitable companies go under because of insufficient cash, due, for example, to having to wait for customers for pay invoices. It just isn't intuitive.

Implementation details are important because that's what makes things happen. Your brilliant strategies and beautifully formatted planning documents are just theory unless you assign responsibilities, with dates and budgets, and lots of following up and tracking of results. Business plans are really about getting results, and improving your company.

Are There Standard Steps to Completion?

I don't recommend developing the plan in the same order you present it as a finished document. For example, although the Executive Summary comes as the first section of a business plan, I recommend writing it after everything else is done. It will appear first, but you write it last.

This book, therefore, discusses the business plan in the recommended order you develop a plan, rather than the order of the document outline.

Is There a Standard Business Plan Outline?

No, there isn't. Every plan should be tailored to your needs. Don't include anything that doesn't help you do your business better. The purpose isn't the document; it's the results of the document.

However, if and when you have a specific audience for a business plan, you should recognize what's standard in that audience's mind. Certainly banks, investors, academics, and seasoned business people have expectations that a business plan should meet.

The business plan outline at the end of this chapter explains in detail where the different tables and topics fall in a standard outline and where you can find the related discussions in this book.

Form Follows Function

As we noted in *Chapter 1: It's About Results,* business planning is about results. Make the contents of your plan match your purpose and adjust the outline to match your type of plan.

For example, if you are developing an internal plan for company use, you don't need to include a section about the company. If your plan focuses on existing products or services and is intended for internal use only, you may not even need to include the details about the products.

Another example that comes up frequently is the level of detail required in your market analysis. Business plans looking for investors need to have some convincing market data, but a plan for a small business, to be used mainly by a small group of people close to the company, may not need as much research. Is there an opportunity to improve the company and the plan by learning more about the market? If so, then do it. If not, it may be overkill.

Investor Summaries and Loan Applications

When a plan is used to back up a loan application or to explain a business to potential investors, it may require a special summary document as well as a complete plan. Many investors like to see a brief summary, and a loan application doesn't always require a complete plan. If you develop your plan in the right way, you can use the summary paragraphs of the main sections — company, market, product, etc. — to create these summary documents.

Timeframes: Is Three Years Enough?

Regarding the span or length of focus of a business plan — its timeframe — opinions vary. I believe a business plan should normally project sales by month for the next 12 months and annual sales for the following two years. This doesn't mean businesses shouldn't plan for a longer term than just three years, not by any means. It does mean, however, that the detail of monthly forecasts doesn't pay off beyond a year, except in special cases. It also means that the detail in the yearly forecasts probably doesn't make sense beyond three years. Plan your business for five, 10, and even 15-year timeframes; just don't do it within the detailed context of business plan financials.

Summary

Although different plans require different sections, almost all need to keep cash planning and implementation at the center. Make the contents of your plan match your business purpose.

Outline order and sequence in a standard business plan.

Where the process is covered in this book.

1.0 Executive Summary

   1.1 Objectives

   1.2 Mission

   1.3 Keys to Success

Chapter 18: Strategy is Focus, helps you write the main summary.

Chapter 3: Initial Assessment, talks about Objectives, Mission, and Keys to Success.

2.0 Company Summary

   2.1 Company Ownership

   2.2 Start-up Plan (for new companies) or Company History (for ongoing companies)

   2.3 Company Locations and Facilities

Chapter 6: Describe Your Company, covers the company text section in your business plan as well as the related tables, either the Start-up or the Past Performance table.

3.0 Products (or Services, or both)

   3.1 Product and/or Service Description

   3.2 Competitive Comparison

   3.3 Sales Literature

   3.4 Sourcing

   3.5 Technology

   3.6 Future Products

This is in *Chapter 7: What You Sell.*

4.0 Market Analysis Summary

   4.1 Market Segmentation

   4.2 Target Market Segment Strategy

      4.2.1 Market Needs

      4.2.2 Market Trends

      4.2.3 Market Growth

   4.3 Industry Analysis

      4.3.1 Industry Participants

      4.3.2 Distribution Patterns

      4.3.3 Factors of Competition

      4.3.4 Main Competitors

This is covered in *Chapter 10: Know Your Market.*

Chapter 12: Your Target Market, also includes the market analysis table and chart.

This is all in *Chapter 9: The Business You're In.*

Outline order and sequence in a standard business plan.

Where the process is covered in this book.

5.0 Strategy and Implementation Summary

    5.1 Strategy Pyramids

    5.2 Value Proposition

    5.3 Competitive Edge

    5.4 Marketing Strategy

        5.4.1 Positioning Statement

        5.4.2 Pricing Strategy

        5.4.3 Promotion Strategy

        5.4.4 Marketing Programs

    5.5 Sales Strategy

        5.5.1 Sales Forecast

        5.5.2 Sales Programs

    5.6 Strategic Alliances

    5.7 Milestones

Much of this is covered in *Chapter 18: Strategy is Focus.*

Chapter 19: Make it Real, also covers the recommended Milestones table.

Implementation and plan vs. actual analysis comes up again in *Chapter 20: Plan for Implementation.*

The sales forecast topics and the forecast itself are discussed in *Chapter 11: Forecast Your Sales.*

6.0 Management Summary

    6.1 Organizational Structure

    6.2 Management Team

    6.3 Management Team Gaps

    6.4 Personnel Plan

Chapter 8: Management Team, covers this text and the Personnel Plan table.

7.0 Financial Plan

    7.1 Important Assumptions

    7.2 Key Financial Indicators

    7.3 Break-even Analysis

    7.4 Projected Profit and Loss

    7.5 Projected Cash Flow

    7.6 Projected Balance Sheet

    7.7 Business Ratios

    7.8 Long-term Plan

Chapter 15: The Bottom Line, covers the Profit and Loss and General Assumptions tables.

Chapter 3: Initial Assessment, includes the Break-even table as part of the Initial Assessment.

Cash Flow and the Cash Flow table are discussed in *Chapter 16: Cash is King.*

The Balance Sheet table is covered in *Chapter 14: About Business Numbers.*

The Business Ratios table appears in *Chapter 17: Finish the Financials.*

Long-term plans are discussed in *Chapter 19: Make it Real.*

This page intentionally blank.

CHAPTER 3:

INITIAL ASSESSMENT

*Start your business plan with a quick assessment. "Feasibility" is the formal term for it, although I prefer to think of it as finding out "is there a **there** there?" Even for an ongoing business, take the time to step away from the business and look at the basics. Do your business numbers make sense? Try to separate your feelings and identity for a while, and ask yourself about its core concepts.*

Quick Count of Customers

What you need most in business is customers. Nothing else is more important. Whether they are individual consumers, families, businesses, government organizations, or whatever, a business needs customers. So ask yourself:

- Who needs or wants what this business offers?

- How much are they willing to pay for it?

Don't worry too much about the difference between wants and needs. We don't want to narrow businesses down to those based on needs, when in the real world wants are just as important as needs. Nobody needs perfume, stuffed mushrooms, or music, for example. Businesses do well supplying non-essential goods and services — as long as somebody is willing to pay for them.

And it doesn't always matter who pays for them, as long as somebody (or some organization) does. Nonprofit organizations normally don't charge money for all services. The free medical clinic, for example, can survive if segments of society — donors, government agencies, etc. — are willing to pay.

Developing Your Mission Statement

Use the mission statement to define your business concept. A company mission statement should define underlying goals (such as making a profit) and objectives in broad strategic terms, including what market is served and what benefits are offered.

Define the Pain Point

Define the **pain point** that drives your business. What customer problem, need, or want does your business address? This is a core concept you'll need to establish with a mission statement. Who is better off because your business exists, and why are they better off?

Sometimes this is obvious. A bakery supplies fresh bread. A car supplies transportation. A commercial jet takes people from one city to another.

Some pain points are less obvious. Does anybody really need hair coloring? Starbucks offers "affordable luxury." That's not an obvious need but it is an obvious want. Does anybody really need an extremely expensive automobile that carries only two people and goes three times faster than the law allows? No, but some people want that, and businesses that supply it do very well.

Here are some other examples:

- Some restaurants solve the problem of getting food cheaply, or fast. Some solve the problem of where people can go out together to celebrate an occasion with a good meal. Which one is likely to be at an airport? Do all restaurants have the same mission? Does the high-end restaurant solve a problem as much as it fills a need and supplies a want?

- A résumé writer solves a specific problem for specific people.

- A pickup truck solves one set of problems for one set of people, and a sports car solves another set of problems for a different set of people. The pickup truck doesn't have to take corners fast, and the sports car doesn't have to carry a lot of cargo.

What Business Are You In?

Ask yourself what business you are in, and don't narrow yourself down. One of the classic business examples is the railroads, which lost a chance to expand in the twentieth century because they misdefined themselves. They thought they were in the business of running trains on tracks. They didn't understand they were in the business of transporting goods and people. When trucks, buses and highways grew, the railroads were left behind.

My company, Palo Alto Software, is not in the business of software development. It is in the business of helping people do business plans by themselves, providing business know-how through software and documentation. The broader definition helps us understand what we're up to.

Customer Satisfaction

Leading experts in developing customer satisfaction look to a mission statement to define customer satisfaction goals. Developing customer care programs depends on spreading the idea and its importance within a company. That should normally start with a goal included in your mission statement.

Workplace Philosophy

Some mission statements also define internal goals, such as maintaining a creative work environment and building respect for diversity. Experts in employee relations look immediately to a mission statement for a definition of a company's stand on some of these fundamental issues.

Value-Based Marketing

Experts developed the value-based marketing framework to help companies understand their business better. This framework starts with a business value proposition, which states what benefits a business offers, to whom, and at what relative price level.

For example:

- This automobile manufacturer offers reliable, safe automobiles for families at a relative price premium.

- This fast-food restaurant offers quick and consistent lunches at a low price.

Put it Together in a Simple Mission Statement

If you don't already have it, you should develop a useful mission statement and make it a foundation of long-term strategy. Make sure it addresses what the company offers to each of three important groups: customers, employees, and owners. Make sure it can last for years.

Keys to Success

Focusing on what I call "keys to success" is a good idea for getting a better view of the priorities in your business. Just about any business imaginable is going to depend a lot on three or four most important factors. In a retail business, for example, the classic joke is that the keys to success are "location, location, and location." In truth, that might be, for example, location, convenient parking, and low prices. A computer store's keys to success might be knowledgeable salespeople, major brands, and newspaper advertising.

Focus is very important, and the keys to success framework helps you develop focus. There is what I call a law of inverse focus. I can't prove it with detailed research but I've seen many times that, beyond three or four key items, the more items on a priority list, the less chance of implementation. Thinking about keys to success is a great way to focus on the main elements that make your business work.

Explore Sales and Costs

You also need to think about prices and costs. Ask yourself:

- How much will the customers pay?

- How many customers are there?

- How many will actually do business with me?

- How much will it cost me to deliver what each customer wants?

You don't need to answer these questions thoroughly or provide back-up research and documentation already — not yet, at least. That comes later as you develop the full business plan. What you do want is to have a good general idea of the answers before you proceed with a plan.

Do worry about cost compared to price. You don't need a detailed study at this point, but you do need to have a good idea. If the frozen dessert costs you $10 to make and you plan to sell it cheap in the summer at the beach, then maybe the business has a problem. You also have to cover wages and salaries, rent, and other fixed costs. Make sure there is an underlying business proposition.

You don't have to be the first of a kind, or the first in your market, to have a good business. Your community probably has lots of some kinds of businesses: restaurants, food stores, clothing. Many different kinds of business are so common, and they don't all have to be first or unique. What you do need is customers.

Break-even Analysis

Some people find a simple break-even analysis is a good way to get a quick view of the underlying running expenses, pricing, and costs in a business. This doesn't have to be a carefully researched and detailed break-even at this point — that will come later as you develop a full plan. For initial assessment, a simple estimated break-even might still be useful. A simple Break-even Analysis table is shown here:

BREAK-EVEN ANALYSIS TABLE

Break Even Analysis	
Monthly Units Break-even	1,222
Monthly Sales Break-even	$397,262
Assumptions	
Average Per-unit Revenue	$343.04
Average Per-unit Variable Cost	$248.15
Estimated Monthly Fixed Costs	$97,778.00

The Break-even Analysis table calculates a break-even point based on fixed costs, variable costs per unit of sales, and revenue per unit of sales.

Make the following three simple assumptions:

- Average per-unit sales price (per-unit revenue):

  The price that you charge per unit. Take into account sales discounts and special offers. For non-unit based businesses, make the per-unit revenue $1 and enter your costs as a percent of a dollar.

- Average per-unit cost:

  The incremental cost of each unit of sale. If you are using a Units-Based Sales Forecast table (for manufacturing and mixed business types), you can project unit costs from the Sales Forecast table. If you are using the basic Sales Forecast table for retail, service and distribution businesses, use a percentage estimate. For example, a retail store running a 50% margin would have a per-unit cost of .5, and a per-unit revenue of 1.

- Monthly fixed costs:

  Technically, a break-even analysis defines fixed costs as costs that would continue even if you went broke. Instead, you may want to use your regular running fixed costs, including payroll and normal expenses. This will give you a better insight on financial realities.

This next illustration shows a Break-even chart. As sales increase, the profit line passes through the zero or break-even line at the break-even point.

BREAK-EVEN CHART

The Break-even chart shows that the company needs to sell about 1,200 units per month to break even.

This chart, based on the table example from the previous page, shows that the company needs to sell approximately 1,200 units in order to cross the break-even line. This is a classic business chart that helps you consider your bottom-line financial realities. Can you sell enough to make your break-even volume?

Of course the break-even analysis depends on assumptions made for average per-unit revenue, average per-unit cost, and fixed costs. These are rarely exact assumptions.

Palo Alto Software's business resource website www.Bplans.com offers an easy-to-use online Break-even Analysis Calculator.

Objectives

Objectives are business goals. Set your market share objectives, sales objectives, and profit objectives. Companies need to set objectives and plan to achieve them.

Make sure your objectives are concrete and measurable. Be specific, such as achieving a given level of sales or profits, a percentage of gross margin, a growth rate, or a market share. Don't use generalities like "being the best" or "growing rapidly."

Broad statements like "maximize customer satisfaction" are not serious business plan objectives, because they cannot really be measured. Much better objectives would set measurable goals, such as holding gross margin to 25 percent as a minimum, or selling more than $3 million, or achieving six percent profit on sales and ten percent return on equity.

If less tangible goals are critical to a plan, find a way to measure them. For example, if image and awareness are vital, then plan for statistically valid surveys to measure the improvements in image and awareness. You can also set goals for market share, and purchase research to measure the actual share. Or, if you want to focus on customer satisfaction, plan for a survey to quantify satisfaction or specify numerical objectives regarding returns or complaints.

Summary

At this point, you've started a plan.

If you're working on a plan for an existing business, then you've probably covered old ground. Your company already has customers, operates in a known market, and has lived through the evolution of sales and costs and expenses. Still, planning is an opportunity to take a new, fresh look at the business. Change is constant. Your business is changing and your market is changing, so the regular fresh looks are important.

If you're working on a plan for a new start-up business, you've taken important steps towards defining your business, your financial break-even point, and your total potential market.

- How does your business look from this viewpoint?
- Does it make sense?
- Can you make the sales you need to break even?
- Is the market big enough?
- Are your projections realistic?
- Can you bring together the keys to success?

Chapter 4:

STARTING A BUSINESS

It's dangerous to fall in love with the idea of starting a business instead of falling in love with the business itself. Go into this with a good idea of reality.

Starting Thoughts

First Things First

A business plan is not the most important single requirement for starting a business. Many other things are much more important. For example:

- **Customers:** The first thing you really need to start a business, maybe even the only thing you really need, is customers. It all starts with at least one customer.

- **Customer needs:** Your business must fulfill some type of customer need in order to be successful. Sometimes customer needs can be intangible, like security or prestige. Some customer needs seem frivolous, but they still matter. Make sure there is a market for your service or product. Your business will fail if it doesn't address a customer need.

Myths About Starting a Business

There are several myths about owning and operating a business that should be avoided at all costs. These common myths cause a lot of problems:

- **The myth of "being your own boss":** You are not your own boss when you own a business. Your customers are your boss. Your bank is your boss. Your fixed costs are your boss.

- **The myth of "independence":** Owning a business doesn't make you independent—not needing money makes you independent. As long as you need money, you can't be independent.

Think it Over

The folklore of business start-ups generally underestimates the risks. Imagine yourself missing mortgage payments when you can't cover your business costs and facing employees when you can't make payroll. Those negative images are also part of business ownership.

Don't go into a business based on the folklore and myths. There are plenty of good reasons to do it. As you start a company, plan ahead. Give yourself the benefit of a real estimate of start-up costs.

- If you can't afford to lose the money, then don't put it at risk.

- If you can't convince somebody else to put up the money, think again about the business you want to start.

Try running through the easy-to-use online starting costs calculator at www.Bplans.com.

About Business Names

We are talking about the name of your business in this section, not your trademarks, or service marks, logos, or slogans. We are not attorneys, we do not give legal advice, so be sure to check with an attorney early on as you build your business. Trademark law protects product names, logos, trade names, and even some slogans as trademarks or service marks. Copyright law protects works of art, fiction, movies, literature, sculpture, and other creative works. Business law, however, does not fully guarantee you the exclusive use of your business name. To get close to exclusivity, you have to be first, you have to be national, and you have to be alert.

Owning and Establishing a Business Name

The most common misunderstanding about business names is about registering, protecting, and reserving business names. You can't reserve a business name completely; you can't have exclusive use. A business name is a lot like a personal name, in that the first or oldest John Smith cannot claim exclusive use of that name. He can't make all the other John Smiths change their names. So too, the first Smith's Restaurant can't stop all other Smith's Restaurants from using that same name. McDonald's Hamburgers can't make McDonald's Hardware Store change its name, and McDonald's Hardware Store in Manhattan can't sue McDonald's Hardware Store in San Francisco.

However, just as you have rights to your own identity, so does your company. One John Smith can sue another John Smith for using his identity, having bills sent to the wrong address, or purposely confusing people. McDonald's Hamburgers can sue just about anybody trying to use McDonald's for a business selling fast foods.

The confusion starts because business names are registered by different authorities in different places and on different levels.

- The first and simplest business name is your own name, which might be enough for John Smith using Smith Consulting or operating Smith's Restaurant. This kind of business name normally requires no additional paperwork, although most business owners end up registering a name anyhow to establish their legal claim to it.

- The second common level of business names is called DBA (for "doing business as") or Fictitious Business Name, which gives an individual the right to operate under a business name with signs, bank accounts, checks, and so on. These are generally registered and legalized by county governments within states. There might be a McDonald's Hardware Store as a DBA in many counties within a given state, and across many different states.

  To register a business with a fictitious business name, call your county government for details. You can expect that you'll have to visit an office in the county government, pay a fee of less than $100, and do some legal advertising, also less than $100, probably using forms you can fill out in the same office.

  Somebody will probably look up the registry to make sure that yours is the first business in the county with that name. Details will vary depending on which state and county you're in.

- The third level is the corporation, regardless of its various corporate entities. Whether they are S Corporations, C Corporations, LLCs, or whatever, a corporation is registered at the state level and only one can have the same name in the same state. However, there is no guarantee that there won't be many businesses registered as McDonald's Hardware Store in several counties in a state, and a corporation registered as McDonald's Hardware Corporation. This kind of duplication happens.

  To establish a corporation, you can use some of the national services such as the Company Corporation (www.corporate.com) or a local attorney. The corporate forms will go to the state, and details will depend on which state you're in.

Even though duplicate business names are possible and quite common, you do still have the right to protect and defend your own business name once you've built the business around it. The key to this is the real or perceived confusion in the mind of the customer. As we said above, one John Smith can sue another John Smith for purposely confusing their identities. So too, McDonald's Hamburgers can and should sue anybody who starts a new restaurant named McDonald's serving any fast foods.

On this point, when one business is confused with another, being first matters. When somebody tries to establish a second McDonald's Hardware where it would confuse people with the first, then the first McDonald's has a legal right to prevent it. If the second store puts up a sign, then the first store should take quick legal action to stop it. The longer the first store ignores the second, the better the case of the second store.

When the whole mess goes to court, the first one to use the name is likely to win, but if the first one sat quietly while the other one built the name, then there is more doubt. An existing business should always watch out for people using the same or confusingly similar names, because the sooner it complains, the better for its legal arguments.

Researching Whether a Name is Available

You can't absolutely guarantee that nobody has the name you want, but you can at least try. You don't want a business name that can cause problems later because it confuses you with some other business. That's obvious, but how do you research a name to make sure there won't be a conflict? There is no single sure way, but here are some suggestions:

- **Search Online.** Start with your favorite search engine and see whether anything turns up on the company name you're considering. You can also go to the U.S. Patent and Trademark Office website, www.uspto.gov or www.knowx.com, or similar sites.

- **Search the Internet domain names.** There are several websites that offer access to the Internet databases using the search term 'whois'. The most traditional site for this is the one at Network Solutions, www.networksolutions.com.

- **See an attorney.** Since you probably want to talk to an attorney about the correct business entities and other start-up matters, you may also ask your attorney about checking on business names. Generally, you want to do your own check first to catch any obvious conflicts.

Ultimately, you really protect your business name by using it. Corporations are registered by states, and fictitious business names are registered in counties. Registering a name doesn't really protect it though, because the same name could legally exist in many other states, many other counties.

You could be Acme Corporation in Illinois and legally own that corporation in that state, but there could be another Acme Corporation in every other state, and every one of them is legal until you win a lawsuit proving that they are trading on the commercial interests you own. When you really get protection is when you find somebody else using the name and you can prove that you had it first, so they are trading on your name. There are lots of McDonald's restaurants around, and McDonald's can't stop them from using that name if they had it early enough, and especially if they aren't pretending to be a fast-foods hamburger joint. The intent and the attempt to confuse is very important.

Choosing a Business Name

The choice of a business name is very important, worth taking time to develop. Don't end up with a name that you can't live with. Look for something that describes your business, is easy to explain, fits on the signs, and works.

Find an Attorney

I'm not an attorney, and I don't give legal advice. I do strongly recommend working with an attorney to go through the details of your company's legal establishment, licenses, and other items covered here. By including this information in this book, I don't mean to imply you should do it yourself.

The trade-offs involved in incorporation vs. partnership vs. other forms of business are significant. Small problems developed at the early stages of a new business can become horrendous problems later on. What's true in one state isn't true in the next one. The cost of simple legal advice in this regard is almost always worth it. Starting a company should not involve a major legal bill except in special cases. Don't skimp on legal costs.

Licenses and Permits are Usually Local Issues

It's hard to generalize on licenses and permits, because some of these depend on where you are and some depend on what you do. When in doubt, you should check with local sources. If you don't want to go straight to the local government and ask your questions directly, then ask at your local Chamber of Commerce, www.chamberofcommerce.com, or Small Business Development Center (SBDC), www.bplans.com/sb/.

For example, many cities have zoning laws that define where you can put retail stores, office space, and industries. Few of these affect the small home-based business, but it's not unusual to have zoning laws prohibit signs on lawns or houses.

Some types of businesses require local or state licenses. This depends on where you are. For example, businesses including day care, hair care, food service, and bars and nightclubs often require special licenses.

Resale Licenses and Sales Taxes

In states that have sales tax, state authorities manage a system that sets reseller businesses into a special category so they don't have to pay sales taxes on items they buy for resale. The required paperwork and the state offices that manage it are different in many states, so you'll have to ask state offices for your state's rules as you establish your business.

Taxpayer ID and Employer Numbers

Employer Identification Numbers (EIN) are assigned by the Internal Revenue Service and state tax authorities. If you don't have employees and you haven't established a corporation, then your social security number is your federal taxpayer ID. If you've established a corporation or you have employees, then you must have a federal EIN, which is assigned by the federal IRS. In most states, the state assigns a separate state number.

The Business Entity

The pros and cons of different business formations are worth understanding. They vary by state — this is not a good area for guesswork, and not a good place to save money — so please go through this with an attorney you can trust. The following is for background information.

Although the details vary, it starts with the choice between sole proprietorship, partnership, corporation, or the more trendy Limited Liability Company, LLC. Within the corporation classification you have some additional choices, between the standard C corporation or the small business S corporation.

Sole Proprietorship

Simply put, your business is a sole proprietorship if you don't create a separate legal entity for it. This is true whether you operate it in your own name, or under a trade name. If it isn't your own name, then you register a company name as a "Fictitious business name," also called a DBA ("Doing Business As"). Depending on your state, you can usually obtain this through the county government. The cost is no more than a small registration fee plus a required newspaper ad, for a total of less than $100 in most states.

The main disadvantage of the sole proprietorship is the lack of a separate entity, which means you have personal responsibility for it. If the business fails, then its creditors can go after your personal assets.

Tax treatment is quite simple; your profit and loss goes straight through to your personal taxes. Your business income is normally on Schedule C of your tax return. This can be good or bad for your tax situation, depending on where you stand with other income.

Partnerships

Partnerships are harder to describe because they change so much. They are governed by state laws, but a Uniform Partnership Act has become the law in most states. That act, however, mostly sets the specific partnership agreement as the real legal core of the partnership, so the legal details can vary widely. Usually the income or loss from partnerships passes through to the partners, without any partnership tax.

The agreements can define different levels of risk, which is why you'll read about some partnerships that have general partners and limited partners, with different levels of risk for each.

The agreement should also define:

- What happens if a partner withdraws
- Buy and sell arrangements for partners
- Liquidation arrangements, should that becomes necessary

If you think a partnership might work for your business, make sure you do this right. Find an attorney with experience in partnerships, and check for references of present and past clients. This is a complicated area and a mistake in the agreement can cause a lot of problems.

Corporations

Corporations are either the standard C corporation or the small business S corporation. The C corporation is the classic legal entity of the vast majority of successful companies in the United States. Most lawyers would agree that the C corporation is the structure that provides the best shielding from personal liability for owners, and provides the best non-tax benefits to owners. This is a separate legal entity, different from its owners, which pays its own taxes. Most lawyers would also probably agree that for a company that has ambitions of raising major investment capital and eventually going public, the C corporation is the standard form of legal entity.

The S corporation is used for family companies and smaller ownership groups. The clearest distinction from C is that the S corporation's profits or losses go straight through to the S corporation's owners, without being taxed separately first. In practical terms, this means that the owners of the corporation can take their profits home without first paying the corporation's separate tax on profits, so those profits are taxed once for the S owner, and twice for the C owner. In practical terms, the C corporation doesn't send its profits home to its owners as much as the S corporation does, because it usually has different goals and objectives. It often wants to grow and go public, or it already is public. In most states an S corporation is owned by a limited number (25 is a common maximum) of private owners, and corporations can't hold stock in S corporations, just individuals.

Corporations can switch from C to S and back again, but not often. The IRS has strict rules for when and how those switches are made. You'll almost always want to have your CPA and in some cases your attorney guide you through the legal requirements for switching.

Limited Liability Company

Be careful with this one, because the Limited Liability Company (LLC) form is different for different states, with some real advantages in some states that aren't relevant in others. An LLC is usually a lot like an S corporation, a combination of some limitation on legal liability and some favorable tax treatment for profits and transfer of assets. This is a newer form of legal entity and often harder to establish than a corporation.

Why would you establish an LLC instead of a corporation? That's a tough legal question, not one we can answer here. In general, the LLC has to be missing two of the four characteristics of a corporation (limited liability, centralized management, continuity of life, and free transferability of ownership interest). Still, with the advisability and advantages varying from state to state, here again, this is a question to take to an attorney who has small business experience.

A Simpler Plan for Start-ups

Don't let me, this book, business-planning software, or any other source force you into doing more of a business plan than you need. A plan can help you move forward, make decisions, and make your business successful. Not every plan is the same, not every business needs the same level of detail.

For a simple example, imagine a woman making jewelry at home and selling it at a local craft market on the weekend. A business plan could give her a chance to step back from the normal flow and look at ways to develop and improve the business. The planning process should help her understand her business. It should help her define what she wants from the business, understand what her customers want, and decide how to optimize her business on her own terms. She might benefit from developing a less detailed sales and expense forecast, maybe even a profit and loss, so she can plan how to use and develop her resources. She might not need to create detailed cash flow, balance sheet, and business ratios. A simple plan may be just what she needs to get going.

Even at the early start-up stage your business plan is very important. The outline below illustrates the contents of a simpler business plan. For many smaller and start-up businesses, this plan outline can cover all the bases.

Simpler Plan Outline

Outline	Topic	Table	Chart
1.0	Executive Summary		Highlights
1.1	Objectives		
1.2	Mission		
1.3	Keys to Success		
2.0	Company Summary	Start-up	Start-up
3.0	Product Description		
4.0	Market Analysis Summary	Market Analysis	Market Forecast
4.1	Market Segmentation		
4.2	Target Market Segment Strategy		
4.3	Market Needs		
4.4	Competitions and Buying Patterns		
5.0	Strategy and Implementation Summary		Annual Sales
5.1	Competitive Edge		
5.2	Sales Strategy	Sales Forecast	Monthly Sales
6.0	Management Summary		
7.0	Financial Plan		
7.1	Break-even Analysis	Break-even	Break-even
7.2	Projected Profit and Loss	Profit and Loss	
7.3	Projected Cash Flow	Cash Flow	Cash Flow

For an example of the very early stages of a plan, review the elements of starting a business plan in the section *Chapter 3: Initial Assessment*. This first stage of a plan focuses only on a few starter elements. The Mission Statement, Keys to Success, Market Analysis, and Break-even Analysis give you a critical head start toward understanding your business.

However, not all start-ups are that simple. Many of them need product development, packaging, retail fittings and signage, office equipment, websites, and sometimes months or even years of payroll before the sales start. Unless you're wealthy enough to finance these expenditures on your own, then you'll need to deal with bank loans or investors or both; and for that you'll need a more extensive business plan. Start-up company or not, the plan has to meet expectations.

One suggestion for getting started is to develop your plan in stages. A few key text topics might be enough to discuss the plan with potential partners and team members, as a first phase. You may then want to add a basic sales and expense forecast, leading to profit and loss, as the next phase. Adding business numbers helps you predict business flow and match spending to income.

Ultimately, the choice of plan isn't based as much on the stage of business as it is on the type of business, financing requirements, and business objective. Here are some important indicators of the level of plan you'll need, even as a start-up:

- Some of the simpler businesses keep a plan in the head of the owner, but every business has a plan. Even a one-person business can benefit from creating a plan document with ideas written down, because the process is valuable. The exercise of producing a plan is a useful process.

- As soon as a second person is involved, the need for planning multiplies. The plan is critical for communicating values, goals, strategies, and detailed implementation.

- As soon as anybody outside the company is involved, then you need to provide more background information as part of the plan. When a plan is for internal use only, you may not need to describe company history and product features, for example. Stick to the topics that add value, that make you think, that help support decisions.

- For discussion purposes, text is enough to get a plan started. Try describing your mission, objective, keys to success, target market, competitive advantage, and basic strategies. How well does this cover your business idea?

- Can you live without a sales and expense forecast? Sometimes the one-person business keeps numbers in its (the owner's) head. However, it's much easier to use tools that can put the numbers in front of you and add and subtract them automatically. That's where a plan helps.

- Do you really know your market? A good market analysis can help you see opportunities that might not otherwise be obvious. Understand why people buy from you. What are the needs being served? How many potential customers are out there?

- Do you manage significant amounts of inventory? That complicates your cash management and requires a more sophisticated plan. You must buy inventory before you sell it.

- Do you sell on credit? If you are a business selling to businesses, then you probably do have to sell on credit, and that normally means you have to manage money owed to you by your customers, called accounts receivable. Making the sale is no longer the same thing as getting the money. That usually requires a more sophisticated plan.

- Do you do your taxes on a cash basis or accrual basis? If you don't know, and you are a very small (one person, maybe two to three people) business, then you're likely to be on a cash basis. That makes your planning easier.

   However, most businesses big enough to work with a CPA and have separate tax statements use accrual accounting because they want to deduct expenses as they are incurred, even if they aren't fully paid for. By the time you are using accrual accounting, you'll probably need more sophisticated cash flow tools and a more extensive business plan.

- As you approach banks and other lending institutions, expect to provide more detail on personal net worth, collateral, and your business' financial position. Some banks will accept a very superficial business plan as long as the collateral looks good. Others will demand to see detailed monthly projections. No bank can lend money on a business plan alone; that would be against banking law. But a bank wants to see a good plan.

- If you're looking for venture investment, take a good look at your plan. Professional investors will expect your plan to provide proof, not just promises. They'll want to see market data, competitive advantage, and management track records. They'll want to see robust and comprehensive financial projections. True, you'll hear stories about investors backing new companies without a plan, but those are the exceptions, not the rule.

So, however you cut it, your business plan is very important, even at the early start-up stage, and even if you can keep it in your head. Before you purchase business stationery, telephones, or rent a location, you should do a business plan.

Realistic Start-up Costs

Start-up expenses are those expenses incurred **before** the business is running. Many people underestimate start-up costs and start their business in a haphazard, unplanned way. This can work, but is usually a harder way to do it. Customers are wary of brand new businesses with makeshift logistics.

Use a start-up worksheet to plan your initial financing. You'll need this information to set up initial business balances and to estimate start-up expenses, such as legal fees, stationery design, brochures, and others. Don't underestimate costs.

This illustration reproduces a typical Start-up table for a home office, service business — in this case a résumé-writing service. The assumptions used in this illustration show how even simple, service-based businesses need some start-up money.

START-UP COSTS

Start-up Plan	
Requirements	
Start-up Expenses	
Legal	$50
Stationery, etc.	$100
Brochures	$450
Consultants	$100
Insurance	$50
Rent	$0
Research and Development	$0
Expensed Computer Equipment	$500
Other	$500
Total Start-up Expenses	**$1,750**
Start-up Assets	
Cash Required	$500
Start-up Inventory	$250
Other Current Assets	$25
Long-term Assets	$0
Total Assets	**$775**
Total Requirements	**$2,525**

Start-up table for a hypothetical home office résumé service.

Understand the Risks

I've spent many years as an entrepreneur and working with entrepreneurs. I understand and sympathize with the urge to create something, to build your own business, and make it work. However, I've also seen the disaster of the business start-up that absorbs more money than it should, and optimistic owners who keep dumping more money into a lost cause, digging themselves deeper into a hole instead of getting out of it.

The illustrations on the following pages are hypothetical examples of three classic types of start-up companies. There is the successful product-based start-up, the successful service start-up, and the failed product start-up. It shows simple lines indicating the cumulative balance for each business, over time. This cumulative balance stands for how much money is spent or received and how much money is at risk. The actual times and actual amounts, shown in the tables, are not as important as the relative relationship between the examples.

Both the successful and the failed product company launches look the same in the beginning. The successful launch turns upward and generates money, but the unsuccessful launch never does. The service company, in contrast, generates less money but also risks less money.

This chart comparison makes two extremely important points about the money at risk in different kinds of businesses:

- Product businesses usually require more investment than service businesses.

- "Bootstrapping" (starting the business without start-up capital) is much harder for product businesses than service businesses.

THE START-UP CURVE AND RISK TO INVESTMENT

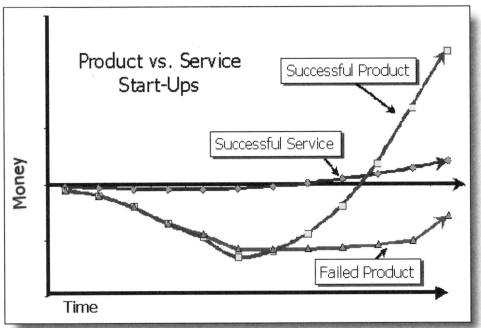

The lines show the cumulative cash positions for two start-up product companies and a start-up service company. The product companies risk more than the service company.

SUCCESSFUL PRODUCT START-UP

Successful Product Example	Jan	Feb	Mar	Apr	May	Jun	Jul	Aug	Sep	Oct	Nov	Dec
Sales												
Sales	$0	$0	$0	$0	$50,000	$75,000	$100,000	$125,000	$150,000	$150,000	$150,000	$150,000
Cost of Sales	$0	$0	$0	$0	$10,000	$15,000	$20,000	$25,000	$30,000	$30,000	$30,000	$30,000
Expenses												
General Start-up Expenses	$4,500	$0	$0	$0	$0	$0	$0	$0	$0	$0	$0	$0
Product Work	$0	$5,000	$5,000	$0	$0	$0	$0	$0	$0	$0	$0	$0
Packaging Work	$0	$0	$5,000	$5,000	$0	$0	$0	$0	$0	$0	$0	$0
Initial Inventory Build	$0	$0	$0	$10,000	$0	$0	$0	$0	$0	$0	$0	$0
Product Release PR	$0	$0	$5,000	$5,000	$5,000	$0	$0	$0	$0	$0	$0	$0
Running Operating Expenses	$5,000	$5,000	$5,000	$10,000	$10,000	$20,000	$20,000	$20,000	$20,000	$20,000	$20,000	$20,000
Total Expenses	$9,500	$10,000	$20,000	$30,000	$15,000	$20,000	$20,000	$20,000	$20,000	$20,000	$20,000	$20,000
Accounts Receivable												
Accounts Receivable	$0	$0	$0	$0	$50,000	$125,000	$175,000	$225,000	$275,000	$300,000	$300,000	$300,000
Deposits from Accts Receivable	$0	$0	$0	$0	$0	$50,000	$75,000	$100,000	$125,000	$150,000	$150,000	$150,000
Payments												
Costs of Sales	$0	$0	$0	$0	$10,000	$15,000	$20,000	$25,000	$30,000	$30,000	$30,000	$30,000
Expenses	$9,500	$10,000	$20,000	$30,000	$15,000	$20,000	$20,000	$20,000	$20,000	$20,000	$20,000	$20,000
Total Payments	$9,500	$10,000	$20,000	$30,000	$25,000	$35,000	$40,000	$45,000	$50,000	$50,000	$50,000	$50,000
Net Cash	($9,500)	($10,000)	($20,000)	($30,000)	($25,000)	($35,000)	$10,000	$30,000	$50,000	$75,000	$100,000	$100,000
Cumulative Cash	($9,500)	($19,500)	($39,500)	($69,500)	($94,500)	($129,500)	($119,500)	($89,500)	($39,500)	$35,500	$135,500	$235,500

FAILED PRODUCT START-UP

Failed Product Example	Jan	Feb	Mar	Apr	May	Jun	Jul	Aug	Sep	Oct	Nov	Dec
Sales												
Sales	$0	$0	$0	$0	$25,000	$27,500	$30,000	$32,500	$35,000	$37,500	$40,000	$42,500
Cost of Sales	$0	$0	$0	$0	$5,000	$5,500	$6,000	$6,500	$7,000	$7,500	$8,000	$8,500
Expenses												
General Start-up Expenses	$4,500	$0	$0	$0	$0	$0	$0	$0	$0	$0	$0	$0
Product Work	$0	$5,000	$5,000	$0	$0	$0	$0	$0	$0	$0	$0	$0
Packaging Work	$0	$0	$5,000	$5,000	$0	$0	$0	$0	$0	$0	$0	$0
Initial Inventory Build	$0	$0	$0	$10,000	$0	$0	$0	$0	$0	$0	$0	$0
Product Release PR	$0	$0	$5,000	$5,000	$5,000	$0	$0	$0	$0	$0	$0	$0
Running Operating Expenses	$5,000	$5,000	$5,000	$10,000	$10,000	$20,000	$20,000	$20,000	$20,000	$20,000	$20,000	$20,000
Total Expenses	$9,500	$10,000	$20,000	$30,000	$15,000	$20,000	$20,000	$20,000	$20,000	$20,000	$20,000	$20,000
Accounts Receivable												
Accounts Receivable	$0	$0	$0	$0	$27,500	$52,500	$57,500	$62,500	$67,500	$72,500	$77,500	$42,500
Deposits from Accts Receivable	$0	$0	$0	$0	$0	$0	$25,000	$27,500	$30,000	$32,500	$35,000	$72,500
Payments												
Costs of Sales	$0	$0	$0	$0	$5,000	$5,500	$6,000	$6,500	$7,000	$7,500	$8,000	$8,500
Expenses	$9,500	$10,000	$20,000	$30,000	$15,000	$20,000	$20,000	$20,000	$20,000	$20,000	$20,000	$20,000
Total Payments	$9,500	$10,000	$20,000	$30,000	$20,000	$25,500	$26,000	$26,500	$27,000	$27,500	$28,000	$28,500
Net Cash	($9,500)	($10,000)	($20,000)	($30,000)	($20,000)	($25,500)	($1,000)	$1,000	$3,000	$5,000	$7,000	$44,000
Cumulative Cash	($9,500)	($19,500)	($39,500)	($69,500)	($89,500)	($115,000)	($116,000)	($115,000)	($112,000)	($107,000)	($100,000)	($56,000)

These two tables demonstrate the difference in cumulative cash and the money at risk between a successful product start-up and a failed product start-up.

SUCCESSFUL SERVICE START-UP

Successful Service Example												
	Jan	Feb	Mar	Apr	May	Jun	Jul	Aug	Sep	Oct	Nov	Dec
Sales												
Sales	$0	$0	$1,000	$3,500	$6,000	$8,500	$11,000	$13,500	$16,000	$18,500	$21,000	$23,500
Cost of Sales	$0	$0	$50	$175	$300	$425	$550	$675	$800	$925	$1,050	$1,175
Expenses												
General Start-up Expenses	$2,500	$0	$0	$0	$0	$0	$0	$0	$0	$0	$0	$0
Product Release PR	$0	$500	$500	$0	$0	$0	$0	$0	$0	$0	$0	$0
Running Operating Expenses	$1,500	$1,500	$1,750	$2,375	$3,000	$3,625	$4,250	$4,875	$5,500	$6,125	$6,750	$7,375
Total Expenses	$4,000	$2,000	$2,250	$2,375	$3,000	$3,625	$4,250	$4,875	$5,500	$6,125	$6,750	$7,375
Accounts Receivable												
Accounts Receivable	$0	$0	$1,000	$3,500	$6,000	$8,500	$11,000	$13,500	$16,000	$18,500	$21,000	$23,500
Deposits from Accts Receivable	$0	$0	$0	$1,000	$3,500	$6,000	$8,500	$11,000	$13,500	$16,000	$18,500	$21,000
Payments												
Costs of Sales	$0	$0	$50	$175	$300	$425	$550	$675	$800	$925	$1,050	$1,175
Expenses	$4,000	$2,000	$2,250	$2,375	$3,000	$3,625	$4,250	$4,875	$5,500	$6,125	$6,750	$7,375
Total Payments	$4,000	$2,000	$2,300	$2,550	$3,300	$4,050	$4,800	$5,550	$6,300	$7,050	$7,800	$8,550
Net Cash	($4,000)	($2,000)	($2,300)	($1,550)	$200	$1,950	$3,700	$5,450	$7,200	$8,950	$10,700	$12,450
Cumulative Cash	($4,000)	($6,000)	($8,300)	($9,850)	($9,650)	($7,700)	($4,000)	$1,450	$8,650	$17,600	$28,300	$40,750

The successful service start-up requires less cash in any month than a product company, and so there is less money at risk.

Summary

I'll always remember a talk I had with a man who had spent 15 years trying to make his sailboat manufacturing business work, achieving not much more than aging and more debt. "If I can tell you only one thing," he said, "it is that you should never leave yourself without an exit. If you have no exit, then you can never get out. Businesses sometimes fail, and you need to be able to close it down and walk away. I wasn't able to do that."

The story points out why the U.S. government securities laws discourage getting business investments from people who aren't wealthy, sophisticated investors. They don't fully understand how much risk there is. Please, as you start your business, make sure that you understand how easily money invested in a business can be lost.

If I could make only one point with budding entrepreneurs, it would be that you should know what money you need and understand that it is at risk. Don't bet money you can't afford to lose. Know how much you are betting.

CHAPTER 5:

GROWING YOUR BUSINESS

Existing businesses should use effective business planning processes to control their destiny, set long-term objectives and vision, and manage the steps towards their future in an organized, strategic, and managed process. The process, not just the plan, is a vital part of managing growth.

Control Your Destiny

Ask the owner of a small-to-medium company about a business plan. Expect the answer: "Business plan? But I'm not a start-up. Why would I want a business plan?"

They don't all answer that way, but too many do, and it's a shame. Creating a business plan is a great tool for growing a business, but so many people dismiss it as a one-time process used only to start a company or raise financing. The myth that a business plan is only for start-ups gets in the way far too often. If you own or run a company, you probably want to grow it. And if you want to grow a company, then you want to plan that growth. And the planning is only the beginning; you want to use the full planning process to manage growth.

Think for just a minute about how many different reasons there are for an existing company to plan (and manage) its growth. There's the need, first of all, to control your company's destiny, to set long-term vision and objectives, and to calculate steps to take to achieve that vision. Without planning, the company is reacting to events, following reality as it emerges. With planning, there's the chance to proactively lead the company towards its future.

For an existing company that wants to grow, the planning process is essential. Everybody wants to control their own destiny. The planning process is the best way to review the market and refresh your marketing, to prioritize and channel growth into the optimal areas, to allocate resources, to set priorities and manage tasks. Bring a team of managers together and develop strategy that the team can implement. Work on dealing with reality, the possible instead of just the desirable, and make strategic choices. Then follow up with regular plan review that becomes, in the end, management.

This normally starts with a plan, but the plan is just the beginning. It takes the full cycle to make a plan into a planning process. Forget planning a start-up or a single plan to overcome some specific business hurdle; what you want is regular planning, full cycle, a complete planning process that becomes a managing tool for growing your business:

- Take a fresh look.
- Develop your team with SWOT Analysis.
- Make strategic choices.
- Create commitment.
- Establish regular plan reviews.

Take a Fresh Look

Back in the 1970s when I was a foreign correspondent living in Mexico City, I dealt frequently with an American diplomat who provided information about Mexico's increasing oil exports, which were a big story back then. We had lunch about once a month and he became a friend.

Then one day he told me he was being transferred to another post because he had been in Mexico too long. I was disappointed for two reasons. "What? But you've only been here for three years," I said, "and you've barely learned the good restaurants!" He explained to me that the U.S. foreign service moved people about every three years on purpose. "Otherwise we think we know everything and we stop questioning assumptions," he said, "and that's dangerous."

I still remember that day because I've seen the same phenomenon many times in the years since, in business. We — business owners and operators — are so likely to fall into the same trap. Our business landscape is constantly changing, no matter what business we're in, but we keep forgetting the fresh look. "We tried that and it didn't work" is a terrible answer to a suggestion when a few years have gone by. What didn't work six years ago might be just what your business needs right now. But you think you don't have to try again what didn't work in the past.

This is why I advocate the "fresh look" at the market at least once a year. Existing businesses that want to grow too often skip the part of business planning that requires looking well at their market, why people buy, who competes against them, what else they might do and what their customers think about them. Think of the artist squinting to get a better view of the landscape. Step back from the business and take a new look. Use the standard techniques and content from *Chapter 10: Know Your Market,* applying it to your existing business, not a new opportunity.

Talking to customers — well, listening to customers, actually — is particularly important. Don't ever assume you know what your customers think about your company. Things change. If you don't poll your customers regularly, do it at least once a year as part of the fresh look. As an owner, you should listen to at least a few of your customers at least once a year. It's a good exercise.

For creativity's sake, think about revising your market segmentation, creating a new segmentation. For example, if you've divided by size of business, divide by region or type of business or type of decision process. If you've always used demographics, use psychographics. For a discussion of psychographics, see *Chapter 10: Know Your Market.*

Remember to stress benefits. Review what benefits your customers receive when they buy from you, and follow those benefits into a new view of your market.

Question all your assumptions. What has always been true may not be true anymore. That's what I call the fresh look.

Develop Your Team with SWOT Analysis

Especially when you're growing an existing business, you want the planning process to pull your team together, to develop commitment and accountability. Managers have to believe in a plan to implement a plan. They also have to believe that results will be tracked and that managers will be held accountable for disappointing results and will be given credit for positive results. The planning process depends on everybody believing that results will make a difference. As an owner or operator of an existing business, recognize this team factor as a vital part of your planning process. Work on bringing the team into the planning at several levels.

SWOT Analysis (assessing internal **S**trengths and **W**eaknesses, and external **O**pportunities and **T**hreats) is an excellent framework that everyone can understand. It is probably the best tool there is for taking a strategic look at a company. It's also a wonderful tool for gathering a team. I recommend the SWOT, as a group discussion leading to strategy, be part of every planning process, and that its summary be a page or two in the business plan. I can recommend some specific steps that will help make this work:

1. At least once a year, go through a strategy review process that begins with a SWOT meeting and SWOT review. Get your key people together and develop bullet points. Keep notes. Keep the discussion open.

2. Digest the results of the SWOT. Consider the responsibility you have as owner or manager of a business. Strategy is not done by committee or by popular vote. Work on a digestion system that combines ownership responsibility with participation and teamwork. Optimize the SWOT.

3. Share the digested, optimized SWOT with your team of key managers. Develop the strategy. Keep in mind that strategy is focus, and remember the principles of long-term consistency, displacement, and priorities.

4. Give the team time to develop detailed strategy, tactics, and programs. You can use the strategy pyramid framework, for example. Keep everybody involved focused on strategic priorities and look for concrete, measurable, detailed specifics. Make sure that everything important is measurable, and that the measure is embedded into the plan. If you can't track it, then you won't be able to manage it later.

5. Merge the team's contributions into a plan. Remember again that strategy isn't done by committee or popular vote. Somebody has to have the last word, and that somebody ought to be somebody who owns the business.

6. Schedule regular implementation and plan review meetings — give them dates and importance from the beginning — at the same time that you approve the plan. Make this schedule very specific, real dates and times, so that every manager knows ahead of time, like the third Thursday of every month. Review plan vs. actual results. Talk about why actual results are different from what was planned — and they always will be — and what should be done about it.

7. Make sure that those review meetings happen. They have to be important. If you're the owner, operator, or manager, make sure you attend and manage those meetings. If the review meetings fall apart, so will the plan.

During my 20+ years as a business plan consultant and 10+ more years running a company, I've seen many times how the SWOT is an icebreaker. It invites people to contribute. It gets people thinking strategically, talking, sharing, and it turns a group of people into a team.

The SWOT also offers a good forum for opening up discussion. I've seen a SWOT discussion bring up problems that needed upper management attention but might otherwise have remained hidden. Middle managers don't always like telling upper managers what's wrong. Even in a healthy company culture, that can be awkward. SWOT makes that easier.

For example, I once saw a 30-year-old software development manager suggest during a SWOT meeting that one company weakness was the 50-year-old president messing with the software code instead of leaving it to the full-time pros. I saw another SWOT meeting in which several managers said ownership was unwilling to hold managers accountable for underperforming.

It's not magic. It's just an easy-to-understand framework that invites anybody who cares about a business to contribute.

Of course you have to manage a SWOT meeting well. Like any other meeting subject, SWOT can degenerate into useless discussion. A SWOT meeting should focus on the SWOT agenda and avoid unrelated side discussions. It should invite contributions without reprisals for negative comments. It's a variation on brainstorming, so contributions — as in suggested bullet points, suggested items on the list — are all positive as long as they are well intentioned.

If you do that, you also get the benefit of bringing people into the discussion. Implementation is much more likely when managers contribute to the plan. They understand the background and they feel like the plan reflects their input.

So use the SWOT both ways — use it to catalyze team commitment and to develop strategy.

Make Strategic Choices

One of the hardest things business owners and operators do is deciding not to do something. It's the art of saying no. Particularly for a growing business, the difference between strategy and chaos is knowing when and how to say no.

This is against the background of the fact that **Strategy is Focus**. Most growing companies want to do far more than they can effectively do. Bright managers want to seize every opportunity in sight, and all at the same time. In the real world, however, displacement is a fact of life. Everything you do in a business rules out something else that you can't do as a result. To grow your business you must focus on well-defined target markets, well-defined products and services, building competitive advantage, capitalizing on your strengths and avoiding your weaknesses.

Yes, all of that seems obvious, and the best strategies are obvious. They come straight from the SWOT. They are maintained over the long term, meaning several years. Successful strategies will be copied by competitors. Better a mediocre strategy consistently applied over several years than a series of brilliant strategies pushed one after the other.

All of which makes focus the key to effective growth strategies. And, furthermore, focus means exercising discipline in management, not trying to do everything.

Create Commitment

There's an old joke about commitment, defining the difference between commitment and involvement in breakfast: the chicken is involved, the pig is committed.

In business planning processes, commitment is essential. Plans need to be implemented, and implementation means commitment. There has to be accountability, and peer pressure. You have to follow up on what was planned to make sure that it was actually carried out. Here are some ways to create commitment within your team:

- Use the SWOT to start discussion. SWOT brings team members into the strategic discussion. It makes strategy understandable. Your managers have to be part of the team that discusses strategy.

- Make the budgeting elements of the planning process visible. Managers should see what their peers are spending and should hear why. One of the best things I ever watched, as a consultant, was a management group that argued over the activity budgets during the planning process. Each manager had to defend his or her budget, showing what sales and marketing budgets would come out of it. There was a lot of peer pressure.

- Make sure people know that actual results will be compared to plan. With time, in a company that uses the planning process, this becomes second nature. In the beginning, however, it is extremely important that the main company owners and operators set the standards by scheduling plan review meetings each month and attending them. This has to be important.

The bottom line here is that the planning process, for a growing company, is about the people more than the plan. Not only does everything have to be measurable, but it also has to be measured after the fact, and tracked, and managed. Your people must be committed to your plan.

Establish Regular Plan Reviews

Each year, as you get ready to publish the next year's plan, schedule the plan review meetings. Use some regular meeting schedule, such as the third or fourth Thursday of every month. All the managers committed to the plan will know about the schedule ahead of time, so there are few reasons to miss a meeting.

Some excuses will come up. There will be events like trade shows or client events that some managers have to attend. However, with a preplanned schedule for review meetings, these problems won't happen that often.

If your planning process includes a good plan — with specific responsibilities assigned, managers committed, budgets, dates, and measurability — then the review meetings become easier to manage and easier to attend. The agenda of each meeting should be predetermined by the milestones coming due soon, and milestones recently due. Managers review and discuss plan vs. actual results, and explain and analyze the difference.

At Palo Alto Software, we review coordinated milestones once a week in about 20 minutes. The monthly plan vs. actual review includes financial results and other measurables — product milestones, support calls, sales events, etc. — and takes just two hours a month.

It doesn't take much time, but there is very little in management more valuable. It makes your plan a planning process.

This page intentionally blank.

CHAPTER 6:

DESCRIBE YOUR COMPANY

A standard business plan needs to lay out the background and history of a company. First review your thinking about your company and its long-term strategy. You should also develop baseline numbers, either start-up costs or past performance, depending on whether you are planning for a start-up or an ongoing company.

You're probably noticing as we proceed through chapters that developing a business plan doesn't really happen in a straight, logical order of steps. It isn't really a sequential process.

As discussed earlier in Chapter 2: Pick Your Plan, *the standard business plan outline includes a chapter topic on your company right after the Executive Summary. I pointed out then that you may not need to include this chapter if you are writing an internal plan. However, any outsiders reading your plan will want to know about your company before they read about products, markets, and the rest of the story.*

Legal Entity and Ownership

In this paragraph, describe the ownership and legal establishment of the company. This is mainly specifying whether your company is a corporation, partnership, sole proprietorship, or some other kind of legal entity, such as a Limited Liability Corporation. You should also explain who owns the company, and, if there is more than one owner, in what proportion.

If your business is a corporation, specify whether it is a C corporation (the more standard type) or an S corporation (more suitable for small businesses without many different owners). Also, of course, specify whether it is privately owned or publicly traded.

Many smaller businesses, especially service businesses, are sole proprietorships. Some are legal partnerships. The protection of incorporating is important, but sometimes the extra legal costs and hassles of turning in corporate tax forms with double-entry bookkeeping are not worth it. Professional service businesses, such as accounting or legal or consulting firms, may be partnerships, although that mode of establishment is less common these days. If you're in doubt about how to establish a start-up company, consult a business attorney.

Locations and Facilities

Briefly describe offices and locations of your company, the nature and function of each, square footage, lease arrangements, etc.

If you are a service business, you probably don't have manufacturing plants anywhere, but you might have Internet services, office facilities, and telephone systems that are relevant to providing service. It is conceivable that your Internet connection, as one hypothetical case, might be critical to your business.

If you are a retail store, then your location is probably a critical factor, so explain the location, traffic patterns, parking facilities, and possibly customer demographics as they relate to the specific location. Your Market Analysis, discussed in *Chapter 11: Your Target Market,* goes elsewhere in the plan, but if your shopping center location draws a particular kind of customer, note that here.

If you are a manufacturer, then you may have different facilities for production, assembly, and offices. You may also have manufacturing and assembly equipment, packing equipment, shipping docks, and other facilities.

Depending on the nature of your plan, its function and purpose, you may want to include more detail about facilities as appendices attached to your plan. For example, if your business plan is intended to help sell your company to new owners and you feel that part of the value is the facilities and locations, then you should include all the detail you can. If you are describing a manufacturing business for bankers or investors, or anybody else trying to value your business, make sure you provide a complete list and all necessary details about capital equipment, land, and building facilities. This kind of information can make a major difference to the value of your business. On the other hand, if your business plan is for internal use in a small company with a single office, then this topic might be irrelevant.

Thinking Strategically About Your Company

One of the most valuable benefits of developing a business plan is thinking in depth about your company. You started that as part of *Chapter 3: Initial Assessment*, as you entered drafts of your objectives, mission statement, and keys to success. A standard plan also includes sections in the strategy chapter that provide deep background for strategy. This is a good point for developing those texts.

Value Proposition

Value-based marketing is a useful conceptual framework. The value proposition is benefit offered less price charged, in relative terms. For example, the auto manufacturer, Volvo, has for years offered a value proposition based on the value of safety, at a price premium. A more detailed discussion of this framework can be found in *Chapter 18: Strategy Is Focus*.

Competitive Edge

So what is your competitive edge? How is your company different from all others? In what way does it stand out? Is there a sustainable value there, something that you can maintain and develop over time? The classic competitive edges are based on proprietary technology protected by patents. Sometimes market share and brand acceptance are just as important, and know-how doesn't have to be protected by patent to be a competitive edge.

For example, Apple Computer for years used its proprietary operating system as a competitive edge, while Microsoft used its market share and market dominance to overcome Apple's earlier advantage. Several manufacturers used proprietary compression to enhance video and photographic software, looking for a competitive edge.

The competitive edge might be different for any given company, even between one company and another in the same industry. You do not have to have a competitive edge to run a successful business — hard work, integrity, and customer satisfaction can substitute for it, to name just a few examples — but an edge will certainly give you a head start if you need to bring in new investment. Maybe it's just your customer base, as is the case with Hewlett-Packard's traditional relationship with engineers and technicians. Maybe it is the quality control and consistency of IBM.

The most understandable competitive edges are those based on proprietary technology. A patent, an algorithm, even deeply entrenched know-how, can be solid competitive edges. In services, however, the edge can be as simple as having the phone number 1 (800) SOFTWARE, which is an actual case. A successful company was built around that phone number.

Baseline Numbers For Ongoing Companies

While we're focusing on the company description, let's establish some starting numbers that form the basis of your cash flow and balance sheet in the following sections. For ongoing companies, your starting balance for the future is the last balance from the past.

Past Performance for Ongoing Companies

Past performance explained here is for ongoing companies. If you are a start-up business, skip to the next section, Baseline Numbers for Start-up Companies.

Ongoing companies need to include a summary of company history, as a topic in your text. If you are an ongoing company, then you'll need to present financial results of the recent past, and this text section is where you explain them.

Explain why your sales and profits have changed. If you've had important events like particularly bad years or good years, or new services, new locations, new partners, etc., then include that background here. Cover the founding of the company, important events, and important changes.

Your first consideration is the needs of your reader. This isn't a history assignment. Give the reader of the business plan the background information he or she needs to understand your business.

The following illustration shows a sample listing of recent financial results for an ongoing company. Generally three years is good enough. You should have these numbers as part of your standard business accounting. You can include them in the body of your plan, or as an appendix.

For your financial analysis as an ongoing company, you will want to make sure you have some very important highlights of your company's past financial performance, as shown in the next table.

PAST PERFORMANCE TABLE

Past Performance	Prior Year 3	Prior Year 2	Prior Year 1
Sales	$3,773,889	$4,661,902	$5,301,059
Gross Margin	$1,189,495	$1,269,261	$1,127,568
Gross Margin %	31.52%	27.23%	21.27%
Operating Expenses	$752,083	$902,500	$1,052,917
Collection Period (days)	39	35	39
Inventory Turnover	6.22	6.19	5.96

Balance Sheet	Prior Year 3	Prior Year 2	Prior Year 1
Current Assets			
Cash	$43,023	$47,650	$55,432
Accounts Receivable	$281,282	$347,468	$395,107
Inventory	$573,159	$708,026	$805,098
Other Current Assets	$15,000	$20,000	$25,000
Total Current Assets	$912,464	$1,123,144	$1,280,637
Long-term Assets			
Capital Assets	$250,000	$300,000	$350,000
Accumulated Depreciation	$5,000	$20,000	$50,000
Total Long-term Assets	$245,000	$280,000	$300,000
Total Assets	$1,157,464	$1,403,144	$1,580,637
Current Liabilities			
Accounts Payable	$159,395	$196,901	$223,897
Current Borrowing	$64,072	$79,149	$90,000
Other Current Liabilities	$10,679	$13,191	$15,000
Total Current Liabilities	$234,146	$289,241	$328,897
Long-term Liabilities	$202,797	$250,516	$284,862
Total Liabilities	$436,943	$539,757	$613,759
Paid-in Capital	$250,000	$350,000	$500,000
Retained Earnings	$186,204	$274,993	$418,355
Earnings	$284,318	$238,395	$48,523
Total Capital	$720,522	$863,388	$966,878
Total Capital and Liabilities	$1,157,465	$1,403,145	$1,580,637

Important past performance items can be typed into the past performance worksheet. They are used for comparing past performance to projected future, and to establish starting balances for your business plan financials.

Baseline Numbers For Start-up Companies

While we're focusing on the company description, let's establish some starting numbers that form the basis of your cash flow and balance sheet in the following sections. For new companies, your plan determines the starting balances for the future.

Start-up Costs for Start-up Companies

The start-up company should include a Start-Up table instead of the Past Performance table. The next illustration is a simple example.

START-UP REQUIREMENTS TABLE

Start-up Plan	
Requirements	
Start-up Expenses	
Legal	$1,000
Stationery, etc.	$3,000
Brochures	$5,000
Consultants	$5,000
Insurance	$350
Expensed Computer Equipment	$3,000
Other	$1,000
Total Start-up Expenses	**$18,350**
Start-up Assets	
Cash Required	$25,000
Other Current Assets	$7,000
Long-term Assets	$0
Total Assets	**$32,000**
Total Requirements	**$50,350**

Use the start-up requirements worksheet to plan your initial financing.

Start-up Expenses

The first portion of the sample start-up table estimates start-up expenses. Make sure, first of all, that you understand expenses, which are different from assets. You can check with the glossary for a detailed definition of expenses, but basically your start-up expenses are only those expenses incurred before the start of the plan. If they come after the start of the plan, they belong in the profit and loss table in the appropriate month. In the example, the total for start-up expenses is $18,350.

Don't confuse expenses and assets. Assets are goods and documents that have transferable value. Assets make the company's balance sheet look better. However, given a choice, most companies prefer to deduct their purchases as expenses rather than store them up as assets. For example, in the United States a computer purchase can be treated either as an asset or an expense, depending on conditions set forth in federal tax law. When you can choose, you normally want to expense your purchases because then you can deduct those expenses from income. This is why we have "Expensed Computer Equipment," a piece of expensed equipment, among the expenses in our example.

The table shows some common types of start-up expenses, such as legal costs, stationery, and brochures. One category that frequently generates questions is office equipment, such as computers and telephones, that the tax authorities allow a business to report as expenses. While these purchases might normally be assets, they are more often expensed for start-ups because that reduces taxable income, and the U.S. government allows using them as expenses instead of assets.

Product development expenses cause some confusion because some people want to make them assets, but they are almost always expenses. The trouble is that although you'd like to think of product expense as developing future assets, that's not the normal tax treatment.

Start-up Assets

The second portion of the sample start-up table estimates the assets your business will have at start-up, including starting cash, inventory (except for service companies), and others. The example shows just two categories, cash and other short-term assets, because it was taken from a service company that had no starting inventory requirements. Office furniture, shelving, and signage are often start-up assets. The total in the example is $32,000.

Your starting cash is your most critical input. Don't expect to get it right the first time without adjustments. Normally you start with an educated guess; an amount equal to what you think should be your business checking account bank balance when you start. After that, you continue working with other tables in your plan, including Sales Forecast, Personnel, and Profit and Loss, developing estimates for the values in those tables.

If you are like most start-ups, as you refine your estimates you'll discover that your Cash Flow table has a negative balance. If you do have this negative balance, that's an indication of typical negative cash flow of start-up companies. To complete your plan, you'll have to go back to the Start-up table and increase the estimate for starting cash until the starting cash is enough to eliminate any negative balances in the cash flow projections for the following months.

For example, if your cash flow indicates a negative balance of -$8,000 in the worst month, and your original estimate of starting cash was $15,000, then you would need to increase your estimated starting cash by $8,000 to cover the estimated deficit in the cash flow for the first few months. That would require a starting cash balance of $23,000 ($15K + $8K). In the example the starting cash is $25,000 instead of $23,000 because that's a round number and adds a slight cash buffer.

Ultimately the cash in the starting balance comes from the money you raise as loans and investments. If you need more cash, you need to raise more money. If you raise more money, then you need to increase your cash. The starting cash is often an important logical check, which you increase or decrease to make your balance correct. In the example, this company is raising $50,350 as a combination of loans and investments, and it has a total of $50,350 combined between start-up expenses and start-up assets, so its start-up table is correctly balanced. If it had raised $100,000, but you only had $50,350 in assets and expenses, then it would have lost $49,650 as accounted-for funding. It could correct that situation by putting an extra $49,650 into its starting cash, which will increase the assets by $49,650.

Important: The cash you want to have in the bank at start-up is different from the money raised to start the business. The total money raised must match what was spent as expenses and assets. The cash at start-up is one of the assets. If you increase the amount of money raised, then you have to increase the start-up assets, usually by increasing the starting cash. You have to fund start-up expenses as well as start-up assets.

Total Start-up Requirements

The Total Requirements row, shown in the start-up expenses and assets table, sums the start-up expenses and start-up assets. This is the money you've decided you need — by estimating start-up expenses and start-up assets — to start the business.

Start-up Funding

Your business plan isn't complete with start-up costs unless it also includes planned start-up funding. You need to explain where you get the money to pay for start-up expenses and start-up assets. Generally accepted accounting (financial) principles (GAAP) require that the spending planned is financed by either debt or investment.

In the Start-Up Funding table example on the next page, the "Additional Investment Requirement" amount (also known as the "left to finance" amount) shows up as a positive number only when you haven't provided enough funding to finance both expenses and assets. If it shows as a zero, you may have exactly the right amount, or too much.

You can tell that you have not accounted for all your incoming financing by looking at the "Loss at Start-up" value. That should be the same number as Total Start-up Expenses (except negative) shown in the Start-up Requirements table. If it is more negative than start-up expenses are positive, then you have brought in funds that haven't been accounted for. You can fix that by adding more money into your starting cash to account for the additional financing.

Investment is money that you or your investors sink into the business for good. You don't expect to get it back. Borrowing is money loaned to the business — including loans as simple as purchases with credit cards and unpaid bills, called unpaid expenses. Loans can be unpaid expenses, short-term loans, or long-term loans. You need to invest and borrow enough money to equal the start-up expenses and start-up assets combined.

START-UP FUNDING TABLE

Start-up Funding	
Start-up Expenses to Fund	$18,350
Start-up Assets to Fund	$32,000
Total Funding Required	$50,350
Assets	
Non-cash Assets from Start-up	$7,000
Cash Requirements from Start-up	$25,000
Additional Cash Raised	$0
Cash Balance on Starting Date	$25,000
Total Assets	$32,000
Liabilities and Capital	
Liabilities	
Current Borrowing	$0
Long-term Liabilities	$0
Accounts Payable (Outstanding Bills)	$350
Other Current Liabilities (interest-free)	$0
Total Liabilities	$350
Capital	
Planned Investment	
Owner	$20,000
Investor	$20,000
Other	$10,000
Additional Investment Requirement	$0
Total Planned Investment	$50,000
Loss at Start-up (Start-up Expenses)	($18,350)
Total Capital	$31,650
Total Capital and Liabilities	$32,000
Total Funding	**$50,350**

Start-up numbers aren't complete until they include plans for funding the start-up requirements, through debt or investment.

You can see from the previous example that the total of debt and investment must account for the total funding requirements. The money coming in must equal money going out. That's a nice match between common sense and accounting principles: you can't spend it if you don't have it.

Loss at Start-up

Because of accounting principles, your loss at start-up will always be exactly equal to your start-up expenses, but in the opposite direction. In the example, the start-up expenses total $18,350, so the loss at start-up should be exactly -$18,350. This is correct accounting. These are expenses taken against future income, and you have no income, so you have a loss. This is normal, since the vast majority of start-up companies start with a loss.

The rule of accounting is that assets are equal to capital plus liabilities. That is the same as capital being equal to assets minus liabilities, which is also your company's net worth. That's the law in accounting: if you have $32,000 in assets and $350 in liabilities, your capital should be $31,650 (assets less liabilities). If you invested $50,000 in this case but your capital should be only $31,650, then your loss at start-up has to be $18,350. The original $50,000 investment minus the $18,350 loss at start-up gives you the correct number for capital, $31,650. Your loss at start-up will always be equal to start-up expenses. Whether you like the loss at start-up or not, it happens whenever a start-up company has expenses before it starts to sell. This makes your balance correct at the start.

- If your loss at start-up is greater than your start-up expenses, this means that you haven't accounted for all of the money you raised in investments and liabilities. Remember, all the money has to be accounted for as either expenses or assets.

- If your loss at start-up is less than your start-up expenses, you haven't raised enough money to meet your funding requirements.

If you don't like the loss at start-up, there is only one way to reduce it: reduce start-up expenses.

Section Overview

Now that you've written the details, go back to the beginning of the section and create a good summary paragraph that you can use as part of a summary memo or a loan application support document. Include the essential details, such as the name of the company, its legal establishment, how long it has been in existence, and what it sells to what markets. Summarize your start-up requirements and funding, or recent financial history, in a sentence or two.

Summary

You should include a good company description, especially if you're developing a plan to be shown to people outside the company.

Don't stop with just legal formation and history; include some strategic topics, such as competitive edge and value proposition.

You need one of two tables, either start-up or past performance, to establish a starting balance for your projected cash flow and balance sheet.

This page intentionally blank.

CHAPTER 7:

WHAT YOU SELL

For the standard plan, this is where you tell your reader about your products or services, or both. This step in the process is much more important for plans going to external readers — like banks and investors — than for internal plans. In all cases, though, it is a good place to focus thoughts about what you sell and why people buy from you.

This part of the plan is mainly description. Sometimes it will include tables that provide more details, such as a bill of materials or detailed price lists. More frequently, however, this section is mainly text. It normally appears as Chapter 3.0 in the plan, after the company description, but before the market analysis.

Start with an Overview

Every section in a business plan should have an opening paragraph that describes the rest of the section. These summary paragraphs can also be used quite effectively in summary memos and loan application support documents. Readers may frequently skip the details, but only when they have an effective summary. It should be a clear and concise single paragraph that can be merged into the executive summary page. For this section, what do you sell, and to whom?

Add Detail as Needed

The previous topic was the summary, so in this topic, you need to provide more detail. List and describe the products or services you sell. Cover the main points, including what the product or service is, how much it costs, what sorts of customers make purchases, and why. You might not want or need to include every product or service in the list, but at least consider the main sales lines.

It is always a good idea to think in terms of customer needs and customer benefits as you define your product offerings, rather than thinking of your side of the equation — how much the product or service costs, and how you deliver it to the customer.

As you list and describe your sales lines, you may run into one of the serendipitous benefits of good business planning, which is generating new ideas. Describe your product offerings in terms of customer types and customer needs, and you'll often discover new needs and new kinds of customers to cover. This is the way ideas are generated.

Competitive Comparison

Use this topic for a general comparison of your offering as one of several choices a potential buyer can make. There is a separate topic, in the market analysis section, for a detailed comparison of the strengths and weaknesses of your specific competitors.

In this topic you should discuss how your product lines and retail offering compare in general to the competition. For example:

- Your ski shop might offer better ski equipment than some other general outdoor store, or perhaps it is located next to the slopes and caters to rental needs.

- Your jewelry store might be mid-range in price but well known for proficiency in appraisals, remounts, and renovation.

- Your hobby shop has by far the largest selection of model trains and airplanes.

In other words, you want to discuss how you are positioned in the market. Why do people buy from your business instead of from others in the same market? What do you offer, at what price, to whom, and how does your mix compare to others?

Think about specific kinds of benefits, features, and market groups, comparing where you think you can show the difference. Do you sell better features, better price, better quality, better service, or some other factor?

Sourcing and Fulfillment

In this section, you want to explain your product sourcing and the cost of fulfilling your service. Manufacturers and assemblers should present spreadsheet output showing standard costs and overhead. Distributors should present discount and margin structures. Service companies should present costs of fulfilling service obligations.

For example, sourcing is extremely important to a manufacturing company. Your vendors determine your standard costs and hold the key to continued operation. Analyze your standard costs and the materials or services you purchase as part of your manufacturing operation. Look for strengths and weaknesses.

Manufacturing companies want to have ample information about resource planning and sourcing of vital materials, especially if you are preparing a plan for outsiders, such as bankers or investors, or for business valuation. In this case, you may have additional documentation you can copy and attach as appendices, perhaps even contracts with important suppliers, standard cost breakdowns, bills of materials, and other information.

Where materials are particularly vital to your manufacturing, you might discuss whether second sources or alternative sources are available, and whether or not you use them or maintain relationships with them. This is also a good time to look at your sourcing strategy, and whether or not you can improve your business by improving your product sourcing.

But sourcing is not just for product-based companies. For example, a professional service company, such as an accounting practice, medical practice, law practice, management consulting firm, or graphic design firm, is normally going to provide the service by employing professionals. In this case, the cost is mainly the salaries of those professionals.

Other service businesses are quite different. The travel agency provides a service through a combination of knowledge, rights, and infrastructure, including computer systems and databases. The Internet provider or telephone company provides a service by owning and maintaining a network of communications infrastructure. A restaurant is a service business whose costs are a combination of salaries (for kitchen and table waiting) and food costs.

Technology

In this section, explain how technology affects your business, the products you sell, the means you use to sell them, and the needs of the customers you serve.

In some cases this might be a change in scanning technology, retail point-of-sale systems, or even video displays. In others, technology changes the nature of the goods or services you sell, such as cellular phones or high-definition TVs that didn't even exist a few years ago. Do you want to include the Internet? Will a website change the way you do business?

Sometimes, technology can be vital to a service company, such as the case of the Internet provider that uses wireless connections as a competitive edge, or the local company that offers conference rooms for video conferencing. An accounting practice might gain a competitive advantage from proprietary software or wide-area network connections to its clients. A medical laboratory might depend completely on certain expensive technologies for medical diagnostics. A travel agency might depend on its connection to an airline reservation system.

Technology can be critical to a manufacturing business in at least two ways: first, the technology involved in assembly or manufacturing, such as in the manufacture of computer chips; and second, the technology incorporated in your product, such as proprietary technology that enhances the value of the product. In either case, technology can be a critical competitive edge. If you are writing a plan for outsiders, then you need to describe the technology and how well or thoroughly you have the technology protected in your business, through contracts, patents, and other protection.

Technology might be a negative factor, something to be included in a plan because a threat should be dealt with. For example, that same travel agency that depends on a computerized reservation system might also note growing competition from Internet reservations systems available to consumers who prefer to buy direct.

Not all businesses depend on technology. Technology might also be irrelevant for your business. If so, you can delete this topic if it doesn't seem important.

Future Products

Now you want to present your outlook for future products or services. Do you have a long-term product strategy? How are products developed? Is there a relationship between market segments, market demand, market needs, and product development?

Here again, what you include depends on the nature of your plan. In some cases future products are the most important point for investors looking to buy into your company's future. On the other hand, a bank is not going to lend you money for product development or hopes for future products; so in a plan accompanying a Loan Application, there would probably be much less stress on this point.

You may also need to deal with the issue of confidentiality. When a business plan includes sensitive information on future products, then it should be carefully monitored, with good documentation of who receives copies of the plan. Recipients might reasonably be asked to sign non-disclosure statements and those statements should be kept on file.

Sales Literature

It is generally a good idea to include specific pieces of sales literature and collateral as attachments or appendices to your plan. Examples would be copies of advertisements, brochures, direct mail pieces, catalogs, and technical specifications. When a plan is presented to someone outside the company, sales literature is a practical way to both explain your services and present the look and feel of the company.

If it is relevant for your business, you should also use this topic to discuss your present situation regarding company literature and your future plans. Is your sales literature a good match to your services and the image your company wants to present? How is it designed and produced? Could you improve it significantly, or cut the cost, or add additional benefits?

Summary

Depending on the purpose of your plan, you should provide good, practical information on the products or services you sell. Give your plan readers what they will need to evaluate the plan. Make sure they understand the need you serve, how well you satisfy that need, and why your customers buy from you instead of somebody else. Ideally, the descriptions in this chapter make your sales forecast seem realistic and even conservative.

CHAPTER 8:

MANAGEMENT TEAM

A management team and bringing people together is a lot more than just résumés and venture capital. It's what makes a company work, or not work.

For example: It's a sunny March Friday in Western Oregon, which is rare; so rare, in fact, that the boss decides to order pizza for lunch for the entire staff.

The controller is a former history major, Phi Beta Kappa into grad school, who discovered midway through her 30s that she really liked making numbers work. As people gather in the main room around the pizza, she announces that all should enjoy her hair that day "because I am having a rare good hair day." Everybody laughs.

The head of tech support turns the attention to the "krinkly hair" of the marketing manager. Everybody laughs again. There are jokes about the pizza and the root beer.

The product manager demonstrates ballroom dancing steps in preparation for his upcoming wedding, and somebody thinks to turn the music-on-hold up, through the phones, as accompaniment.

The documentation manager emerges from her sunny office in the back and announces that she has a new couch in her office so people can escape from all the administration in the front.

These people seem happy. The technical support manager really likes to explain to people on the telephone; the documentation manager loves teaching and writing. The admin department includes a college student and a soccer mom, both of whom understand the accounting system very well and usually forgive it its flaws. The office manager, a former teacher, says managing this diversity is nothing compared to dealing with a classroom full of adolescents. The product manager and marketing manager both earned their business degrees while working part-time in tech support, and joined full-time as soon as they graduated. These people like their jobs and they like each other. They work together well.

Flash back to the same company four years earlier, with a totally different staff. Back then, the controller was worried sick about the integrity of the computer system. The former technical support person was tired of technical support and upset that the controller had a better computer. The sales manager spent half of her day settling disputes between the controller and the technical support person.

The point here is that the jobs need to be done and the people need to match their job functions and preferences. A manufacturing company can't survive without a production manager, a software company can't live without technical support, and most companies also need office management and administration.

If we jump straight into personnel plans and résumés and business jargon related to the management team, we can inadvertently forget that there is something much more vital and alive than just looking good for investors. A company is where its employees come together most every day, for the major part of the day. If it isn't a good place to work, then it won't be successful. Keep this in mind as you plan your management and develop this part of your plan.

Cover the Bases in Text

Summarize Your Management Chapter

The management chapter starts, like the other chapters, with a good summary. Cover the main points. Consider what you'd say about your management team if you had one or two paragraphs to say it.

Make sure you cover the basic information first. That would include how many employees the company has, how many managers, and how many of the managers are founders. Is your team complete, or are there gaps still to be filled? Is your organizational structure sound, with job descriptions and logical responsibilities for all the key members?

Particularly with start-up companies, you may not have the complete team as you write the plan. In that case, be sure to point out the gaps and weaknesses and how you intend to fill them.

Explain Your Organizational Structure

The organizational structure of a company is what you frequently see as an organizational chart, also known as an "org chart." If you have access to a graphic of an organizational chart (from a drawing program, or one of the specialized organizational charting software packages available), that works really well at this point. If not, you can just use the text to describe the organizational structure in words, without a chart.

Make sure you explain how job descriptions work and how the main company functions are divided up. Are your organizational lines drawn clearly? Is the authority properly distributed? Do you have jobs that include responsibility without authority? Do your resources seem in line with your organizational needs?

List Team Members and Their Backgrounds

List the most important members of the management team. Include summaries of their backgrounds and experience, using them like brief résumés. Describe their functions with the company. Résumés should be attached to the back of a plan.

Discuss Your Management Gaps

You may have obvious gaps in the management, especially in start-up companies, but even in ongoing companies. For example, the manufacturing company without a production manager has some explaining to do, and the computer company without service has some problems. It is far better to define and identify a weakness than to pretend it doesn't exist. Specify where the team is weak because of gaps in coverage of key management functions. How will these weaknesses be corrected? How will the more important gaps be filled?

Other Management Team Considerations

Applicability depends on your company. Some questions that should be answered include:

- Do any managers or employees have "noncompete" agreements with competitors?
- Who is on your board of directors?
- What do the members contribute to the business?
- Who are your major stockholders?
- What is their role in management?

At this point you should normally include a Personnel table to project personnel costs, including direct compensation and indirect costs. The indirect costs include vacation pay, sick pay, insurance benefits, education, and of course, payroll taxes and some other costs. There are different terms for all of this, but my favorite is "personnel burden," which is a cost over and above the direct wages and salaries.

Special Treatment for Home Offices

If you are working as a sole proprietor in a home office, you should still include your own compensation as part of your business plan. What you pay yourself should be added into the profit and loss as an expense. However, in this case you don't really need to include payroll burden, because these additional expenses are irrelevant until you include additional employees.

Standard Personnel Variations

A good personnel plan varies according to your business and business plan needs. You may want a simple list of names, titles, or groups, each of which is assigned a monthly cost. This model is shown in the next illustration.

STANDARD PERSONNEL PLAN

Personnel Plan					
	Jan	Nov	Dec	Year 1	Year 2
Partners	$12,000	$12,000	$12,000	$144,000	$175,000
Consultants	$0	$0	$0	$0	$50,000
Editorial/graphic	$0	$6,000	$6,000	$18,000	$22,000
VP Marketing	$0	$5,000	$5,000	$20,000	$50,000
Sales people	$0	$0	$0	$0	$30,000
Office Manager	$0	$2,500	$2,500	$7,500	$30,000
Secretarial	$0	$1,750	$1,750	$5,250	$20,000
Other	$0	$0	$0	$0	$0
Total People	3	7	7	7	14
Total Payroll	$12,000	$27,250	$27,250	$194,750	$377,000

The standard personnel plan is a simple list of names, titles, or categories. The sum transfers into your profit and loss statement. This illustration shows three months and first two years of a sample plan.

The simpler model totals all payroll only. It is perfectly appropriate for a lot of small businesses. You can use each of the lines in the table to describe specific individuals, or groups and departments. When you have the list complete, just add up the totals for personnel costs in your Profit and Loss, discussed in *Chapter 15: The Bottom Line*. Multiply that total times your burden rate — say 15 or 20 percent — to calculate your personnel burden. The burden goes into the profit and loss as a separate line.

The next illustration shows the more detailed personnel plan that divides the rows into categories, such as sales and marketing, general and administrative, and so forth. The more detailed model shown here totals the planned payroll for each of the four departments, and then calculates total payroll.

DETAILED PERSONNEL PLAN

Personnel	Jan	Nov	Dec	Year 1	Year 2
Production Personnel					
Manager	$3,000	$3,000	$3,000	$36,000	$40,000
Assistant	$1,000	$1,000	$1,000	$12,000	$13,000
Technical	$2,000	$2,000	$2,000	$24,000	$27,500
Fulfillment	$1,500	$1,500	$1,500	$18,000	$22,000
Subtotal	$7,500	$7,500	$7,500	$90,000	$102,500
Sales and Marketing Personnel					
Manager	$6,000	$6,000	$6,000	$72,000	$76,000
Technical Sales	$5,000	$5,000	$5,000	$60,000	$63,000
Salesperson	$2,500	$2,500	$2,500	$30,000	$55,000
Salesperson	$2,500	$2,500	$2,500	$30,000	$50,000
Subtotal	$16,000	$16,000	$16,000	$192,000	$244,000
General and Administrative Personnel					
President	$5,500	$5,500	$5,500	$66,000	$69,000
Finance	$0	$0	$0	$0	$29,000
Admin Assistant	$2,000	$2,000	$2,000	$24,000	$26,000
Clerical	$0	$0	$0	$0	$0
Subtotal	$7,500	$7,500	$7,500	$90,000	$124,000
Other Personnel					
Programming	$3,000	$3,000	$3,000	$36,000	$40,000
Other Technical	$0	$0	$0	$0	$30,000
Other	$0	$0	$0	$0	$0
Subtotal	$3,000	$3,000	$3,000	$36,000	$70,000
Total People	11	11	11	11	13
Total Payroll	$34,000	$34,000	$34,000	$408,000	$540,500

The more detailed personnel plan shown here divides personnel expenditures into classifications including production, sales and marketing, administration, and other.

An alternative plan estimates total people per department, and the average salary per department. This can be a useful way to project growth of personnel in a high-growth mode requiring rapid addition of people. The next illustration shows an example of this personnel projection method.

HEADCOUNT-BASED PERSONNEL PLAN

Personnel Plan	Jan	Nov	Dec	Year 1	Year 2
Fulfillment Personnel					
People	4	4	4	4	5
Average per Person	$1,875	$1,875	$1,875	$22,500	$24,000
Subtotal	$7,500	$7,500	$7,500	$90,000	$120,000
Sales and Marketing Personnel					
People	4	4	4	4	6
Average per Person	$4,000	$4,000	$4,000	$48,000	$50,000
Subtotal	$16,000	$16,000	$16,000	$192,000	$300,000
General and Administrative Personnel					
People	2	2	2	2	2
Average per Person	$3,750	$3,750	$3,750	$15,000	$18,000
Subtotal	$7,500	$7,500	$7,500	$30,000	$36,000
Other Personnel					
People	1	1	1	1	2
Average per Person	$3,000	$3,000	$3,000	$36,000	$39,000
Subtotal	$3,000	$3,000	$3,000	$36,000	$78,000
Total People	11	11	11	11	15
Total Payroll Expenditures	$34,000	$34,000	$34,000	$348,000	$534,000

This personnel plan shows personnel expenditures by people per department and spending per person.

For any of these three personnel tables, you also want to calculate a payroll burden as a percentage of the total, and make sure to include the personnel burden amount among the operating expenses, usually as a separate line in Profit and Loss.

The payroll assumptions in this model will also be used for the other financial projections. The Profit and Loss (also called income statement) will use personnel plan numbers.

Summary

Your personnel plan is actually just an educated guess. It is hard to make this kind of guess if you aren't used to forecasting, but you can do it by breaking the assumptions down into rows and thinking it through. If you're having trouble with it, remember that a real business plan is frequently revised to accommodate changes in sales, marketing, and finances.

This page intentionally blank.

CHAPTER 9:

THE BUSINESS YOU'RE IN

In addition to the information you've already developed, you also need to explain the type of business you're in: not just your company, but the business environment around you. This is one step in a business plan's comprehensive marketing analysis.

Industry Analysis

A standard business plan should explain the general state of the industry and the nature of the business. You might be able to skip this for an internal plan because most of the target readers already know the industry, but even in this case, taking a step away and taking a fresh look can be valuable.

Whether you're a service business, manufacturer, retailer, or some other type of business, you should do an industry analysis, describing:

- Industry Participants
- Distribution Patterns
- Competition

There is plenty of information available, too much, in fact; your hardest task is sifting through it all. There are websites for business analysis, financial statistics, demographics, trade associations, and just about everything you'll need for a complete business plan. We'll look at that in this chapter after going through some of the topics to cover. I'll also include some of the old-fashioned reference works, just in case you really need them. Remember though, that websites are always changing. Your most effective tools are good search techniques.

Industry Participants

You can't easily describe a type of business without describing the nature of the participants. There is a huge difference, for example, between an industry like long-distance telephone services, in which there are only a few huge companies in any one country, and one like dry cleaning, in which there are tens of thousands of smaller participants.

This can make a big difference to a business and a business plan. The restaurant industry, for example, is what we call "pulverized," which, like the dry cleaning industry, is made up of many small participants. The fast-food business, on the other hand, is composed of a few national brands participating in thousands of branded outlets, many of them franchised.

Economists talk of consolidation in an industry as a time when many small participants tend to disappear and a few large players emerge. In accounting, for example, there are a few large international firms whose names are well known and tens of thousands of smaller firms. The automobile business is composed of a few national brands participating in thousands of branded dealerships. In computer manufacturing, for example, there are a few large international firms whose names are well known, and thousands of smaller firms.

Distribution Patterns

Explain how distribution works in your industry. Is this an industry in which retailers are supported by regional distributors, as is the case for computer products, magazines, or auto parts? Does this industry depend on direct sales to large industrial customers? Do manufacturers support their own direct sales forces, or do they work with product representatives?

Some products are almost always sold through retail stores to consumers, and sometimes these are distributed by distribution companies that buy from manufacturers. In other cases, the products are sold directly from manufacturers to stores. Some products are sold directly from the manufacturer to the final consumer through mail campaigns, national advertising, the Internet, or other promotional means.

In many product categories there are several alternatives, and distribution choices are strategic. Encyclopedias and vacuum cleaners were traditionally sold door-to-door, but are now also sold in stores and direct from manufacturer to consumer through radio, television, and Sunday newspaper print ads.

Many products are distributed through direct business-to-business sales, and in long-term contracts such as the ones between car manufacturers and their suppliers of parts, materials, and components. In some industries companies use representatives, agents, or commissioned salespeople.

Technology can change the patterns of distribution in an industry or product category. The Internet, for example, is changing the options for software distribution, books, music, and other products. Cable communication is changing the options for distributing video products and video games.

The Distribution Patterns topic may not apply to most service companies, because distribution is normally about physical distribution of specific physical products. If you are a restaurant, graphic artist, architect, or some other service that doesn't involve distribution, just delete this topic from your plan.

For a few services, distribution may still be relevant. A phone service or cable provider or Internet provider might describe distribution related to physical infrastructure. Some publishers may prefer to treat their business as a service rather than a manufacturing company, and in that case distribution may also be relevant.

Competition and Buying Patterns

Explain the nature of competition in this market. This topic is still in the general area of describing the industry, or type of business. Explain the general nature of competition in this business, and how the customers seem to choose one provider over another.

What are the keys to success? What buying factors make the most difference? Price? Product features? Service? Support? Training? Software? Delivery dates? Are brand names important?

In the computer business, for example, competition might depend on reputation and trends in one part of the market, and on channels of distribution and advertising in another. In many business-to-business industries, the nature of competition depends on direct selling, because channels are impractical. Price is vital in products competing with each other on retail shelves, but delivery and reliability might be more important for materials used by manufacturers in volume, where a shortage can affect an entire production line.

In the restaurant business, competition might depend on reputation and trends in one part of the market, and on location and parking in another.

In many professional service practices, the nature of competition depends on word of mouth, because advertising is not completely accepted. Is there price competition between accountants, doctors, and lawyers? How do people choose travel agencies or florists for weddings? Why does someone hire one landscape architect over another? Why choose Starbucks, a national brand, over the local coffee house? All of this is the nature of competition.

Main Competitors

List the main competitors. What are the strengths and weaknesses of each? Consider their products, pricing, reputation, management, financial position, channels of distribution, brand awareness, business development, technology, or other factors that you feel are important. In what segments of the market do they operate? What seems to be their strategy? How much do they impact your products, and what threats and opportunities do they represent?

Gathering Information

A great deal of business information and small business or entrepreneurial help is readily available on the Internet. Market research firms and industry experts publish much of their information on websites, and in trade and business magazines. Reference sites index these magazines, many offer the texts online, and if not, then libraries stock them. Trade associations publish many listings and statistics on their websites as well as in hard-copy publications. Public stock laws require detailed reporting of financial results, and stock market information sources compile industry statistics from financial reports.

I'm old enough to remember when gathering information was a problem. Business consultants could make money just collecting the kind of information you need for a good business plan market analysis. These days, however, the problem is much more about sorting through all the information than it is gathering information. The Internet has completely changed research, especially practical business research.

This is far too large a topic to cover here, but it is still vital to modern business. By the time you're looking at developing a business plan, I think you should know how to use the Internet to gather information. At the very least, know how to search at Google and how to find Yahoo! and sort through its catalog of business information.

As an example, the illustrations on the next page show the main pages of Google and Yahoo!. Of course, they will have changed by the time you read this.

Google and Yahoo!

SEARCHING WITH GOOGLE

The Google site, www.google.com, is probably the best-known Internet search site.

SEARCHING YAHOO!

The Yahoo! site, www.yahoo.com, is probably the best-known Internet catalog. It sorts and catalogs the World Wide Web according to logical categories, and also includes a powerful search engine.

New search engines and new searching techniques appear all the time, so even if it seems hard to keep up, please try to stay current.

Business Plan Sites

Palo Alto Software maintains two Internet websites that offer free downloadable sample plans, tips, outlines, and discussions of topics related to developing a business plan.

WWW.BPLANS.COM

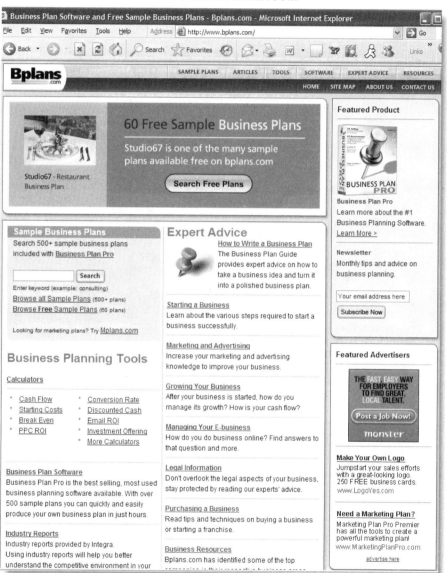

Bplans.com also includes many suggested links to other sources of small business information, including the Small Business Administration (SBA), Small Business Development Centers (SBDCs), and many other valuable sites. It is stocked with the latest available information, and references to information that might be available elsewhere.

WWW.PALOALTO.COM

The Palo Alto Software website provides valuable product information to our customers, an online store, business planning resources, and links to sample plans and other information sources.

Both these sites have links to the Ask the Experts team of volunteer experts who respond to general questions about business planning, entrepreneuring, and marketing planning. You can post your question and receive an answer as an email reply. There are more than 4,000 answers currently available in the database.

Government Sites

We describe the U.S. Census Bureau site in the upcoming sections on market analysis, *Chapter 10: Know Your Market* and *Chapter 12: Your Target Market*. Also, be sure to visit the Small Business Administration (SBA) website at: www.sba.gov.

U.S. SMALL BUSINESS ADMINISTRATION WEBSITE

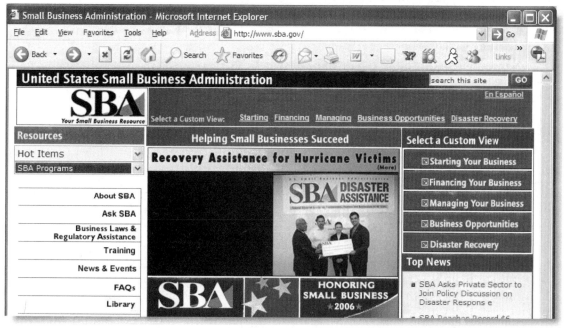

The Small Business Administration website offers a wealth of free information, and links to other sources as well.

And Many Others

There's no easy way to keep track of all the business information sites on the Web. New sites appear every day, existing sites change, and old sites sometimes close. Use your main search engines and go from there, learning to search, looking for leads.

Financial Profiles and Ratios

There's no substitute for composite industry data showing standard financials for your type of business. For example, Business Plan Pro®, www.paloalto.com/sp/bp/, includes thousands of industry data reports showing average sales growth over five years, average profitability, and balance sheet numbers for different types of businesses classified according to the Standard Industrial Classification (SIC) listings and the North American Industry Classification System (NAICS). The data is tied into the ratios table of the product, so users can automatically compare their own numbers to standard industry profiles.

This information can be very valuable. It tells me, for example, that shoe retailers selling less than $1 million per year make an average of 42 percent gross margin, they spend an average of 40 percent on operating expenses, and they net about one percent of sales as profits. The source of this data, Integra Information Systems, maintains its website at www.integrainfo.com where it sells additional data reports including standard industry profiles, in-depth industry profiles, valuation reports, and others.

The Risk Management Association (formerly the Robert Morris Associates) is a membership organization sponsored by banks which publishes an annual listing of standard financial ratios, developed by polling member banks, for actual business results of thousands of different companies in the small business arena.

Two of RMA's publications, called *Annual Statement Studies* and *Financial Ratios Benchmarks*, are other very valuable sources of information. Like Integra's data, it lists standard financial profiles according to SIC and NAICS codes. This information is available in print, on CD-ROM, or online and at this writing sells for less than $129 to members or $400 to nonmembers. Separate industry profiles are also available online. You can find out more by calling (215) 446-4000, or visiting their website at www.rmahq.com.

Trade Associations

Many industries are blessed with an active trade association that serves as a vital source of industry-specific information. Such associations regularly publish member directories and the better ones publish statistical information that track industry sales, profits, economic trends, etc.

If you don't know which trade associations apply to your industry, find out. Search the Internet with Yahoo!, Google, and other search engines. Look for the website of the trade association for your industry. Ask at the reference section of your library for listings of industry associations. Ask someone else in the same industry. Consult an industry-specific magazine. Look in the *Readers' Guide to Periodicals Index* or the *Business Periodicals Index* (in the following section, Business Publications) or *Ayer's Directory*, which lists periodicals.

As a specific example, since we mentioned a hypothetical shoe store, the National Shoe Retailers Association publishes a biennial *Business Performance Report*, a statistical review of more than 1,700 independent shoe retail companies. They sell it for $50 to members, or $100 to non-members. It covers men's, women's, children's, and family shoe companies, and includes standard financials, statistics, and other information.

Business Publications

Business magazines are an important source of business information. Aside from the major general-interest business publications such as *Business Week, Wall Street Journal*, etc., there are many specialty publications that look at specific industries.

Specialization is an important trend in the publishing business. Dingbats and Widgets may be boring to the general public, but they are exciting to Dingbat and Widget manufacturers who read about them regularly in their specialized magazines. The magazines are an important medium for industry-specific advertising, which is important to readers as well as advertisers.

The editorial staffs of these magazines have to fill the space between the ads. They do that by publishing as much industry-specific information as they can find, including statistics, forecasts, and industry profiles. Paging through one of these magazines can sometimes produce a great deal of business forecasting and economic information.

Several good reference sources list magazines, journals, and other publications. They also offer indices to published articles, which you can use to search for the exact references you need. These will be kept in the reference section of most libraries:

- *Readers' Guide to Periodical Literature* indexes popular magazines. It is published by H.W. Wilson of New York, www.hwwilson.com. Hard copies are available in most library reference sections, but the website is more immediate.

- *Business Periodicals Index,* also published by H.W. Wilson of New York. Indexes business magazines and journals only.

Use the indices to identify published information that might help your business plan. When you find an index listing for an article that forecasts your industry or talks about industry economics or trends, jot down basic information on the publication and ask the library for a copy of the publication.

Reference Libraries

Reference librarians follow reference sources as a profession. They are excellent sources of good advice and tips on reference materials that may help you acquire the information your business plan requires.

Small Business Administration

In the United States, the SBA is best known for its small business loans. However, it also provides business training, business information, and business services, including workshops, counseling, publications, and videotapes. It has program offices in every state, the District of Columbia, the U.S. Virgin Islands, and Puerto Rico. It has business development specialists stationed in more than 100 field offices nationwide. We noted its website, www.sba.gov, with an illustration, a few sections back.

The SBA publishes many business booklets and information products. These products are free, many as electronic files, but the SBA suggests a small donation (under $3.00 for most of them) for hard copy. They answer many frequently-asked questions and provide important information for business owners and would-be business owners.

If you don't have Internet access, you can find out about SBA business development programs and services by calling the SBA Small Business Answer Desk at 1-800-UASKSBA (1-800-827-5722). The answer desk "hotline" provides an information and referral service staffed by the organization's office of business initiatives, education, and training. It operates during normal office hours five days a week.

SCORE Association

The SCORE Association, "Counselors to America's Small Business" is a resource partner with the SBA. This Service Corps of Retired Executives includes more than 10,000 volunteers who provide training and one-on-one counseling at no charge, in 389 offices all over the country. You can find out about SCORE at www.score.org.

Small Business Development Centers

SBDCs are funded in part by the SBA and also work with local colleges and some other funding agencies. Every state has at least one SBDC, and most states have several offices in several cities. Visit our website at www.bplans.com/sb/ for a list of several hundred local SBDC addresses.

We've found the SBDCs to be an excellent resource for businesses, offering high quality, professional advice at very low prices. SBDCs also work closely with local colleges to participate in and provide courses in business topics, such as business planning, bookkeeping, employee management, sales, marketing, and other vital subjects. SBDCs also publish books, surveys, and studies, and in some cases even audio tapes, videotapes, and workshops. Palo Alto Software has worked with SBDCs in the past, to provide software and seminar courses related to business planning.

U.S. Census Bureau

The United States Census Bureau, part of the Department of Commerce, has a wealth of information available for business and educational purposes. I refer to it, specifically and with examples, in the market analysis portion of *Chapter 10: Know Your Market.*

Most of the Census Bureau's reports cover the entire United States and summarize data for the nation. However, the Bureau also publishes information on states, counties in states, and even cities within counties. Among the more valuable special reports are city and county reports that list the number of business establishments by type of establishment. These are special reports available directly from the Bureau and also from some libraries and electronic database services. Many of these reports are also available through online services. The Census Bureau has an electronic edition called CENDATA. It also has an Internet website at www.census.gov.

The U.S. Department of Commerce has a website at www.osec.doc.gov.

Business Assistance

The Federal Government Agencies

The information gathering process will take you through several sources of business assistance. The best of them are the government agencies we've just discussed as sources of information: the SBA, SCORE, and SBDCs.

New businesses, small businesses, and business planning are good for the economy. Governments, higher education institutions, and business organizations know that and try to help businesses as much as possible. For you and your business, there is probably a great deal of help available. But you need to know where to ask.

In these pages, I only describe the United States organizations offering help to small business and start-ups. In other markets, similar organizations exist. Check with your Chambers of Commerce and industry organizations, government development organizations, and business schools.

Consultants, Accountants, and Attorneys

Consultants, accountants, and attorneys are the first line of business assistance. They aren't really the main focus of this chapter, however, and not because they aren't, in general, excellent sources of information. We have the utmost respect for the value of professional advice. In this discussion, however, we deal with relatively low-cost sources of business assistance, such as development agencies, local adult education and continuing education schools, and online information services. We don't have a lot to add to the general doctrine of how to choose a good business professional. Let the buyer beware. A good business professional is always worth the money, if you have the money. Unfortunately, not all professionals are good, and it's hard to know who's good until you've committed money.

Always try to get some good references on professionals — other clients, satisfied clients — before you use them, and don't forget to check those references. Furthermore, it is not always true that with business consultants you get what you pay for. In our experience, there is not always a direct correlation between the fees charged and the value provided.

The SBA says consultants "can be a great asset to a small business owner. A business consultant's fees typically range between $25 and $250 an hour. If you decide to retain the services of a consultant, make sure he/she is reputable and be certain that you understand the fee schedule up front."

Business Organizations

Explore what's available through local business organizations such as the Chamber of Commerce. Many areas have entrepreneurial interest groups, such as a new enterprise forum, entrepreneurs' association, or industry associations. Some also have municipal or county development organizations whose main goal is to help companies get started.

Schools and Colleges

Many local community colleges work directly with the SBA to house the Small Business Development Centers (SBDCs) discussed as part of the government resources in the previous section. The community college/SBDC combination is often an excellent resource for workshops, classes, and even business consulting, all of it with experts whose job involves helping small businesses and start-ups. SBDCs are funded, in part, by the school and the government. Call your local community college and ask about business classes.

Libraries

Local libraries regularly carry business periodicals and business books. Reference sections are frequently staffed by experts who are happy to help you find what you need. Look for magazine indices, trade association annual publications, and government publications.

Banks

Banks are often involved in local development activities, and even when they don't directly offer business help (some do), they will usually know where else you can go for help in the local area. The SBA says "many bank officers have a broad understanding of finance, business operations, and the local economic climate. Do not be afraid to ask your banker questions."

State Development Agencies

Most states have development agencies of one kind or another. They also offer information related to small businesses and start-ups, and can be valuable resources. Check with your other resource providers about state agencies. You can also look in your telephone directory for government agencies under the State category.

Summary

We are in a brave new world of too much information, not too little. It will be hard for you to sort through all the information you'll find on your business or your industry, hard to summarize, hard to decide what is most important. As you do, keep in mind that the business plan is supposed to guide decisions. It is not a school report or even a graduate thesis. If it doesn't have a business purpose — which might be describing the industry for a bank or investor, or for your own team, for example, but certainly not just to prove you can — then you shouldn't include it.

CHAPTER 10:

KNOW YOUR MARKET

What's the first thing, the most essential element, you need in business? No, not a plan: you need customers.

Market Research

In *Chapter 3: Initial Assessment*, you took a good first look at whether or not your business has (or will have) enough customers to keep it healthy. For the next step, you need to go further into a market analysis. It doesn't have to be academic, necessarily, and it doesn't have to be a huge project that stalls your planning process. What you want, ultimately, is to know your customers.

Some of the best market research is simple, practical, and even obvious. You don't get it from reference sections in libraries, or even from the Internet. You get it from real people, particularly customers or potential customers. Here are some practical examples.

Simple and Practical Market Research

Look at existing, similar businesses. This is a very good first step. If you are planning a retail shoe store, for example, spend some time looking at existing retail shoe stores. Park across the street and count the customers that go into the store. Note how long they stay inside, and how many come out with boxes that look like purchased shoes. You can probably even count how many pairs of shoes each customer buys. Browse the store and look at prices. Look at several stores, including the discount shoe stores and department store shoe departments.

Find a similar business in another place. If you are planning a local business, find a similar business far enough away that you won't compete. For the shoe store example, you would identify shoe stores in similar towns in other states. Call the owner, explain your purpose truthfully, and ask about the business.

Scan local newspapers for people selling a similar business. Contact the broker and ask for as much information as possible. If you are thinking of creating a shoe store and you find one for sale, you should consider yourself a prospective buyer. Maybe buying the existing store is the best thing. Even if you don't buy, the information you gain will be very valuable. Why is the owner selling? Is there something wrong with the business? You can probably get detailed financial information.

Always shop the competition. If you're in the restaurant business, patronize your competition once a month, rotating through different restaurants. If you own a shoe store, shop your competition once a month, and visit different stores.

Talk to Customers

If you're considering starting a new business, talk to potential customers. In the shoe store example, talk to people coming out of the stores. Talk to your neighbors, talk to your friends, talk to your relatives. Ask them how often they buy shoes, what sizes, where, at what price, and whatever else you can think of. If you're starting a restaurant, landscape architecture business, butcher shop, bakery, or whatever, talk to customers.

At most business schools, when they teach business planning, students have to do a market survey as part of the plan. The plan isn't complete unless they go out and ask a credible number of people what they want, why, where they get it, how much they pay, and so forth. Although you may not go through the formality of a customer survey for your business, this information is vital.

At Palo Alto Software, we frequently put a customer survey on two of our websites. People who are browsing the Internet looking for materials and information on business plans can visit us at www.PaloAlto.com or www.bplans.com.

One of those sites does no selling. Instead, it provides free information, including free downloadable sample plans, outlines, and discussions, including answers to several hundred specific questions about details of developing a business plan. We sometimes ask people stopping by our websites to answer a few quick questions that concern us. The invitation promises just a few questions, and promises also that we won't ask their names or e-mail addresses, and we won't follow up with sales information. When we run one of these surveys we get about 300 responses a month, which provides us with valuable information about the concerns people have as they consider writing a business plan.

If you have an ongoing business, the process of developing a plan should include talking to customers. Take a step away from the routine, dial up some of your customers, and ask them about your business. How are you doing? Why do they buy? How do they feel about your competitors? It is a good idea to take a customer to lunch once a month, just to keep yourself in touch.

Count Potential Customers

Most business plans contain an analysis of potential customers. We saw that in *Chapter 3: Initial Assessment*. As an essential first step, you should have a good idea of how many potential customers there are. The way you find that out depends on your type of business. For example, a retail shoe store needs to know about individuals living in a local area, a graphic design firm needs to know about local businesses, and a national catalog needs to know about households and companies in an entire nation.

What constitutes good sources depends on what you need. Government and commercial statistics are usually more than enough, but for some plans you may end up purchasing information from professional publishers or contract researchers.

For general demographic data about a local area, if you have no easier source, ask the reference desk at a local library. A local university library is even better, particularly a business library. Chambers of Commerce usually have general information about a local market. In the United States, there is the federal government's U.S. Census Bureau. Nowadays the quickest route to the census bureau is their Internet website at www.census.gov.

Before the Internet became so ubiquitous, I frequently turned to vendors of mailing lists for general information about people and types of business. The mailing list vendors often have catalogs listing total numbers of types of people and types of business. For example, to find out how many attorneys or CPA offices there are in the United States, I might look at the lists for sale at a list broker.

Magazines provide another good source of demographics. If you're selling to computer stores, for example, call *Computer Retail Week* and *Computer Reseller News* and ask both publications for a media kit. The media kit is intended to sell pages of advertising to potential advertisers. They are frequently full of demographics on the readers. For information on any specific type of business, get the media kits for the magazines that cater to those types of businesses as readers.

Just browsing the Census Bureau website while preparing this draft, it took me about 10 minutes to discover that my home county has 378 general contractors, of which 360 have fewer than 20 employees and the remaining 18 have between 20 and 100. There are 238 legal businesses in my county, of which only 12 have more than 20 employees. Also, following the shoe store example, there are 32 shoe stores in the county, none of them having more than 20 employees. There are 111,000 households in the county, 61 percent of them owner occupied, and an average of 2.49 people per household. Some 22 percent of adults in the county are college graduates, and the median household income is $26,000. All of this information was available for free at the U.S. Census Bureau website.

Know Your Customers

Aside from just counting the customers, you also want to know what they need, what they want, and what makes them buy. The more you know about them, the better. For individuals as customers, you probably want to know their average age, income levels, family size, media preferences, buying patterns, and as much else as you can find out that relates to your business. If you can, you want to divide them into groups according to useful classifications, such as income, age, buying habits, social behavior, values, or whatever other factors are important. For the shoe store example, shoe size is good, but you might also want activity preferences and even — if you can find it — psychographics.

Psychographics divides customers into cultural groups, value groups, social sets, motivator sets, or other interesting categories that might be useful for classifying customers. For example, in literature intended for potential retailers, First Colony Mall of Sugarland, Texas, describes its local area psychographics as including:

- 25% Kid & Cul-de-Sacs (upscale suburban families, affluent)

- 5.4% Winner's Circle (suburban executives, wealthy)

- 19.2% Boomers and Babies (young white-collar suburban, upper middle income)

- 7% Country Squires (elite ex-urban, wealthy).

Going into more detail, it calls the Kids & Cul-de-Sacs group "a noisy medley of bikes, dogs, carpools, rock music and sports." The Winner's Circle customers are "well-educated, mobile, executives and professionals with teen-aged families. Big producers, prolific spenders, and global travelers." The Country Squires are "where the wealthy have escaped urban stress to live in rustic luxury. No. 4 in affluence, big bucks in the boondocks."

SRI Consulting-Business Intelligence (formerly Stanford Research Institute) provides another example. Its VALS service (values and lifestyles) offers information on U.S. customers classified according to the value sets shown in the SRI illustration above. Customers and potential customers are divided into groups, including fulfilleds, achievers, experiencers, and others. More information about that is available from SRI from their website at www.sric-bi.com/VALS/types.shtml

SRIC-BI's VALS PSYCHOGRAPHICS

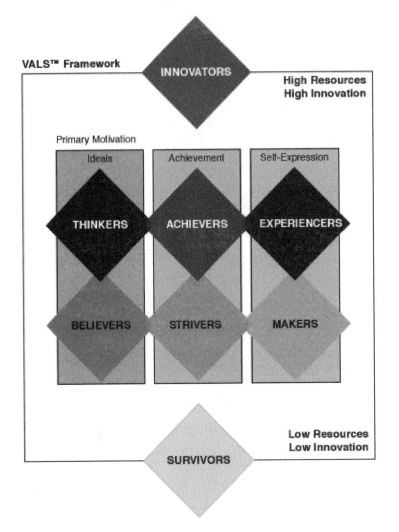

The diagram illustrates SRI's VALS, values and lifestyles psychographics research that divides the U.S. market into various types of potential customers.

Back to the Web

And of course for market research, as with business industry research in the previous chapter, you go very quickly back to the Web. Here, too, it's impossible to keep up, but we can give you some starting points:

www.marketresearch.com MarketResearch.com is a commercial site aggregating published market research.

www.jjhill.org/ Hill Research Library, an excellent nonprofit library resource, offers market research at accessible rates.

www.business.gov This is the U.S. government hub site for market research.

www.clickz.com/stats/ ClickZ Network offers up-to-date statistics on Web usage.

www.census.gov The U.S. government statistical site.

www.knowthis.com KnowThis.com is a marketing information site.

www.marketingpower.com American Marketing Association (AMA) main market information site.

www.hoovers.com Hoovers is a database of American companies.

www.ceoexpress.com Offers a wealth of additional links for additional information sites.

www.bea.gov The Bureau of Economic Analysis is part of the U.S. Department of Commerce, offering business statistics.

Summary

Projecting market growth is particularly important when your plan is related to finding investors or supporting a loan application, because market growth enhances the implied value of your business.

Cite growth rates in terms that fit the available information, whether growth in the number of potential customers, projected dollar sales, meals served, website projects, tax reporting hours, yards to landscape, or whatever you have.

This page intentionally blank.

CHAPTER 11:

FORECAST YOUR SALES

Forecasting is more art than science. Don't fear—it isn't as hard as most people think. Think of your sales forecast as an educated guess. Forecasting takes good working knowledge of your business, which is much more important than advanced degrees or complex mathematics. Whether you have business training or not, don't think you aren't qualified to forecast. If you can run a business, then you can forecast its sales. Most people can guess their own business' sales better than any expert device, statistical analysis, or mathematical routine. Experience counts more than any other factor.

Developing a Sales Forecast

If you've been following along with this book, you've been through some Internet sites and other information sources to know your customers and your industry. You've probably been thinking about your sales forecast while you went through that information. The research for a good forecast is almost always harder than the final process of actually making the detailed educated guesses. You've probably already done the research.

When the research is already done, the mechanics of sales forecasting are relatively simple. Break your sales down into manageable parts, and then forecast the parts. Guess your sales by line of sales, month by month, then add up the sales lines and add up the months. This first illustration shows you a simple sales forecast which estimates total value for each sales category.

VALUE-BASED SALES FORECAST

Sales Forecast	Jan	Dec	Year 1	Year 2
Sales				
Retainer Consulting	$10,000	$20,000	$200,000	$350,000
Project Consulting	$0	$15,000	$270,000	$325,000
Market Research	$0	$20,000	$122,000	$150,000
Strategic Reports	$0	$0	$0	$50,000
Total Sales	$10,000	$55,000	$592,000	$875,000
Direct Cost of Sales	Jan	Dec	Year 1	Year 2
Retainer Consulting	$2,500	$2,500	$30,000	$38,000
Project Consulting	$0	$2,500	$45,000	$56,000
Market Research	$0	$14,000	$84,000	$105,000
Strategic Reports	$0	$0	$0	$20,000
Subtotal Direct Cost of Sales	$2,500	$19,000	$159,000	$219,000

This example of a value-based sales forecast includes simple price and cost forecasts to calculate projected sales and direct cost of sales.

Forecasting is usually easier when you break your forecast down into components. As an example, consider a forecast that projects $1,000 in sales for the month, compared to one that projects 100 units at $10 each for the month. In the second case, when the forecast is price x units, as soon as you know the price is going up, you also know that the resulting sales should also increase. Thinking of the forecast in components is easier.

The illustration below shows the first part of a units-based sales forecast. It takes assumptions for sales in units, then the assumed average prices, and multiplies them to calculate sales dollar values.

UNITS-BASED SALES FORECAST

Sales Forecast	Jan	Dec	Year1	Year 2
Unit Sales				
Systems	85	275	2,255	2,500
Service	200	343	3,128	6,000
Software	150	490	3,980	5,000
Training	145	200	2,230	4,000
Other	160	200	2,122	2,500
Total Unit Sales	740	1,508	13,715	20,000
Unit Prices	Jan	Dec	Year 1	Year 2
Systems	$2,000.00	$1,984.50	$1,980.80	$1,984.50
Service	$75.00	$67.00	$68.54	$84.00
Software	$200.00	$207.00	$212.87	$195.00
Training	$37.00	$50.00	$46.54	$72.00
Other	$300.00	$300.00	$394.21	$300.00
Sales				
Systems	$170,000	$545,736	$4,466,708	$4,961,240
Service	$15,000	$22,981	$214,388	$504,000
Software	$30,000	$101,430	$847,220	$975,000
Training	$5,365	$10,000	$103,795	$288,000
Other	$48,000	$60,000	$836,520	$750,000
Total Sales	$268,365	$740,147	$6,468,631	$7,478,240

The sales forecast multiplies unit forecasts by per-unit prices to calculate projected sales.

Cost of Sales

Cost of sales, sometimes called Cost of Goods Sold (COGS) or direct costs, is traditionally the costs of materials and production of the goods a business sells. Cost of Sales or COGS belongs in accounting in the month in which the goods or services are actually sold, regardless of when they were purchased.

For a manufacturing company this is materials, labor, and factory overhead. For a retail shop it would be what it pays to buy the goods that it sells to its customers. For service businesses, that don't sell goods, the same concept is normally called "cost of sales," which shouldn't be confused with "sales and marketing expenses." The cost of sales in this case is directly analogous to cost of goods sold. For a consulting company, for example, the cost of sales would be the remuneration paid to the consultants plus costs of research, photocopying, and production of reports and presentations.

The illustration on the following page shows how a second part of the same forecast makes assumptions for unit costs and uses them, along with unit sales assumptions above, to calculate direct cost of sales.

UNITS-BASED COSTS OF SALES

Sales Forecast	Jan	Dec	Year 1	Year 2
Unit Sales				
Direct Unit Costs	Jan	Dec	Year 1	Year 2
Systems	$1,700.00	$1,700.00	$1,700.00	$1,686.82
Service	$30.00	$30.00	$30.00	$30.00
Software	$120.00	$120.00	$120.00	$120.00
Training	$11.10	$11.10	$11.10	$11.10
Other	$90.00	$90.00	$90.00	$90.00
Direct Cost of Sales				
Systems	$144,500	$467,500	$3,833,500	$4,217,050
Service	$6,000	$10,290	$93,840	$180,000
Software	$18,000	$58,800	$477,600	$600,000
Training	$1,610	$2,220	$24,753	$44,400
Other	$14,400	$18,000	$190,980	$225,000
Subtotal Direct Cost of Sales	$184,510	$556,810	$4,620,673	$5,266,450

The sales forecast multiplies unit forecasts by unit cost forecasts to calculate projected cost of sales.

This example shows two months of a forecast that actually includes 12 months and then annual projections for a two-year period. The first year column totals the sales of the first 12 months.

Graphics as Forecasting Tools

Business charts are an excellent tool for understanding and estimating numbers. Use them to evaluate the projected numbers. When you view your forecast on a business chart, does it look real? Does it make sense? It turns out that most humans sense the relative size of shapes better than they sense numbers, so we see a sales forecast differently when it shows up in a chart. Use the power of the computer to help you visualize your numbers.

For example, consider the monthly sales chart below. You can look at this chart and immediately see the ebbs and flows of sales during the year. Sales go up from January into April, then down from Spring into Summer, then up again beginning in September. When you look at a chart like that, you should ask yourself whether that pattern is correct. Is that the way your sales go?

MONTHLY SALES CHART

This chart shows planned sales for each month of the first 12 months of the plan.

The next chart shows a comparison of three years of annual sales. Here again you can sense the relative size of the numbers in the chart. If you knew the company involved, you'd be able to evaluate and discuss this sales forecast just by looking at the chart. Of course you'd probably want to know more detail about the assumptions behind the forecast, but you'd have a very good initial sense of the numbers.

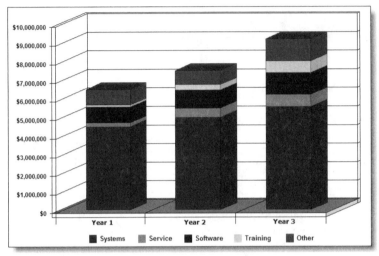

This chart shows planned sales for each of the years included in the plan.

Explain the Forecast

Although the charts and tables are great, you still need to explain them. A complete business plan should normally include some detailed text discussion of your sales forecast, sales strategy, sales programs, and related information. Ideally, you use the text, tables, and charts in your plan to provide some visual variety and ease of use. Put the tables and charts near the text covering the related topics.

In my standard business plan text outline, the discussion of sales goes into Chapter 5.0, Strategy and Implementation. You can change that to fit whichever logic and structure you use. In practical terms, you'll probably prepare these text topics as separate items, to be gathered into the plan as it is finished.

Sales Strategy

Somewhere near the sales forecast you should describe your sales strategy. Sales strategies deal with how and when to close sales prospects, how to compensate sales people, how to optimize order processing and database management, and how to maneuver price, delivery, and conditions.

- How do you sell?

- Do you sell through retail, wholesale, discount, mail order, phone order?

- Do you maintain a sales force?

- How are sales people trained, and how are they compensated?

Don't confuse sales strategy with your marketing strategy, which goes elsewhere. Sales should close the deals that marketing opens.

To help differentiate between marketing strategy and sales strategy, think of marketing as the broader effort of generating sales leads on a large scale, and sales as the efforts to bring those sales leads into the system as individual sales transactions. Marketing might affect image and awareness and propensity to buy, while sales involves getting the order.

Sales Programs

Details are critical to implementation. Use this topic to list the specific information related to sales programs in your milestones table, with the specific persons responsible, deadlines, and budgets. How is this strategy to be implemented and measured? Do you have concrete and specific plans?

Business plans are about results, and generating results depends in part on how specific you are in the plan. For anything related to sales that is supposed to happen, include it here and list the person responsible, dates required, and budgets. All of that will make your business plan more real.

Forecast Details

Your business plan text should summarize and highlight the numbers you have entered in the Sales Forecast table. Make sure you discuss important assumptions in enough detail, and that you explain the background sufficiently. Try to anticipate the questions your readers will ask. Include whatever information you think will be relevant, that your readers will need.

How Many Years?

I believe a business plan should normally project sales by month for the next 12 months, and annual sales for the following three years. This doesn't mean businesses shouldn't plan for a longer term than just three years. It does mean, however, that the detail of monthly forecasts doesn't pay off beyond a year, except in special cases. It also means that the detail in the yearly forecasts probably doesn't make sense beyond three years.

It does mean, of course, that you still plan your business for five, 10, and even 15-year timeframes; just don't do it within the detailed context of business plan financials.

Summary

A sales forecast is hard for many people because they are unsure of how to forecast. Don't worry; if you know your business, you can give an educated guess of future sales. Remember, one thing harder than forecasting is running a business without a forecast.

This page intentionally blank.

CHAPTER 12:

YOUR TARGET MARKET FORECAST

The market segmentation concept is crucial to market assessment and market strategy. Divide the market into workable market segments — age, income, product type, geography, buying patterns, customer needs, or other classifications. Define your terms, and define your market. And of course, markets change. Don't assume you know your market because you've been in business a few years. Take a step back for a fresh look.

Market Segmentation is Critical

Segmentation can make a huge difference in understanding your market. For example, when a local computer store defines its customer segments as "high-end home office" and "high-technology small business," its segmentation says a lot about its customers. The segmentation helps the company plan its focus on the different types of potential customers.

MARKET ANALYSIS PIE CHART

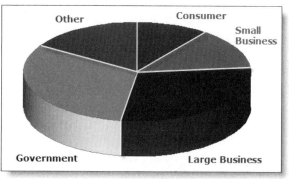

The pie chart shows the potential market and the relative sizes of different target market groups.

When I was consulting for Apple Computer in the middle 1980s, we divided the markets into workable categories, including home, education, small business, large business, and all others. Some other groups in Apple also focused on government as a specific market segment. As you define the segment you point toward an understanding of the market.

In the 1970s, I knew a company that was selling candy bars through retail channels. They segmented the market in a way that defined a range of products as "oral satisfacters" (their term, not mine) that included candy, cookies, soft drinks, and bagged chips. The segmentation helped the marketers understand their real competition, which wasn't just other candy bars, but also other products targeting the same customer money. That understanding improved the marketing and sales programs.

In today's business it's easy to see segmentation in action. Consider the different tone, content, and media for ads that sell products to kids, compared to those that sell the same product to parents. Car companies change their advertising substantially from one type of program to another. Stand-up comedian Robert Klein used to joke about the beer company ads that changed the style of the music to match the audience. He complained that he kept getting the country music version, but he liked the blues version better. The company that did those ads used the styles of music to address different target customer groups.

In developing segmentation, consider what factors make a difference in the purchasing, media, and value patterns of your target groups. Does age matter in choice of restaurants, or is style and food preference more important? Is income level a key factor? Education? I suspect some restaurants will sell more meals to college graduates than others. Is this because of education, age, or income levels? That depends on your business.

In your initial assessment you may have already developed your first basic Market Analysis worksheet for analyzing potential customers. It will help you define your market and understand your key market segments. As you complete your market analysis, look at your segmentation critically and strategically. Is this the best segmentation? Be sure to revise and polish your numbers.

The Market Analysis Table

As part of the business plan, you should generate enough information to develop a basic Market Analysis table. The illustration below gives you an example of a list of market segments, implemented as a spreadsheet table. Each segment is a group of customers that are classified according to the market segments you define.

MARKET ANALYSIS TABLE

H5		f_x =IF(C5<>0,(G5/C5)^(1/4)-1,0)						
	A	B	C	D	E	F	G	H
2	Market Analysis							
3			Year 1	Year 2	Year 3	Year 4	Year 5	
4	Potential Customers Growth							CAGR
5	Consumer	2%	12,000	12,240	12,485	12,735	12,990	2.00%
6	Small Business	5%	15,000	15,750	16,538	17,365	18,233	5.00%
7	Large Business	8%	33,000	35,640	38,491	41,570	44,896	8.00%
8	Government	-2%	36,000	35,280	34,574	33,883	33,205	-2.00%
9	Other	0%	19,000	19,000	19,000	19,000	19,000	0.00%
10	Total		2.78%	115,000	117,910	121,088	124,553	128,324	2.78%

This table shows a simple classification of market segments, each segment defined by its total potential customer count and its estimated growth rate.

To calculate compound average growth rate (CAGR), the standard formula is:

(last number/first number)^(1/periods)-1

You can see that formula at work in the illustration, in the formula shown in the edit bar of the spreadsheet, calculating the CAGR from the two numbers. Average growth in the Consumer segment during that period was 2%.

In the illustration you can see how the spreadsheet works. It is pointing to cell H5, and the formula in the edit bar is the formula in that cell. It identifies the last year in row-column notation as G5, and the first year as C5. The growth rate calculation produces the number showing in H5, 2%.

As you can probably guess, the formulas in the rest of this row take the growth rate assumption in column B and apply it to the other cells, after the initial value in column C. You add 1 to the growth rate and multiply it by the previous year to get the next year's calculated amount.

You can create a simple market analysis by estimating the number of potential customers for each segment and the growth rate, as shown in this example. Once you have those numbers, it should be a simple step to develop a corresponding chart, such as the pie chart shown on page 12.1.

Filling Out the Text

After you find out about your market for a business plan, you also want to communicate that knowledge to the readers of your plan. Keep your explanations clear and concise. The depth of detail in market analysis will depend a lot on the type of plan. You may not need to provide a complete market study in a plan developed for internal use, when all of your team knows the market well. Maybe you'll just cite the type of customers you attract, and the part of town you serve. The market analysis section in a business plan is the section that is most likely to require research for information from outside your business, while most others require thinking and analysis of factors within your business.

This is a good point to add a word of caution about the level of detail required. Please remember that planning is about making good decisions, applying focus and enforcing priorities. A useful business plan doesn't necessarily include a market analysis suitable for a Ph.D. candidate in market research. Planning is not about testing your knowledge. If you are looking for investment, then you may have to use this section to display your wisdom and understanding of your industry, but don't overdo it. If you are planning an internal plan and have no audience other than your own team, I recommend enough market research to make sure you're not missing key points.

The value of information is limited by its impact on decisions. If more market information is not going to help you do something better, then don't bother.

Explain your Segmentation

Make sure to explain and define the different segments in your table, particularly since you refer to them and they are the basis of your strategy. What distinguishes small business from large business, if this is part of your segmentation? Do you classify them by sales, number of employees, or some other factor? I've seen segmentations that define customers by the channels they buy in, as in the retail customer compared to the wholesale or direct customer, also compared to the Internet download customer. Have you defined which segment is which, and why?

As you deal with segmentation, you should also introduce the strategy behind it and your choice of target markets. Explain why your business is focusing on these specific target market groups. What makes these groups more interesting than the other groups that you've ruled out? Why are the characteristics you specify important? This is more important for some businesses than others. A clothing boutique, for example, might focus on one set of upper-income customers instead of another, for strategic reasons. An office equipment store might focus on certain business types with needs that match the firm's expertise. Some fast food restaurants focus on families with children under driving age. Strategy is focus; it is creative and it doesn't follow pre-written formulas.

Explain Market Needs, Growth, and Trends

All marketing should be based on underlying needs. For each market segment included in your strategy, explain the market needs that lead this group to buy your product or service. Did the need exist before the business was there? Are there other products or services or stores that offer different ways to satisfy this same need? Do you have market research related to this market need?

It is always a good idea to try to define your retail offering in terms of target market needs, so you focus not on what you have to sell, but rather on the buyer needs you satisfy. As a shoe store, for example, are you selling shoes or are you satisfying the customer needs for covered feet? Are there additional underlying needs, such as style and prestige for fashion footwear, or padding for runners, or jumping for basketball players, that relate to selling shoes? Are kids buying status with their basketball shoes?

Understand and explain market trends. What factors seem to be changing the market, or changing the business? What developing trends can make a difference? Market trends could be changes in demographics, changes in customer needs, a new sense of style or fashion, or something else. It depends on what business you are in.

For example, a building supply store might note the trend toward remodeling older homes instead of buying new homes, or a trend toward more rooms in larger houses, despite smaller families, because of home offices, dens, and exercise rooms.

A grocery store might note a trend toward Asian foods or spicier foods, or toward fresher, healthier foods, or development of a new shopping area in a different part of town.

A credit and investment counselor might note demographic trends, such as baby boomers aging, leading to a greater need for estate planning and retirement planning. Look to market trends as a way to get ahead of the market, to know where it is going before it gets there.

You should also understand and explain market growth in each segment. Ideally you cite experts: a market expert, market research firm, trade association, or credible journalist.

Section Overview

Your market section should begin with an overview describing the different groups of target customers in your market analysis and why you are selecting these as targets. You may also want to summarize market growth, citing highlights of some growth projections.

This paragraph might be included in a loan application or summary memo, so you need it to highlight the rest of the section. Select information as though you had only one brief topic to include about your market. Write the highlights into this topic after you have finished the rest of the section.

Summary

Projecting market growth is particularly important when your plan is related to finding investors or supporting a loan application, because market growth enhances the implied value of your business.

Cite growth rates in terms that fit the available information, whether growth in the number of potential customers, projected dollar sales, meals served, website projects, tax reporting hours, yards to landscape, or whatever you have.

Whenever you can, relate the growth rates cited in expert forecasts to the growth in potential customers that you included in the market analysis table.

Chapter 13:

EXPENSE BUDGET

Budgets are plans. They are spending plans, activity plans, sales plans, marketing plans, all linked to the disciplines of careful projection and resource allocation.

Simple Math, Simple Numbers

The expense budget is built on common sense and reasonable guesses, without statistical analysis, mathematical techniques, or any past data. The mathematics are simple; sums of the rows and columns.

In the example below, each line of expense occupies a row, and months and years occupy columns. The Total expense row sums the individual monthly expense columns. The annual expense column sums the months for each row, including the Total row.

SIMPLE EXPENSE BUDGET

	Jan	Feb	Nov	Dec	Year 1
Payroll	$12,000	$12,000	$27,250	$27,250	$194,750
Advertising	$13,500	$13,500	$13,500	$13,500	$162,000
Leases	$500	$500	$500	$500	$6,000
Utilities	$1,000	$1,000	$1,000	$1,000	$12,000
Insurance	$300	$300	$300	$300	$3,600
Rent	$1,500	$1,500	$1,500	$1,500	$18,000
Payroll Tax	$1,680	$1,680	$3,815	$3,815	$27,265
Other	$0	$100	$200	$300	$1,000
Total	$30,480	$30,580	$48,065	$48,165	$424,615

As you develop a budget, think of it as the part of your plan you can most easily control. Consider your plan objectives, your sales and marketing activities, and how you'll relate your spending to your strategy. Remember as you budget that you want to prioritize your spending to match your priorities in sales and target marketing. The emphasis in your strategy should show up in your actual detailed programs. That's your budget.

An expense budget can be as simple or complex as you wish. Greater detail in your plan will give you more information about, and more control over, how you spend your money.

Budgeting is About People More Than Numbers

While budget numbers are simple, budget management isn't. To make a budget work, you need to add real management:

1. **Understand that it's about people:** Successful budgeting depends on people management more than anything else. Every budgeted item must be "owned" by somebody, meaning that the owner has responsibility for spending, authority to spend, and the belief that the spending limit is realistic. People who don't believe in a budget won't try to implement it. People who don't believe that it matters won't worry about a budget either.

2. **Budget ownership is critical:** To "own" a budget item is to have the authority to spend, and the responsibility for that spending.

3. **Budgets need to be realistic:** Nobody really owns a budget item until they believe the budget amount is realistic. You can't really commit to a budget you don't believe in.

4. **It's also about following up:** Unless the people involved know that somebody will be tracking and following up, they won't honor a budget. Publishing budget plan vs. actual results will make a world of difference. Rewards for budget success and penalties for budget failures can be as simple as peer group managers sharing results.

The Budgeting Process

Here's a simple step-by-step way to increase the importance of budgeting and implementation within your business.

1. **Budget preliminary meeting:** Start your budgeting process with a preliminary meeting that brings your main managers together. Discuss strategy and priorities, realistic amounts, and the planning process. Distribute a simple template and ask each manager to prepare a proposed budget for his or her area. Ask the managers to create a proposal that includes monthly numbers, and descriptions of the programs and activities involved.

2. **Budget development:** Allow a period for managers to develop their budgets, working with the standard template. Enforce deadlines for preliminary proposal and revisions. Consolidate the proposed budgets into a single budget table that lists all of the proposed programs and activities. In most cases the total of all proposals will be 2-3 times the real amount your company can spend. Share that consolidated table with all managers. Share with them the difference between proposed budgets and actual spending limits, and ask them to think about it.

3. **Budget discussion:** Bring your managers back together to discuss the budget table. Ideally you set up a conference room with a projector and the consolidated proposed budget. Then you go through the budget, item by item, and pare it down to a realistic amount. Your managers will be together in a group, so they will have to defend different proposals, and as they do they will build up their personal commitments and their ownership of budget items and programs. They will explain why one program is more valuable than another, they will argue about relative value, and they will increase the level of peer-group commitment.

When this process works well, you have a more accurate, more realistic, and more useful budget. You also have a high level of commitment from your managers, who are now motivated to implement the budget as well as possible.

As you build your expense budget you are also creating your projected profit and loss. The profit and loss includes sales, cost of sales, and expenses. With the way business numbers work, your expense budget will eventually become part of your Profit and Loss table, which we discuss in *Chapter 15: The Bottom Line*. If you're using a personal computer with spreadsheet or business plan software, you should expect to see automatic linking so the expense budget is absorbed in the Profit and Loss tables. The illustration below shows a standard profit and loss, with the expense budget showing as the Expenses portion of the larger statement.

STANDARD PROFIT AND LOSS STATEMENT

	Jan	Feb	Mar
Sales	$70,000	$71,300	$72,600
Direct Cost of Sales	$15,000	$15,000	$15,000
Other	$1,000	$1,000	$1,000
Total Cost of Sales	$16,000	$16,000	$16,000
Gross Margin	$54,000	$55,300	$56,600
Gross Margin %	77.14%	77.56%	77.96%
Expenses			
Payroll	$29,750	$29,750	$29,750
Advertising	$14,000	$14,000	$14,000
Depreciation	$0	$0	$0
Leases	$500	$500	$500
Utilities	$1,100	$1,100	$1,100
Insurance	$300	$300	$300
Rent	$1,600	$1,600	$1,600
Payroll Tax	$4,500	$4,500	$4,500
Other	$0	$0	$0
Total Operating Expenses	$51,750	$51,750	$51,750
Interest Expenses	$617	$617	$617
Taxes Incurred	$408	$733	$1,058
Net Profit	$1,225	$2,200	$3,175

This example is a simple budget that doesn't divide expenses into categories. This is ideal for smaller businesses with only a few employees. By the time you have workgroups and a slightly larger business, however, you'll probably end up dividing expenses into categories such as sales and marketing expenses, administrative expenses, and other expenses. We will look at the Profit and Loss statement in more detail in *Chapter 15: The Bottom Line*.

Budgets and Milestones Work Together

Ideally, every line in a budget is assigned to somebody who is responsible for managing that budget. In most cases you'll have groups of budget areas assigned to specific people, and a budgeting process that emphasizes commitment and responsibility. You'll also need to make sure that everybody involved knows that results will be followed up. The ideal plan relates the budgets to the Milestones table, discussed in *Chapter 19: Make it Real*. The Milestones table takes all the important activities included in a business plan and assigns them to specific managers, with specific dates and budgets. It also tracks completion of the milestones and actual results compared to planned results.

THE MILESTONES TABLE

Milestones					
Milestone	**Start Date**	**End Date**	**Budget**	**Manager**	**Department**
Corporate Identity	28-Nov	14-Dec	$10,000	Tamzin J	Marketing
Seminar Implementation	29-Dec	7-Jan	$1,000	Irminsul R	Sales
Business Plan Review	30-Dec	8-Jan	$0	Reggie J	GM
Upgrade Mailer	30-Dec	14-Jan	$5,000	Irminsul R	Sales
New Corporate Brochure	30-Dec	14-Jan	$5,000	Tamzin J	Marketing
Delivery Vans	29-Dec	22-Jan	$12,500	Sepp D	Service
Direct Mail	30-Jan	14-Feb	$3,500	Isuldur R	Marketing
Advertising	30-Jan	14-Feb	$115,000	Reggie J	GM
X4 Prototype	29-Jan	22-Feb	$2,500	Geoffrey S	Product
Service Revamp	29-Jan	22-Feb	$2,500	Soren D	Product
6 Presentations	30-Jan	23-Feb	$0	Irminsul R	Sales
X4 Testing	27-Feb	4-Mar	$1,000	Geoffrey S	Product
3 Accounts	27-Feb	15-Mar	$0	SorenD	Sales
L30 Prototype	30-Mar	24-Mar	$2,500	Pamyla R	Product
Techo-Expo	30-Mar	10-Apr	$15,000	Todd B	Marketing
VP Sales & Marketing Hired	30-May	9-Jun	$1,000	Jemma K	Sales
Mailing System	29-Jun	23-Jul	$5,000	Sepp D	Service
Totals			**$181,500**		

These are the milestones, the heart and core of the business plan. Using the Milestones table will assign responsibility and authority to the expense budget plans.

Summary

Regardless of which budget style you choose, you make very important choices as you plan your profit and loss. This is where you plan your expenses. You are estimating expenditures across the business, from rent and overhead to marketing expenses such as advertising, sales commissions, and public relations. Decisions you make here are as important as the mathematics are simple. Your sum of expenses ultimately determines your company's profitability. This is the business plan equivalent to budgeting, as you set your sights on the levels of expenditures you expect your company will need.

CHAPTER 14:

ABOUT BUSINESS NUMBERS

A business plan depends on both words and numbers. You can't describe a business in words alone, and the numbers don't work without the words. In this chapter, we go through the basics of how the numbers come together.

Words and Numbers Make a Complete Plan

Allow me to tell a personal story about words and numbers, and why you need both to make a complete plan.

In 1974, I switched from general journalism, writing for United Press International from Mexico City, to business journalism, writing for Business International and McGraw-Hill World News. With the switch, I found myself covering business and economics instead of general news, writing for (among others) *Business Week* and *Business Latin America*. Because I thought it would be nice to have some idea what I was writing about, I went to the local graduate school at night for courses in general economics, accounting, finance, and marketing.

As I learned about macroeconomics, and how to read financial statements, I discovered that the truth in business is almost always a combination of words and numbers, and can't be explained with either one without the other. For example, when a Central American government announced a new federal budget that it said was going to both develop growth and reduce inflation, the numbers said that was a contradiction. You can't do both; you can do one or the other. You could only see that by dealing with both words and numbers.

A business plan is like that, too. You can't describe a plan without both text and tables, both words and numbers. The single most important analysis in a business plan is a cash flow plan, because cash is the most critical element in business. With the way the numbers work, however, you can't do a cash flow plan without looking at the income statement and balance sheet as well.

You really can't do the income statement without looking at sales, cost of sales, personnel expenses and other expenses, so you need those too. And you'd have trouble doing a sales forecast without understanding your market, so a market analysis is recommended.

And then you have the break-even as part of the initial assessment, and tables for business ratios, general assumptions, and other numbers. Step by step, the business plan becomes a collection of tables and charts around the text.

Although cash is critical, people think in terms of profits instead of cash. We all do. When you and your friends imagine a new business, you think of what it would cost to make the product, what you could sell it for, and what the profits per unit might be. We are trained to think of business as sales minus costs and expenses, which results in profits.

Unfortunately, we don't spend the profits in a business. We spend cash. Profitable companies go broke because they had all their money tied up in assets and couldn't pay their expenses. Working capital is critical to business health. Unfortunately, we don't see the cash implications as clearly as we should, which is one of the best reasons for proper business planning. We have to manage cash, as well as profits.

Know These Words

You don't have to be an accountant or an MBA to do a business plan, but you will be better off with a basic understanding of some essential financial terms. Otherwise, you're doomed to either having somebody else develop and explain your numbers, or having your numbers be incorrect. This is a good point to note the advantage of teams in business — if you have somebody on your team who knows fundamental financial estimating, then you don't have to.

It isn't that hard, and it's worth knowing. If you are going to plan your business, you will want to plan your numbers. So there are some terms to learn. I'm not going to get into formal business or legal definitions, and I will use examples:

- **Assets**: cash, accounts receivable, inventory, land, buildings, vehicles, furniture, and other things the company owns are assets. Assets can usually be sold to somebody else. One definition is anything with monetary value that a business owns.

- **Liabilities**: debts, notes payable, accounts payable, amounts of money owed to be paid back.

- **Capital** (also called equity): ownership, stock, investment, retained earnings. Actually there's an iron-clad and never-broken rule of accounting: Assets = Liabilities + Capital. That means you can subtract liabilities from assets to calculate capital.

- **Sales**: exchanging goods or services for money. Most people understand sales already. Technically, the sale happens when the goods or services are delivered, whether or not there is immediate payment.

- **Cost of Sales** (also called Cost of Goods Sold (COGS), Direct Costs, and Unit Costs): the raw materials and assembly costs, the cost of finished goods that are then resold, the direct cost of delivering the service. This is what the bookstore paid for the book you buy, it's the gasoline and maintenance costs of a taxi ride, it's the cost of printing and binding and royalties when a publisher sells a book to a store for resale.

- **Expenses** (usually called operating expenses): office rent, administrative and marketing and development payroll, telephone bills, Internet access, all those things a business pays for but doesn't resell. Taxes and interest are also expenses.

- **Profits** (also called Income): Sales minus cost of sales minus expenses.

Assets vs. Expenses

Many people can be confused by the accounting distinction between expenses and assets. For example, they would like to record research and development as assets instead of expenses, because those expenses create intellectual property. However, standard accounting and taxation law are both strict on the distinction:

- Expenses are deductible against income, so they reduce taxable income, but expenses cannot be depreciated, ever.

- Assets are not deductible against income, but assets whose value declines over time (usually long-term assets) can be depreciated.

Some people are also confused by the specific definition of start-up expenses, start-up assets, and start-up financing. They would prefer to have a broader, more generic definition that includes, say, expenses incurred during the first year, or the first few months, of the plan. Unfortunately, this would also lead to double counting of expenses and non-standard financial statements. All the expenses incurred during the first year have to appear in the Profit and Loss statement of the first year, and all expenses incurred before that have to appear as start-up expenses.

This treatment is the only way to correctly deal with the tax implications and the proper assigning of expenses to the time periods in which they belong. Tax authorities and accounting standards are clear on this.

What a company spends to acquire assets is not deductible against income. For example, money spent on inventory is not deductible as an expense at the point when you buy it. Only when the inventory is sold, and therefore becomes cost of goods sold or cost of sales, does it reduce income.

Why You do not Want to Capitalize Expenses

Sometimes people want to treat expenses as assets. Ironically, that is usually a bad idea, for several reasons:

- Money spent buying assets is not tax deductible. Money spent on expenses is deductible.

- Capitalizing expenses creates the danger of overstating assets.

- If you capitalize the expense, it appears on your books as an asset. Having useless assets on the accounting books is not a good thing.

Debits and Credits

You don't have to know debits and credits to do a business plan. As I say elsewhere, planning is not accounting. You don't need to be an MBA or CPA to develop business plan financials. You need to be able to make reasonable assumptions and follow the financials, preferably using Business Plan Pro® software.

Still, some simple understanding is useful, and easy. Debits and credits originally appeared as part of the double-entry bookkeeping system that supports the entire world of financial accounting, planning, and analysis.

It starts out with a simple accounting sheet, as you see here. You write the item in one column, the debit in another, and the credit in a third.

Item	Debit	Credit
Sales		$635.32
Cash	$635.32	

You'll notice that the single transaction has two entries, one of $635.32 for the sale and the other for the related $635.32 for the cash.

Here's another:

Item	Debit	Credit
Rent	$975.00	
Cash		$975.00

It can get a lot more complicated than that, but with these examples you can see the foundations of the system. Here are some built-in standards that might help.

- Every transaction has to have equal amounts for debits and credits. Accounting must always balance debits and credits. That's where the word "balance" comes from.

- The amount of a sale is normally a credit. A debit to sales is the same as a refund. It reduces sales.

- Costs and expenses are normally debits. You debit the expense account and credit the way it was paid (as in the checking balance or cash) or not paid (as in Accounts Payable).

- An increase in an asset is always a debit. An increase in a liability is always a credit.

- An increase in capital (for example, a new investment) is always a credit. A new investment is a credit to capital and a debit to the checking account.

Three Main Statements

Most financial analysis, including the financials in a standard business plan, revolves around three main statements. Two of them, the Income Statement and Balance Sheet, put to use the basic financial building blocks from the previous section. The third, the Cash Flow, brings the other two forward from accounting semi-fiction to the real world of actual money.

Pro Formas

Elsewhere in this book we discuss the huge difference between planning and accounting. With the three main financial statements, specifically, financial analysts use the term pro forma to describe projected statements, projections, and predictions. An Income Statement, for example, is about past results. A pro-forma Income Statement is a projected income statement.

The Income Statement

The Income Statement is also called Profit and Loss. People often refer to the bottom line as profits, the bottom line of the Income Statement. It has a very standard form. It shows Sales first, then Cost of Sales (or COGS, or Cost of Goods Sold, or Direct Costs, which are essentially the same thing). Then it subtracts Costs from Sales to calculate Gross Margin (which is defined as Sales less Cost of Sales). Then it shows Operating Expenses, usually (but not always) subtracting Operating Expenses from

Gross Margin to Show EBIT (Earnings Before Interest and Taxes). Then it subtracts Interest and Taxes to show Profit.

Sales – Cost of Sales (or COGS, Cost of Goods Sold, or Direct Costs) = Gross Margin

Gross margin – Expenses = Profits

Notice that the Income Statement involves only four of the seven fundamental financial terms we defined in a previous section of this chapter. While an Income Statement will have some influence on Assets, Liabilities, and Capital, it includes only Sales, Costs, Expenses, and Profit.

The Income Statement is about the flow of transactions over some specified period of time, like a month, a quarter, a year, or several years.

We discuss the Income Statement in detail in *Chapter 15: The Bottom Line*.

The Balance Sheet

The Balance Sheet shows a business' financial position, which includes Assets, Liabilities, and Capital, on a specified date. It will always show Assets on the left side or on the top, with Liabilities and Capital on the right side or the bottom.

Balance Sheets must always obey the underlying formula:

Assets = Liabilities + Capital

Unless that simple equation is true, the Balance doesn't balance and the numbers are not right. We discuss the Balance Sheet in detail in *Chapter 17: Finish the Financials* later in this book.

The Cash Flow

The Cash Flow statement is the most important and the least intuitive of the three. In mathematical and financial detail it reconciles the Income Statement with the Balance Sheet, but that detail is hard to see and follow. What is most important is tracking the money. By cash we mean liquidity, as in the balance in checking and related savings accounts, not strictly bills and coins. And tracking that cash is the most important thing a business plan does. The underlying truth is:

Ending Cash = Starting Cash + Money Received – Money Spent

What's particularly important in planning is that neither the Income Statement alone nor the Balance Sheet alone is sufficient to plan and manage cash. We discuss the Cash Flow in much greater detail in *Chapter 16: Cash is King*.

A Simple Example

One of the best ways to understand the dilemma of cash vs. profits is to follow an otherwise-profitable company going broke because it can't meet its obligations. This is a quick and simple example. It also leads us into the relationship between income statement, balance sheet, and cash.

Start with $100, which we'll call capital. At the beginning of this exercise, your balance sheet has assets of $100 — the money — and capital of $100. Assets are equal to capital plus liabilities. A summary of the simple financial statement at this point is shown in this first illustration, Case Starting Point.

SIMPLE CASE STARTING POINT

	Income			Balance
Sales	$0	Assets		
Cost of Sales	$0		Bank Balance	$100
Profit	$0	Total		$100
		Liabilities		
		Capital		
			Paid-In	$100
			Earnings	
		Total		$100

The simple financials show a hypothetical widgets business as it starts.

If you buy a widget for $100 and sell it for $150, you should end up with $50 profit, which is what your income statement covers. Sales minus costs are profit. You should have $150 in the bank. Now your balance sheet shows the same $100 in original capital plus $50 in earnings, which are equal to the $150 you have in cash as an asset. The next illustration shows you how the financials look right after that sale.

Buy another widget for $100 and sell it again for $150, and now you have $200 in the bank. Do it again, you have $250 in the bank. Your income statement shows sales of $450, cost of sales of $300, and profit of $150. At this point your business has sold three units and made $150 profit. In theory it has $250 in the bank.

ONE WIDGET SOLD

	Income			Balance
Sales	$150	Assets		
Cost of Sales	$100		Bank Balance	$150
Profit	$50	Total		$150
		Liabilities		
		Capital		
			Paid-In	$100
			Earnings	$50
		Total		$150

This table shows the financials after the first sale.

NOW WITH THREE WIDGETS SOLD

	Income			Balance
Sales	$450	Assets		
Cost of Sales	$300		Bank Balance	$250
Profit	$150	Total		$250
		Liabilities		
		Capital		
			Paid-In	$100
			Earnings	$150
		Total		$250

Now the company has sold three widgets and made a profit.

Adding Some Realism

Now go back a step and make the situation more realistic. For example, most sales of products to businesses are on terms, with the money generally due in 30 days. So if you sold that widget on credit you don't have $150 in the bank. You still have $50 in your bottom line, but now you have nothing in the bank. Instead, a customer owes you $150, which is what we call "Accounts Receivable."

Compare the One Widget Sold illustration to the Selling on Credit illustration on the next page. This is what really happens to the huge number of businesses that sell to other businesses.

Knowing you can buy a widget for $100 and sell it for $150, you get your widget supplier to sell to you on the same terms you sell, net 30, instead of for cash. Now you have $100 that you owe to suppliers, which is called "Accounts Payable." You also have $100 worth of widgets in inventory.

This gives you the case in the following illustration, Buying on Credit, in which you are now poised to sell another widget and make more profit.

You have an extra $100 in assets (the widget in inventory) and an extra $100 as liabilities (Accounts Payable), so you are still in balance. Also, you still have no money.

SELLING ON CREDIT

	Income			Balance
Sales	$150	Assets		
Cost of Sales	$100		Bank Balance	$0
Profit	$50		Accounts Receivable	$150
		Total		$150
		Liabilities		
		Capital		
			Paid-In	$100
			Earnings	$50
		Total		$150

Sales and profits are the same, but now there's no money.

BUYING ON CREDIT

	Income			Balance
Sales	$150	Assets		
Cost of Sales	$100		Bank Balance	$0
Profit	$50		Accounts Receivable	$150
			Inventory	$100
		Total		$250
		Liabilities		
			Accounts Payable	$100
			Total liabilities	$100
		Capital		
			Paid-In	$100
			Earnings	$50
		Total		$250

Business looked good, so you borrowed the money to buy another widget and continue.

The Buying On Credit illustration shows the financial picture with sales to businesses on credit and purchase of inventory on credit as a short-term debt.

Now the case is more like what you have with real business numbers, in which you have to manage your cash very carefully, and the amounts sitting in inventory and accounts receivable are significant.

NUMBERS MOUNT UP

	Income			Balance
Sales	$450	Assets		
Cost of Sales	$300		Bank Balance	$0
Profit	$150		Accounts Receivable	$450
			Inventory	$100
		Total		$550
		Liabilities		
			Accounts Payable	$100
			Short-term debt	$200
			Total liabilities	$300
		Capital		
			Paid-In	$100
			Earnings	$150
		Total		$550

You have the same sales and profits as in the earlier Three Widgets Sold example, but the balance sheet is more complex.

WORKING CAPITAL

	Income			Balance
Sales	$450	Assets		
Cost of Sales	$300		Bank Balance	$300
Profit	$150		Accounts Receivable	$450
			Inventory	$100
		Total		$850
		Liabilities		
			Accounts Payable	$100
			Short-term debt	$200
			Total liabilities	$300
		Capital		
			Paid-In	$400
			Earnings	$150
		Total		$850

In this illustration the business has enough working capital to survive the unexpected.

More Realism: Working Capital

Even in the case of the Numbers Mount Up illustration above, the example is completely unrealistic.

- Where are the running expenses, such as rent, salaries, telephones, or even advertising those widgets?

- How would they affect the cash situation?

- How far would we get if we couldn't pay the rent or the telephone bill while waiting for customers to pay us?

- Furthermore, what supplier would give us a widget on credit when we have no history and no assets?

- What bank would loan us money in this situation? Banks do loan against inventory and receivables, but only to a certain percentage of total value.

What was missing here, all along, was working capital.

> **Important:** *In strict accounting terms, working capital is equal to short-term assets minus short-term liabilities. In real terms, however, working capital is the glue that holds your cash flow together. Get it into the bank before you need it, or you won't survive the unexpected.*

The Working Capital illustration on the previous page goes back to the beginning of this whole example and does it right, with enough capital in the beginning to finance the company.

Instead of starting with $100 as capital, this business looks a lot better with starting capital of $400. With this additional capital from the start, buying on credit and borrowing against assets is more realistic. In this scenario, working capital is up to $550. Now it has a proper input of working capital at the beginning. With even the barest of business plans, we could tell that $100 wasn't enough to get this business going.

As you can see from the examples, the numbers in a normal business analysis and in a business plan are interrelated. In previous chapters we did the sales forecast and personnel plan, which then reappeared in the income statement, also called the profit and loss. You can see from the examples how the income statement links to the balance sheet. We'll go into cash flow and balance in following chapters, but the point here is that the assumptions and estimates in the standard business plan tables link up to each other in a complex system of relationships. You can see how these relationships work in the following illustrations.

A More Realistic Case

Now let's look at the implications in a real case. The real case is a computer reseller (that is, a retail computer store) in a medium-sized local market, with sales of about $6 million per year. The charts and underlying financial analysis are taken from the sample plan for American Management Technologies (AMT) included with Business Plan Pro®, and posted on our sample plan website www.Bplans.com.

The first chart, in this next illustration, shows a representative sample business plan cash flow for 12 months, given standard assumptions for sales, costs, expenses, profits, and cash management. The sample company is profitable and growing. It sells about $6 million annually, produces about eight percent net profit on sales, and is self supporting. The chart shows a 12-month projection of AMT cash resources.

AS THE CASH CASE STARTS

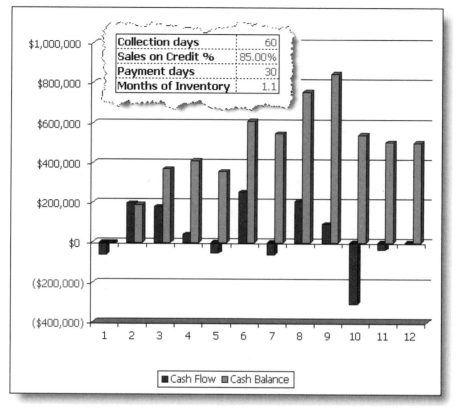

Collection days	60
Sales on Credit %	85.00%
Payment days	30
Months of Inventory	1.1

With the first take of the cash case, the business looks good and the cash plan is acceptable.

The light gray (or green if you are viewing this in pdf or online) colored bars represent the checkbook balance at the end of each month, and the dark bars (red) represent the cash flow, which is how much the balance changes in a month. The first set of bars should never drop below zero, because if your checkbook balance is less than zero, then you are bouncing checks. The mathematics don't care, but the banks do. Cash flow simply tells us how much cash is coming into or flowing out of the business over a particular period. The cash flow bars, on the other hand, can drop below zero without major problems, as long as the balance stays above zero. For example, in this case the company's projected cash flow is negative in January, May, July, October and November. The light gray bar stays positive, but the dark one is negative.

In the illustration on the next page, only one assumption has changed: that same company now waits an extra month, on average, to receive money from customers on invoices presented. The average wait, which is called "collection days," goes from 60 days to 90 days. The impact on the company's cash position at the end of the year is about half a million dollars, from about $400,000 positive (in the Cash Case Starts illustration) to more than $150,000 negative in this second chart. **Nothing else changes — no new employees, no change in costs, no additional expenses.** By the way, accountants call money owed by customers "Accounts Receivable."

CHANGING COLLECTION DAYS ONLY

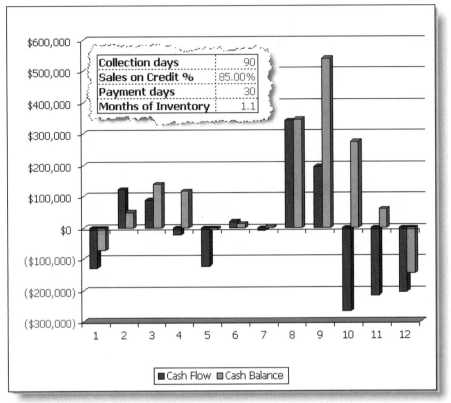

Collection days	90
Sales on Credit %	85.00%
Payment days	30
Months of Inventory	1.1

A single change, from 60 to 90 days, makes a half-million-dollar difference in the cash flow.

Notice here the critical importance of cash, and the critical difference between cash and profits. With this single change in assumptions, the company is still as profitable as it was, down to the last dollar. Now, however, the company needs at least $200,000 in additional financing.

This is new money needed; new investment or new borrowing. The problem can't be solved by reducing expenses or increasing sales.

Companies go out of business for problems like these. Even otherwise-healthy companies can go out of business for lack of cash. The projection shows how this kind of cash crisis can kill a company if it sneaks up by surprise, but can be easily managed when there is a plan for it. This is an eloquent argument for good business planning.

In the third case, shown in the following illustration, we set the collection days back to the original assumption of 60 days, but change the assumption for inventory. Where previously it kept an average of about five weeks' worth of inventory on hand, in this changed assumption it now keeps two months of inventory on hand. Accountants call this Inventory Turnover. The changed assumption creates about as large a cash flow problem as the extra month of collection days.

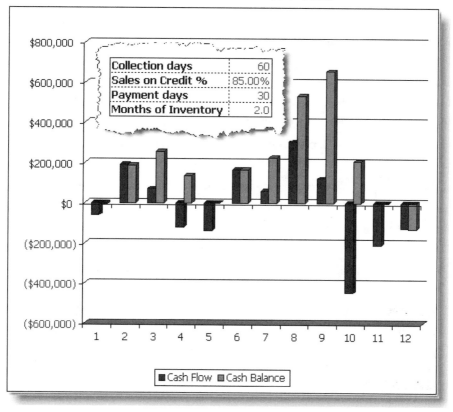

CHANGING INVENTORY ONLY

Collection days	60
Sales on Credit %	85.00%
Payment days	30
Months of Inventory	2.0

The change in inventory assumption shows the cash balance is again well below zero.

The implications of this chart are massive. This is still a profitable company, but it has a critical financial problem. You see how the cash balance bar falls to zero in November, and almost $200,000 below zero in December. That means that this company needs new money, new loans or new capital investment, to make up its cash deficit, even though it is still profitable. This is hard to swallow until you see it happen in real business, but it is the truth and it will happen.

Linking the Numbers

As the chart suggests and the previous examples show, there is a logical link between the business numbers in a standard analysis.

- Your sales forecast should show sales and cost of sales. The same numbers in the sales forecast are the ones you use in the profit and loss.

- As with sales, you should normally have a separate personnel table, but the numbers showing in that table should be the same numbers that show up for personnel costs in your profit and loss table.

- Your profit and loss table should show the same numbers as sales and personnel plan tables in the proper areas. It should also show interest expenses as a logical reflection of interest rates and balances of debt.

- Your cash flow has to reflect your profit and loss, plus changes in balance sheet items and non-cash expenses such as depreciation, which are on the profit and loss. The changes in the balance sheet are critical. For example, when you borrow money, it doesn't affect the profit or loss (except for interest expenses later on), but it makes a huge difference to your checking account balance.

- The balance sheet has to reflect the profit and loss and the cash flow.

- Your business ratios should calculate automatically, based on the numbers in sales, profit and loss, personnel, cash flow, and balance sheet.

LOGIC OF BUSINESS STATEMENTS

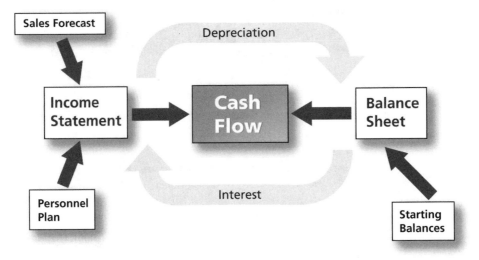

The business plan tables and charts should be linked together to reflect the practical realities of business numbers.

Summary

Use the charts together with the tables to illustrate and enhance your analysis. For example, keeping the Cash Flow chart visible while changing assumptions gives you an instant picture of whether or not you have exceeded available cash resources as you plan your operations.

CHAPTER 15:

THE BOTTOM LINE

The familiar phrase "the bottom line," often used synonymously with the conclusion or the underlying truth, is actually taken from the standard Income Statement in accounting, which subtracts costs and expenses from sales and shows profits as the bottom line of the statement.

The Profit and Loss Statement

The Income Statement is the same as the Profit and Loss statement. You'll also find them called "pro forma," meaning projected, as in "pro forma income" or "pro forma profit and loss." The pro forma income is the same as a standard income statement, except that the standard statement shows real results from the past, while a pro forma statement is projecting the future.

Now that you have projected sales and cost of sales (discussed in *Chapter 11: Forecast Your Sales*), personnel expenses (*Chapter 8: Management Team*), and your operating expenses estimates (*Chapter 13: Expense Budget*) it is time to compare your expenses to your sales.

The following illustration shows a simple income statement. This example doesn't divide operating expenses into categories. The format and math starts with sales at the top.

STANDARD PROFIT AND LOSS STATEMENT

	Jan	Feb	Mar
Sales	$70,000	$71,300	$72,600
Direct Cost of Sales	$15,000	$15,000	$15,000
Other	$1,000	$1,000	$1,000
Total Cost of Sales	$16,000	$16,000	$16,000
Gross Margin	$54,000	$55,300	$56,600
Gross Margin %	77.14%	77.56%	77.96%
Expenses			
Payroll	$29,750	$29,750	$29,750
Advertising	$14,000	$14,000	$14,000
Depreciation	$0	$0	$0
Leases	$500	$500	$500
Utilities	$1,100	$1,100	$1,100
Insurance	$300	$300	$300
Rent	$1,600	$1,600	$1,600
Payroll Tax	$4,500	$4,500	$4,500
Other	$0	$0	$0
Total Operating Expenses	$51,750	$51,750	$51,750
Interest Expenses	$617	$617	$617
Taxes Incurred	$408	$733	$1,058
Net Profit	$1,225	$2,200	$3,175

This is a partial graphic, showing only three months of a 12-month table.

First, subtract cost of sales from sales. This gives you gross margin, an important ratio for comparisons and analysis. Acceptable gross margin levels depend on the industry. According to the 2005 Industry Profile Analysis from *Integra Information*, www.integrainfo.com, an average shoe store has a gross margin of 47 percent. A hat manufacturer has a gross margin of 37 percent, and a grocery store about 18 percent. Then subtract expenses to calculate profits or losses.

Costs, COGS, Direct Costs, Gross Margin

Although we discussed cost of sales or COGS in *Chapter 14: Forecast Your Sales*, you should know that it is important to Gross Margin. In standard accounting, the cost of sales or cost of goods sold are subtracted from sales to calculate gross margin. These costs are distinguished from operating expenses, because gross profit is gross margin less operating expenses. Costs are not expenses.

The division between costs and expenses doesn't change profits. Some very simple bookkeeping systems ignore the distinction altogether. Whether you call it a direct cost or operating expenses, the amount still reduces income. A few service businesses have either tiny direct costs or even no specific costs of sales, which creates a Gross Margin of 100%. For example, a business consultant, attorney, or tax accountant might easily have no specific cost of sales for an engagement, because the deliverable is expertise. Even in these cases, however, there probably is a small cost of sales, such as photocopying expenses or paper or burned CDs. Because computers have difficulty with dividing by zero, you might be better off to estimate Gross Margin at 99% instead of 100%.

A good calculation of Gross Margin depends on properly dividing costs and expenses, and a good calculation of Gross Margin will help you compare your business to others like it. Industry databases including the ones included with Business Plan Pro® track gross margin by type of business. This is always useful to provide at least a rough idea of what things generally cost, and how much things are marked up. For example, retail sporting goods stores make a Gross Margin around 33%, which means that what they buy for about $100 they sell for about $150.

Timing of costs is very important. A bookstore's costs for a book it sells goes into accounting as COGS when the book is sold, not when the bookstore buys it. For example, if a book purchased in October sells in March, the COGS applies to March sales. Remember that you can't calculate the correct Gross Margin unless you correctly apply the direct costs for what you sold in a given period without regard to timing of acquisition or payment.

Unit projections can help calculate both sales and costs.

Expenses

Expenses start with personnel, shown as Payroll. Then you have rent, utilities, equipment, payroll taxes, and probably some advertising, maybe commissions, public relations, and other expenses.

What we're leading to is profits. Profits are what is left over after you start with sales, then subtract cost of sales, expenses, and taxes.

An example of a more detailed Profit and Loss is shown in the illustration below. This example divides operating expenses into categories, including Sales and Marketing expenses and General and Administrative expenses. It provides a breakdown of the business expenses and what they stand for.

DETAILED PROFIT AND LOSS STATEMENT

Pro Forma Profit and Loss	Jan	Feb	Mar	Year 1	Year 2
Sales	$268,365	$342,025	$415,635	$6,468,631	$7,478,240
Direct Costs of Goods	$184,510	$243,061	$301,612	$4,620,673	$5,266,450
Fulfillment Payroll	$9,500	$9,500	$9,500	$139,000	$202,500
Other	$500	$500	$500	$6,000	$6,000
Cost of Goods Sold	$194,510	$253,061	$311,612	$4,765,673	$5,474,950
Gross Margin	$73,856	$88,965	$104,024	$1,702,958	$2,003,290
Gross Margin %	27.52%	26.01%	25.03%	26.33%	26.79%
Operating Expenses					
Sales and Marketing Expenses					
Sales and Marketing Payroll	$24,000	$24,000	$24,000	$344,000	$422,000
Ads	$5,000	$5,000	$7,000	$125,000	$140,000
Catalog	$2,000	$3,000	$2,000	$25,000	$19,039
Mailing	$3,000	$11,800	$5,500	$113,300	$120,000
Promo	$0	$0	$0	$16,000	$20,000
Shows	$0	$0	$0	$20,200	$25,000
Literature	$0	$7,000	$0	$7,000	$10,000
PR	$0	$0	$0	$1,000	$1,250
Seminar	$1,000	$0	$0	$31,000	$45,000
Service	$2,000	$1,000	$1,000	$10,250	$12,000
Training	$450	$450	$450	$5,400	$7,000
Total Sales and Marketing Expenses	$37,450	$52,250	$39,950	$698,150	$821,289
Sales and Marketing %	13.95%	15.28%	9.61%	10.79%	10.98%
General and Administrative Expenses					
General and Administrative Payroll	$10,000	$10,000	$10,000	$155,000	$179,000
Depreciation	$1,000	$1,010	$1,020	$12,681	$13,315
Leased Equipment	$2,500	$2,500	$2,500	$30,000	$31,500
Utilities	$750	$750	$750	$9,000	$9,450
Insurance	$500	$500	$500	$6,000	$6,300
Rent	$7,000	$7,000	$7,000	$84,000	$88,200
Other	$500	$505	$510	$6,331	$6,648
Payroll Taxes	$7,440	$7,440	$7,440	$107,840	$139,760
Total General and Administrative Expenses	$29,690	$29,705	$29,720	$410,852	$474,173
General and Administrative %	11.06%	8.69%	7.15%	6.35%	6.34%
Other Expenses:					
Other Payroll	$3,000	$3,000	$3,000	$36,000	$70,000
Contract/Consultants	$125	$125	$125	$1,500	$5,000
Total Other Expenses	$3,125	$3,125	$3,125	$37,500	$75,000
Other %	1.16%	0.91%	0.75%	0.58%	1.00%
Total Operating Expenses	$70,265	$85,080	$72,795	$1,146,502	$1,370,462
Profit Before Interest and Taxes	$3,591	$3,885	$31,229	$556,456	$632,828
EBITDA	$4,591	$4,895	$32,249	$569,137	$646,143
Interest Expense	$2,597	$2,576	$2,663	$38,562	$71,870
Taxes Incurred	$298	$262	$5,713	$103,678	$112,192
Net Profit	$695	$1,047	$22,852	$414,216	$448,767

This illustration shows the more detailed profit and loss statement that divides operating expenses into categories. This is a partial graphic, showing three months of a 12-month table, plus two years of annual data.

Regardless of which statement style you choose, you make very important choices as you plan your profit and loss. This is where you estimate expenditures across the business, from rent and overhead to advertising, sales commissions, and public relations. Decisions you make here are as important as the mathematics are simple. Your sum of expenses ultimately determines your company's profitability. This is the business plan equivalent to budgeting, as you set your sights on the levels of expenditures you expect your company will need.

Summary

Your profit and loss statement is where you budget and forecast your expenses. You also absorb the more important numbers of your sales forecast and personnel plan, to create a planned bottom line for profit. This is educated guessing. Keep it on a computer so you can revise often as the business changes.

CHAPTER 16:

CASH IS KING

———————◇━◆━◇———————

As we looked at business numbers in the previous two chapters, we focused on the critical difference between cash and profits. This chapter looks at how to plan for cash in a business plan, understanding the critical elements that affect cash flow. You don't want to be one of those businesses that goes broke even while producing profits.

Direct Cash Flow Technique

Let's start again with a simple example. Compared to the examples in the previous chapter, *Chapter 15: The Bottom Line*, this first illustration looks at the business from a completely different point of view; money coming in and money flowing out. Sales and profits are out of the picture (although sales influences money in, and costs and expenses influence money out).

BASIC CASH PLAN

Cash Flow				
Money Received	Start	Month 1	Month 2	Month 3
Cash Sales	$0	$0	$0	$0
Payments Received	$0	$0	$75	$188
New Loans	$200	$0	$0	$0
New Investment	$300	$0	$0	$0
Total Received	$500	$0	$75	$188
Money Spent				
Cash Spending	$0	$0	$25	$50
Bill Payment	$0	$0	$300	$250
Repay Loans	$0	$0	$0	$0
Purchase Assets	$0	$0	$0	$0
Total Spent	$0	$0	$325	$300
Cash Flow	$500	$0	($250)	($113)
Cash Balance	$500	$500	$250	$138

This sample shows examples of incoming cash and expenditures for our sample company.

In this very simple model, your sources of money are cash sales, payments received (for sales on credit, also called accounts receivable), new loan money, and new investment. Your expenditures include buying widgets in cash, paying interest, paying bills as they come due (i.e., paying accounts payable), and paying off loans.

Even at this basic level, you can see the potential complications and the need for linking up the numbers using a computer. Your estimated receipts from accounts receivable must have a logical relationship to sales and the balance of accounts receivable. Likewise, your payments of accounts payable have to relate to the balances of payables and the costs and expenses that created the payables. Vital as this is to business survival, it is not nearly as intuitive as the sales forecast, personnel plan, or income statement. The mathematics and the financials are more complex.

A More Realistic Example

The cash plan can get complicated quickly when you deal with a more realistic business example. In the following illustrations, we're going to look at the cash planning for the company whose cash balances were described in *Chapter 14: About Business Numbers.* This was the company whose cash flow varied widely, depending on cash assumptions.

Beginning Assumptions

With the next illustrations we set the starting points, which are the projected income and the starting balances. We see a simple example of business income, which we'll use as a first step for planning cash. The example already divides sales between cash sales and sales on credit. We also have a simplified version of wages and operating expenses so that we can focus on the cash plan instead of the income statement.

SAMPLE CASE STARTING INCOME STATEMENT

Income Statement	Jan	Feb	Mar	Apr
Sales				
Cash Sales	$40	$51	$62	$106
Sales on Credit	$228	$291	$354	$596
Total Sales	**$268**	**$342**	**$416**	**$702**
Direct Cost of Sales	$183	$242	$301	$392
Personnel in Cost of Sales	$10	$10	$10	$10
Other Cost of Sales	$1	$1	$1	$1
Total Cost of Sales	**$194**	**$253**	**$312**	**$402**
Gross Margin	**$74**	**$89**	**$104**	**$300**
Operating Expenses				
Wages and Salaries	$37	$37	$37	$37
Depreciation	$1	$1	$1	$1
Other Operating Expenses	$32	$47	$35	$48
EBIT	**$4**	**$4**	**$31**	**$214**
Interest	$3	$3	$3	$3
Taxes	$0	$0	$5	$43
Net	**$1**	**$1**	**$23**	**$168**

SAMPLE CASE STARTING BALANCE

Balance Sheet	
Current Assets	
Cash	$55
Accounts Receivable	$395
Inventory	$805
Other Current Assets	$25
Total Current Assets	**$1,280**
Long-term Assets	$350
Accumulated Depreciation	$50
Total Long-term Assets	**$300**
Total Assets	**$1,580**
Liabilities and Capital	
Current Liabilities	
Accounts Payable	$224
Current Borrowing	$90
Other Current Liabilities	$15
Subtotal Current Liabilities	**$329**
Long-term Liabilities	$285
Total Liabilities	**$614**
Paid-in Capital	$500
Retained Earnings	$418
Earnings	$49
Total Capital	**$967**
Total Liabilities and Capital	**$1,581**
Net Worth	**$967**

In these two projected statements, Income (above), and Balance (right), we set the starting points for a detailed cash example taken from the sample company used as a case in the previous two chapters. In both cases the numbers are shown in thousands, and may be affected by rounding. You can compare this simplified Income to the Detailed Profit and Loss example in the previous chapter.

Cash Flow Breakdown

In the following sections, I will explain the Cash Flow table (also called pro forma Cash Flow), row by row, and how the numbers in your Cash Flow have a direct impact on the Balance Sheet, to help you better understand the direct relationship of one table to another, and how changes in one table directly affect the other. For the purpose of discussion, I divided a standard Cash Flow table into separate sections, Cash Received and Expenditures.

Cash Received

The following illustration lists possible cash sources for our sample company. Most of these have balance sheet impact, and several come from the income statement. For now, we'll focus just on the cash flow. After dealing with cash, before we go on to the balance in *Chapter 17: Finish the Financials*, we'll also look briefly at the specific cash flow implications on the balance sheet.

SAMPLE CASE CASH RECEIVED

Cash Flow			
Cash Received	Jan	Feb	Mar
Cash from Operations			
Cash Sales	$40	$51	$62
Cash from Receivables	$198	$205	$230
Subtotal Cash from Operations	$238	$256	$292
Additional Cash Received			
Non Operating (Other) Income	$0	$0	$0
Sales Tax, VAT, HST/GST Received	$0	$0	$0
New Current Borrowing	$0	$0	$0
New Other Liabilities	$0	$0	$0
New Long-term Liabilities	$0	$0	$100
Sales of Other Current Assets	$0	$0	$0
Sales of Long-term Assets	$0	$0	$0
New Investment Received	$0	$25	$0
Subtotal Cash Received	$238	$281	$392

In this section of the Cash Flow table, we list money received, such as cash sales and monies received from accounts receivable. (Amounts shown in thousands. Numbers may be affected by rounding.)

1. The first row, "Cash Sales," is a simple estimate. It should link with your sales forecast and income statement to avoid inconsistencies. Normally, credit card sales are grouped into cash sales because the business gets the money in a day or two. Cash in this case means cash, check, and credit card, everything except the real sales on credit, in which the product or service changes hands in advance of the payment.

2. The second row, "Cash from Receivables," is an estimate of the dollar amount received from customers as payments of accounts receivable. This is critical to your cash flow. Estimating money from receivables is vital. You should estimate receivables using assumptions nimble enough to offer a useful estimate, but simple enough to manage. For example, in the sample case illustration here, we use estimated collection days to calculate amounts received as a manner of estimating the time that passed between making the sale and receiving the payment.

SAMPLE CASE RECEIVABLES DETAIL

Receivables Detail			
	Mar	Apr	May
Estimated Collection Period in Days	60	60	60
Sales on Credit %	85.00%	85.00%	85.00%
Receivables			
Beginning Receivables Balance	$511	$636	$942
Plus Sales on Credit	$353	$596	$547
Less Cash from Receivables	$228	$291	$353
Ending Receivables Balance	$636	$942	$1,136

The collection days estimator sets the amounts received. (Amounts shown in thousands. Numbers may be affected by rounding.)

The calculation in the Receivables Detail example on the previous page is relatively simple. You can see how each month starts with beginning balance, adds new sales on credit, subtracts money received, and then calculates ending balance. Notice that the amounts received in March are the same as the sales on credit for January (shown in the Starting Income Statement illustration on page 16.2) because the collection days estimator is set to 60 days.

To emphasize the importance of collection days as an estimator, look at the following example with the same logic, but set to 90 days instead of 60 days. In this case sales on credit from January are received a month later, in April:

IMPORTANCE OF COLLECTIONS

Receivables Detail			
	Mar	Apr	May
Estimated Collection Period in Days	90	90	90
Sales on Credit %	85.00%	85.00%	85.00%
Receivables			
Beginning Receivables Balance	$651	$865	$1,233
Plus Sales on Credit	$353	$596	$547
Less Cash from Receivables	$139	$228	$291
Ending Receivables Balance	$865	$1,233	$1,489

In this second view, when collection days are stretched, less cash comes in from receivables. The difference affects cash flow. (Amounts shown in thousands. Numbers may be affected by rounding.)

This simple change turns acceptable cash flow into cash problems (see the discussion on Collection Days in *Chapter 14: About Business Numbers*).

Now take a look back at the illustration on page 16.3 (**Sample Case Cash Received**). The first two rows in the cash received section are directly related to standard operations. Cash Sales plus Cash from Receivables (sales on credit) equals total Cash from Operations (also known as Total Sales). The following rows are less direct and less readily available from simple assumptions. So we set these aside as "Additional Cash Received."

3. The third row, "Non Operating (Other) Income," gives you a place to show money received from special operations, such as interest income in a company whose main business isn't making interest. A lot of businesses won't use this one.

4. The next row shows money received from charging customers sales-related and value-added (VAT) taxes that really belong to the government, and must be paid later. These taxes aren't normally part of a sales forecast, so they don't affect the Income statement, but they do affect cash flow.

5. The next three rows are where you estimate amounts of money coming into the company as new borrowed money. The difference between each of the three is a matter of type of borrowing and terms.

   • The row named "New Current Borrowing" (also called short-term debt) is for money you get by borrowing through normal lending institutions, as standard loans, with interest payments.

   • The row named "New Other Liabilities" is for items like accrued taxes and accrued salaries and wages, money owed that will have to be paid, but isn't formally borrowed. Normally there are no interest expenses associated with this row.

- The row named "New Long-term Liabilities" is for new money borrowed on longer terms. This type of borrowing usually requires interest payments.

6. The sixth and seventh additional cash rows are "Sales of Other Current Assets" and "Sales of Long-term Assets." Selling short-term or long-term assets is another possible way to generate cash.

7. The last row in cash received, "New Investment Received," is for new money coming into the company as investment.

The result of this section is the sum of cash received. These are amounts received from normal operations (cash sales and cash from receivables), and additional amounts from assumptions outside the normal operations. Now let's look at spending, the other side of the cash equation.

Estimating Expenditures

SAMPLE CASE CASH SPENT

Cash Flow			
Expenditures	Jan	Feb	Mar
Expenditures from Operations			
Cash Spending	$47	$47	$47
Bill Payment	$225	$36	$59
Subtotal Spent on Operations	$272	$83	$106
Additional Cash Spent			
Non Operating (Other) Expense	$0	$0	$0
Sales Tax, VAT, HST/GST Paid Out	$0	$0	$0
Principal Repayment of Current Borrowing	$0	$0	$90
Other Liabilities Principal Repayment	$0	$0	$0
Long-term Liabilities Principal Repayment	$3	$3	$3
Purchase Other Current Assets	$0	$0	$0
Purchase Long-term Assets	$25	$0	$15
Dividends	$0	$0	$0
Subtotal Cash Spent	$300	$86	$213

The cash plan has to deal with the real flow of money spent. (Amounts shown in thousands. Numbers may be affected by rounding.)

1. The first row is "Cash Spending," which is money spent immediately to pay expenses that are not invoiced (due at a later date). The most obvious example is the spending for wages and salaries and other compensation-related payments you make every month to your employees and the government. These obligations don't go into accounts payable. Instead, you pay them every month. In most companies you can assume that wages and related personnel expenditures are paid the same month incurred.

2. The second obvious use of cash is "Bill Payment." This accounts payable balance is money you owe. Every month, you pay off most of this, depending on how quickly you pay. I recommend estimating payments based on some simple calculations that key on estimated average payment days, as shown in the illustration on the following page:

PAYMENT DETAIL

Payment Detail	Jan	Feb	Mar
Payment Delay in Days	30	30	30
Payables			
Beginning Payables Balance	$224	$34	$49
Plus New Payment Obligations	$82	$97	$346
Less Cash Spending	$47	$47	$47
Less Bill Payments	$225	$36	$59
Ending Payables Balance	$34	$49	$290

Payment delays affect cash flow. The calculations here estimate payments made based on the assumption that payments are made 30 days after bills are received. (Amounts shown in thousands. Numbers may be affected by rounding.)

In the example here, the calculations start with the ending balance of accounts payable from the previous month, then add new obligations, then subtract obligations paid directly in cash, as well as this month's bill payments, to calculate this month's ending balance. This month's bill payments depend on the assumption of waiting 30 days, on average, before paying bills.

The first two rows, cash spending and bill payment, are spending from normal operations. They can be linked to spending in the income statement through assumptions for bill payments and inventory management. The other ways to spend money happen beyond and outside of the Profit and Loss.

3. The "Non Operating (Other) Expenses" row is the complement of the Non Operating (Other) Income in the first part of the cash flow. These are expenses outside of normal operations. They are there to accommodate companies that have "Other Expenses" sections in their normal accounting statements. You know who you are, and if this isn't you, it doesn't affect you.

4. There is a row for spending related to sales tax and value-added tax (VAT), which is money a company holds because it collects it for the government, but which must, in turn, be repaid. Normal cash flow tracks these tax-related amounts as they enter and leave the company.

5. The next three rows, "Principal Repayment of Current Borrowing," "Other Liabilities Principal Repayment," and "Long-term Liabilities Principal Repayment" are for principal repayments of debt. When you pay off your loans, you lose cash. In the example, there is a regular payoff of $3,000 long-term debt, and a single pay off of $90,000 of the current (short-term) debt.

6. In the third row from the bottom, you record the purchase of new Other Current Assets. You'll have to know how much you purchase in new assets in order to estimate your Balance Sheet. While in real life these might also be recorded as Accounts Payable and paid a few weeks later, we make them explicit here as if they were paid immediately in cash. That makes for better cash planning.

7. Logically, this next row is one for purchases of new Long-term Assets. These also reduce cash.

8. The last row in spending tracks dividends. Dividends are the distribution of profits to owners and investors. They reduce cash but don't appear anywhere else.

Planning for Inventory

Inventory is the accounting term for goods or materials a company holds temporarily and then sells to its customers. For example, inventory in a bookstore is the value of the books the store owns and intends to sell to its customers. Inventory in a car dealership is unsold cars. Inventory in a steel manufacturing plant includes iron ore and coal to be made into steel.

Inventory goes into the financials as an asset when it's purchased. It leaves the company as cost of goods sold when it's sold. The cost of inventory shows up in the cash flow when it's paid for, regardless of when it's sold, usually as cash spending or bill payments.

Not all companies manage inventory. Product-related companies normally do have inventory, and service-related companies normally don't. There are many exceptions, though, so if you have doubt, ask your accountant or somebody connected to your company who knows.

ESTIMATING INVENTORY

Inventory Detail			
	Jan	Feb	Mar
Months of Inventory On-hand	1.1	1.1	1.1
Minimum Inventory Purchase	$1,000		
Inventory Balance			
Beginning Inventory Balance	$805	$621	$378
Less Inventory Used as COGS	$185	$243	$302
Plus Inventory Purchase	$0	$0	$256
Ending Inventory Balance	$621	$378	$332

Use simple assumptions to estimate inventory flow and inventory purchases. (Amounts shown in thousands. Numbers may be affected by rounding.)

Inventory gets into your cash flow when you pay for it. Estimate your inventory needs as months of inventory on hand, then estimate inventory flow as a matter of estimating sales and inventory purchases. Payments depend on the rest of your payments policy, because inventory purchase amounts enter the system when an invoice is received, but they are paid when the related invoices are paid.

In the illustration above, the beginning inventory balance supplies the amounts required until the third month, when additional inventory is purchased. That purchase goes into accounts payable, and is paid as part of the normal flow of bill payments. Inventory purchase is the bulk of the $346,000 new obligations in March shown in the Payments Details illustration on the previous page.

Calculating the Cash Balance

When you're done with both sections — receipts and spending — then you can calculate cash flow by subtracting spending from receipts. Cash flow is the change in the balance from one month to another. You calculate cash balance by taking the ending balance from the previous period and adding (or subtracting) cash flow. The sample cash plan shown here below does just that.

CALCULATING THE CASH BALANCE

Cash Flow			
Cash Received	Jan	Feb	Mar
Cash from Operations			
Cash Sales	$40	$51	$62
Cash from Receivables	$198	$205	$230
Subtotal Cash from Operations	$238	$256	$293
Additional Cash Received			
New Other Liabilities	$7	$0	$0
New Long-term Liabilities	$0	$0	$100
New Investment Received	$0	$25	$0
Subtotal Cash Received	$245	$281	$393
Expenditures	Jan	Feb	Mar
Expenditures from Operations			
Cash Spending	$47	$47	$47
Bill Payment	$225	$36	$59
Subtotal Spent on Operations	$272	$83	$106
Additional Cash Spent			
Principal Repayment of Current Borrowing	$0	$0	$90
Long-term Liabilities Principal Repayment	$3	$3	$3
Purchase Long-term Assets	$25	$0	$15
Subtotal Cash Spent	$300	$86	$213
Net Cash Flow	($55)	$195	$180
Cash Balance	$1	$196	$376

Calculating cash flow and cash balance isn't always intuitive, but understanding its two main sections is important. (Amounts shown in thousands and may be affected by rounding.)

What you end up with here is a relatively simple cash plan using the direct method to calculate the cash. The direct method means that you add the new sources of cash and subtract the uses of cash, and you have an estimated ending Cash Balance for each month.

Indirect Cash Flow Method

An alternative cash flow method, called indirect, projects cash flow by starting with net income and adding back depreciation and other non-cash expenses, then accounting for the changes in assets and liabilities that aren't recorded in the income statement.

This methodology produces a Sources and Uses of Cash statement as shown on the following page. The results should be identical, for either direct or indirect methods, because the underlying cash flow is identical.

THE INDIRECT METHOD PRODUCES SOURCES AND USES OF CASH

Sources and Uses of Cash (Indirect Cash Flow Method)	Jan	Feb	Mar
Sources of Cash			
Net Income	$1	$1	$23
Depreciation	$1	$1	$1
Increase in Accounts Payable	$0	$14	$241
Decrease in Accounts Receivable	$0	$0	$0
Decrease in Inventory	$185	$243	$46
New Loans	$7	$0	$100
New Investment	$0	$25	$0
Sales Taxes (VAT/GST) Collected	$0	$0	$0
Sale of Assets	$0	$0	$0
Subtotal Sources of Cash	$194	$284	$411
Use of Cash	Jan	Feb	Mar
Decrease in Accounts Payable	$189	$0	$0
Increase in Accounts Receivable	$31	$86	$123
Increase in Inventory	$0	$0	$0
Repay Loans	$3	$3	$93
Purchase Other Assets	$25	$0	$15
Distributions	$0	$0	$0
Sales Tax Payment	$0	$0	$0
Subtotal Uses of Cash	$248	$89	$231
Net Cash Flow	($54)	$195	$180
Cash Balance	$1	$196	$376

The indirect method starts with net income and then adjusts for all the sources and uses of cash that aren't part of the income calculation. Results should be the same for either direct or indirect. (Amounts shown in thousands. Numbers may be affected by rounding.)

Direct vs. Indirect: Which to Use?

What's most important in cash planning is the forecast of the cash balance. The experts can argue about direct vs. indirect (and theory and fashions DO change), but in the end either method will come to the same cash balance, if properly applied. Choose whichever method seems more natural to you. Some people are comfortable with estimating balances, others prefer to estimate payments made or payments received. For example:

- Suppose you prefer to estimate ending balances using simple assumptions. If you wait an average of 60 days (called collection days) to receive money from customers, then your normal end-of-month accounts receivable will be twice the month's sales on credit. That calculation tool and estimator makes the indirect method better.

- However, you might prefer to estimate payments received by making the payments received in March equal to sales on credit in January. That calculation favors the direct method.

Ultimately, the choice of method doesn't matter. As long as you're consistent and careful with assumptions, the results should be the same.

Links with the Balance Sheet

Even though I cover the balance sheet in the next chapter, I can't talk about cash without relating the cash flow to the balance. The three most important financial statements in a plan, income statement (profit and loss), cash flow, and balance sheet, are all related to each other.

This next illustration shows the sample balance sheet linked to the cash flow in the previous illustration. Most of the rows on this balance sheet are directly affected by the cash flow, and need to change every time the cash changes. To close the circle in this chapter, let's look in detail at the balance:

RELATED BALANCE SHEET

Pro Forma Balance Sheet				
	Starting Balances	Jan	Feb	Mar
Assets				
Current Assets				
Cash	$55	$1	$197	$376
Accounts Receivable	$395	$426	$511	$634
Inventory	$805	$621	$378	$332
Other Current Assets	$25	$25	$25	$25
Total Current Assets	$1,280	$1,073	$1,111	$1,367
Long-term Assets				
Long-term Assets	$350	$375	$375	$390
Accumulated Depreciation	$50	$51	$52	$53
Total Long-term Assets	$300	$324	$323	$337
Total Assets	$1,580	$1,397	$1,434	$1,704
Liabilities and Capital		Jan	Feb	Mar
Current Liabilities				
Accounts Payable	$224	$34	$49	$290
Current Borrowing	$90	$90	$90	$0
Other Current Liabilities	$15	$22	$22	$22
Subtotal Current Liabilities	$329	$146	$161	$312
Long-term Liabilities	$285	$282	$279	$376
Total Liabilities	$614	$428	$440	$688
Paid-in Capital	$500	$500	$525	$525
Retained Earnings	$418	$467	$467	$467
Earnings	$49	$1	$2	$25
Total Capital	$967	$968	$994	$1,017
Total Liabilities and Capital	$1,581	$1,396	$1,434	$1,705
Net Worth	$966	$969	$994	$1,016

The information on the balance sheet should follow from the income statement and the cash flow. Notice, for example, how Long-term Liabilities, above, respond in March to a new loan and a regular principal payment of an existing loan shown in the cash flow table on page 16.8.

1. The "Cash" row is the balance in your checkbook. You calculate this with the cash flow, the subject of this chapter.

2. "Accounts Receivable" is the money owed to you by customers for sales already made. The balance increases with sales on credit, and decreases with payments of accounts receivable. For any month, the ending balance is the sum of the previous ending balance, plus new sales on credit, minus payments received. The details are in the Receivables Detail table on page 16.3.

3. Calculate the "Inventory" balance as the previous balance minus direct cost of sales plus new inventory purchases. The details are in the Inventory Detail table shown on page 16.7.

4. Calculate "Other Current Assets" as the previous balance plus new assets purchased (from the cash spent section of the direct cash flow table) minus sale of assets (from the cash received section).

5. "Long-term Assets" are the depreciable assets, such as plant and equipment, vehicles, etc. This month's balance is equal to last month's balance plus new assets purchased, minus sale of assets.

6. "Accumulated Depreciation" decreases the value of the capital assets. This month's balance is last month's balance plus new depreciation, from the income statement.

7. "Accounts Payable" will be last month's balance plus additions (a subset of costs and expenses) minus payments of payables. New payables will include new inventory not paid for when purchased, plus indirect costs of sales not paid as incurred, operating expenses not paid as incurred, and similar items. The details are in the Payment Detail table shown on page 16.6.

8. "Current Borrowing" will be equal to last month's balance plus new borrowing minus principal payments. Interest payments are not included, because they go into the income statement and don't affect the balance. Principal payments and new borrowing should come from the cash flow.

9. "Other Current Liabilities" are things like accrued taxes and accrued salary; liabilities you know you have but haven't paid. These usually don't cost interest.

10. "Long-term Liabilities" increase when you borrow and decrease with payment of principal. The balance is going to be last month's balance plus new borrowing as a source of cash, minus principal payments as a use of cash. In the sample case, the March balance shows a $100 increase for a new loan, minus a $3 decrease for payment of principal, so that the $376 at the end of March is exactly $97 more than the $279 at the end of February.

11. "Paid-in Capital" is money invested. The balance should be last month's balance plus new investment from sources of cash, minus dividends from uses of cash.

12. "Retained Earnings" is the accumulated earnings reinvested in the company, not taken out as dividends. Normally this changes once a year when the annual statements are prepared.

13. "Earnings" are the accumulated earnings since the end of the last year. This month's balance should be equal to last month's balance plus this month's earnings. At the end of the year, with an annual adjustment, earnings still left in the business become retained earnings.

How to Plan Cash Flow

1. When you reach the Cash Flow table, after filling in profits and assumptions, and again whenever you change profits or assumptions, look at the cash balance row at the very bottom.

2. If all entries are positive numbers, then your cash plan works.

3. If you have one or more negative numbers showing in the bottom row, go to the column for the first month showing a negative cash balance and adjust the cash to make it positive.

4. Here are some things you can do to make a negative cash balance positive:

- Invest more money. In the cash plan, find the row for "New Investment Received" and type a positive number.

- Borrow money. Find a row named "New Current Borrowing," or "New Other Liabilities" for interest-free loans, or "New Long-term Borrowing" for long-term loans, and type a number to represent a new loan.

- Increase your estimated payment days. Go to your Payment Detail table and change your payment days estimator. This indicates that you are paying slower, not making your vendors happy, but sometimes this is necessary.

- Decrease Sales on Credit % in the Receivables Detail table.

- Decrease Collection Days in the Receivables Detail table.

- Decrease the estimated average inventory on hand estimate in the Inventory Detail table.

5. To repay loan principal, type a positive number into the proper repayment of liabilities row in the cash flow.

6. To take money out of the company as dividends, type a positive number into the Dividends row of the cash flow.

These are just a few examples. Cash is the most sensitive portion of business management, so of course there are many other options you might choose. Remember, cash is critical.

Understanding Loans, Interest, and Repayment

A business plan should handle loans, interest, and repayment following standard accounting convention. Amounts of new loans (after start-up) go into the Cash Flow table in the upper section as money received. Interest, which is an expense deductible against income, goes into the Profit and Loss statement. Principal repayments go into the Cash Flow table in the lower section, as spending.

Some people are confused by the concept of separating the payment into interest and principal. A common example, at least in the United States, is making payments on a mortgage. Most lending institutions clearly separate payments into interest and principal components. Even if you write a single check each month to repay the mortgage loan, the payment is divided into interest and principal.

Detailed Principal Payments Function

Your software is likely to have functions to calculate principal and interest payments from assumptions, so you can project payments over time without having to estimate each one. In the following illustration, the spreadsheet uses a built-in financial calculator to estimate the principal payments required for the sample case we've been using. (Note: For this illustration, we display the numbers in dollars, not thousands of dollars, as they are displayed in other illustrations in this chapter.)

USING THE PRINCIPAL PAYMENTS FUNCTION (PPMT)

Cash Flow Table   Show Wizard Instructions

Table	Cash Flow	▼	Full Columns	▼	⇐ ⇒ 🗎 🖾 ✂ 🖹

C33	=-PPMT(long_term_interest_rate/12,COLUMN()+44,120,400000)

	A	C	▲
31	Principal Repayment of Current Borrowing	$0	
32	Other Liabilities Principal Repayment	$0	
33	Long-term Liabilities Principal Repayment	$2,942	
34	Purchase Other Current Assets	$0	
35	Purchase Long-term Assets	$25,000	
36	Dividends	$0	
37	**Subtotal Cash Spent**	$299,527	↕

Use the computer to calculate principal payments for the cash flow table. (This table is taken from Business Plan Pro®, and shown in dollars, not thousands of dollars).

In the sample, the company borrowed $400,000 in a 10-year loan at 8.5% per year several years ago. During the sample plan period, it is making regular payments of just under $5,000 per month. The interest portion of the payment is calculated automatically in the Profit and Loss table. The principal portion of the payment is calculated using the formula below, which you can copy into your own worksheet. The formula for the first month's principal payment is:

=-PPMT(long_term_interest_rate/12,column()+44,120,400000)

- The formula starts with a negative sign ("-") because the cash flow row uses positive numbers for spending amounts, while many spreadsheet functions assume cash flow calculations use negatives for spending.

- The first element of that formula (=PPMT) is a standard function call, used in Business Plan Pro® as well as in Microsoft Excel and compatible spreadsheet software.

- The "long_term_interest_rate/12" is the annual interest rate from a general assumptions table, divided by 12 (because this is monthly interest). The range is named "long_term_interest_rate" using standard spreadsheet range naming.

- The "column()+44" portion represents the 47th payment. "Column()" is a built-in number that equals 3 in the third column.

- The 120 in the formula is the total number of payments (120 for a 10-year loan).

- The 400000 at the end of the formula represents the original loan amount, $400,000.

You can use this special payment function to calculate your own principal payments, if you wish. Or you can get the number from loan papers or from your banker.

Summary

Your cash plan is the most critical element of your business projections. If it is going to be useful at all, a business plan helps you develop a realistic cash estimate, based on the underlying relationships we explored in the previous chapter. Whenever you change an assumption in sales forecast, personnel plan, profit and loss, or balance sheet, it affects your cash flow.

The examples in this and the previous chapters pointed the way toward cash flow, and the way cash works. Profits are very important to cash, of course, and they work in obvious ways — the more profits, the better the cash, because profits are sales (that generate cash) minus costs and expenses (that cost cash). What is less obvious, however, is the impact of balance sheet items:

- An increase in assets decreases your cash. A decrease in assets increases cash.

- An increase in liabilities increases cash. A decrease in liabilities decreases cash.

These two principles lead eventually to the impact of receivables, inventory, and payables. As you look at your assumptions for the cash flow, keep in mind that every extra dollar of receivables or inventory as assets is a dollar that you don't have in your cash balance. Every dollar in payables is a dollar that you have in cash, too. Although this simple cash model doesn't show the critical impact as clearly as our examples in the previous chapter, the mathematics and financial principles are the same.

Your business plan should help you develop a realistic cash estimate with mathematically and financially correct cash tables, in which all the key tables are linked to the cash flow correctly.

Use the Cash Flow Chart as a Cash Pilot

Every plan should have a monthly cash flow chart, which the computer draws from your cash flow table. The chart takes the data from the financial worksheet in the rows for net cash flow and cash balance. Use this chart as an illustration of your cash flow projection.

As an example of how useful the cash chart can be, revisit the series of cash scenarios presented in *Chapter 14: About Business Numbers*. You can see how the estimated cash varies radically depending on critical assumptions for collections, payments, and inventory; and also how the cash chart shows you those variations instantly.

When I am actually working with a business plan, I usually keep the cash chart visible as I change my assumptions. That way I know immediately when I need to revise numbers further because my cash balance is negative.

CHAPTER 17:

FINISH THE FINANCIALS

If you've followed through with the cash plan, your financials are almost done. The balance sheet should be completed by the time you have a cash flow working. Business ratios should be almost automatic too, because they draw their information from tables you've already finished.

The Balance Sheet

I showed you some basic balance sheets in *Chapter 14: About Business Numbers* and *Chapter 16: Cash is King.* You've seen then that the Balance Sheet table shows the financial position of the business, its assets and liabilities, at a specified time. The ironclad rule of Western double-entry bookkeeping and accounting is that assets are equal to capital and liabilities. This is what balance means. The following illustration shows the Balance Sheet table, or pro forma Balance Sheet.

BALANCE SHEET TABLE

Pro Forma Balance Sheet				
		Jan	Feb	Mar
Assets	**Starting Balances**			
Current Assets				
Cash	$55	$1	$197	$376
Accounts Receivable	$395	$426	$511	$634
Inventory	$805	$621	$378	$332
Other Current Assets	$25	$25	$25	$25
Total Current Assets	$1,280	$1,073	$1,111	$1,367
Long-term Assets				
Long-term Assets	$350	$375	$375	$390
Accumulated Depreciation	$50	$51	$52	$53
Total Long-term Assets	$300	$324	$323	$337
Total Assets	$1,580	$1,397	$1,434	$1,704
Liabilities and Capital		Jan	Feb	Mar
Current Liabilities				
Accounts Payable	$224	$34	$49	$290
Current Borrowing	$90	$90	$90	$0
Other Current Liabilities	$15	$22	$22	$22
Subtotal Current Liabilities	$329	$146	$161	$312
Long-term Liabilities	$285	$282	$279	$376
Total Liabilities	$614	$428	$440	$688
Paid-in Capital	$500	$500	$525	$525
Retained Earnings	$418	$467	$467	$467
Earnings	$49	$1	$2	$25
Total Capital	$967	$968	$994	$1,017
Total Liabilities and Capital	$1,581	$1,396	$1,434	$1,705
Net Worth	$966	$969	$994	$1,016

This illustration shows the Balance Sheet table for AMT, Inc., the sample company first introduced in Chapter 14: About Business Numbers (numbers displayed in thousands).

Standard Industry Profiles

Whenever possible, a business plan should compare projected numbers to standard industry numbers of the type we discussed earlier in *Chapter 9: The Business You're In*. We show an example here, in which the sample case's main business numbers for Year 1 through Year 3 are compared to a standard industry profile, shown in the column named "Industry Profile."

STANDARD INDUSTRY COMPARISON

Ratio Analysis	Year 1	Year 2	Year 3	Industry Profile
Sales Growth	22.03%	15.61%	22.93%	10.50%
Percent of Total Assets				
Accounts Receivable	47.20%	46.95%	44.82%	19.20%
Inventory	20.70%	20.30%	18.19%	38.00%
Other Current Assets	2.54%	2.18%	1.69%	20.80%
Total Current Assets	87.24%	83.59%	78.54%	78.00%
Long-term Assets	12.76%	16.41%	21.46%	22.00%
Total Assets	100.00%	100.00%	100.00%	100.00%
Current Liabilities	33.95%	31.31%	26.39%	44.60%
Long-term Liabilities	11.77%	8.94%	5.95%	14.10%
Total Liabilities	45.72%	40.25%	32.34%	58.70%
Net Worth	54.28%	59.75%	67.66%	41.30%
Percent of Sales				
Sales	100.00%	100.00%	100.00%	100.00%
Gross Margin	26.33%	26.79%	31.67%	37.20%
Selling, General & Administrative Expense	19.94%	20.80%	21.33%	22.30%
Advertising Expenses	1.93%	1.87%	1.91%	4.10%
Profit Before Interest and Taxes	8.60%	8.46%	13.68%	1.50%

This sample table compares the plan to industry standard financial profiles.

Don't expect your business to fit exactly into any standard category. For example, is the corner service station also a convenience store? Which category should it use? General profiles are based on averages, and no real business is ever average. As you include standard ratios in your plan, it is more important to explain how your company is different than to be able to match your company exactly to industry averages. *Chapter 9: The Business You're In* lists sources for more information on business ratios, including standards for your type of business.

Our sample company, for instance, has much higher Accounts Receivable than average, but less Inventory, and also lower Other Current Assets. Its Gross Margin is lower than the rest of the industry, but Profit Before Interest and Taxes is higher. In this case the plan text should explain why a well-run company might vary from average numbers. Some readers might worry about unrealistic financial forecasts.

Business Ratios

Aside from profiles, there are also standard business ratios that people use to evaluate a specific business, regardless of its relationship to other businesses of the same kind. Gross margin, debt to equity, return on investment, and other ratios are widely used as general indicators of business performance or business health. After you've developed projections for sales, profits, cash, assets, liabilities, and capital, then you can generate many standard business ratios automatically.

Business ratios are often misunderstood. They aren't magic. Appropriate results vary from industry to industry. For example, a large manufacturing plant is going to have enormous assets compared to a small consulting company. Generally, the most important insight gained from ratios is the change in a ratio over time, rather than the specific number at any given time.

While we do explain the standard financial ratios used here, there are better explanations available in financial management textbooks. Experts will almost always agree on the importance of following changes in a ratio over time, and on the wide variations of standards depending on the type of business.

PROFITABILITY RATIOS

Ratio Analysis	Year 1	Year 2	Year 3	Industry Profile
Main Ratios				
Current	2.57	2.67	2.98	1.78
Quick	1.96	2.02	2.29	0.75
Total Debt to Total Assets	45.72%	40.25%	32.34%	58.70%
Pre-tax Return on Net Worth	32.25%	27.30%	39.68%	3.80%
Pre-tax Return on Assets	17.50%	16.31%	26.85%	9.30%
Additional Ratios	Year 1	Year 2	Year 3	
Net Profit Margin	6.40%	6.00%	10.24%	n.a
Return on Equity	25.79%	21.84%	31.42%	n.a
Percent of Sales				
Sales	100.00%	100.00%	100.00%	100.00%
Gross Margin	26.33%	26.79%	31.67%	37.20%
Selling, General & Administrative Expense	19.94%	20.80%	21.33%	22.30%
Advertising Expenses	1.93%	1.87%	1.91%	4.10%
Profit Before Interest and Taxes	8.60%	8.46%	13.68%	1.50%

Most business plans include some standard business ratios.

- **Gross Margin:** sales minus cost of sales, expressed as a percentage of sales.

- **Net Profit Margin:** net profit divided by sales, as a percentage.

- **Return on Assets:** net profit divided by the total assets.

- **Return on Equity:** also return on investment (ROI). This ratio divides net profit by net worth.

Return on Equity or Return on Investment (ROI) is probably the most important of these ratios. A business is an investment and it should yield profits comparable to alternative investments, unless there is additional compensation (such as salaries for the owners). In theory, at least, if ROI is low, you should sell the business and put your investment money to better use.

Return on Assets and the Net Profit Margin provide a good basis for comparison between your company and the rest of the industry. They are also good indicators of company performance from year to year.

ACTIVITY RATIOS

Activity Ratios	Year 1	Year 2	Year 3	
Accounts Receivable Turnover	3.94	3.94	3.94	n.a
Collection Days	58	86	84	n.a
Inventory Turnover	9.88	8.04	8.08	n.a
Accounts Payable Turnover	11.77	12.17	12.17	n.a
Payment Days	28	28	28	n.a
Total Asset Turnover	2.19	2.17	2.08	n.a

Activity ratios focus on financial performance.

These ratios are generally used to compare a company's performance to the average for its industry. Levels of acceptability tend to vary widely between different industries. For example, large manufacturing companies might have a very low assets turnover, but retail stores should have a high turnover.

- **Accounts Receivable Turnover:** sales on credit divided by accounts receivable. This is a measure of how well your business collects its debts.

- **Collection Days:** accounts receivable multiplied by 360, then divided by annual credit sales is another measure of debt collection and value of receivables. Generally, 30 days is exceptionally good, 60 days is bothersome, and 90 days or more is a real problem. This varies by industry.

- **Inventory Turnover:** cost of sales divided by the average balance of inventory. The higher the turnover, the better for cash flow and working capital requirements.

- **Accounts Payable Turnover:** a measure of how quickly the business pays its bills. It divides the total new accounts payable for the year by the average accounts payable balance.

- **Total Assets Turnover:** sales divided by total assets.

DEBT RATIOS

Debt Ratios	Year 1	Year 2	Year 3	
Debt to Net Worth	0.84	0.67	0.48	n.a
Current Liab. to Liab.	0.74	0.78	0.82	n.a

Debt ratios look at what you owe.

- **Debt to Net Worth:** total liabilities divided by total net worth.

- **Short-term Debt to Liabilities:** short-term debt divided by total liabilities. This is a measure of the depth and term of debt.

LIQUIDITY RATIOS

Main Ratios				
Current	2.57	2.67	2.98	1.78
Quick	1.96	2.02	2.29	0.75
Liquidity Ratios	Year 1	Year 2	Year 3	
Net Working Capital	$1,576,649	$1,798,188	$2,309,442	n.a
Interest Coverage	14.43	8.81	18.41	n.a

Liquidity ratios focus on cash position and ability to meet obligations.

- **Current Ratio:** short-term assets divided by short-term liabilities. This gives a view of a business' cash position and ability to meet short-term commitments.

- **Quick Ratio:** this is the same as the current ratio, except that inventories are first subtracted from short-term assets before they are divided by short-term liabilities. Many financial experts consider this a better measurement of liquidity than the current ratio, because inventory is so often not convertible to real cash in a short period of time.

- **Net Working Capital:** subtract short-term liabilities from short-term assets. This is another measure of cash position.

- **Interest Coverage:** profit before interest and taxes (operating profit) divided by total interest payments. A measure of how much a business is burdened by servicing its own debt.

These are all measures of the overall financial position of a company and its ability to pay its debt. They are very important to bankers and for loan applications. The acid test (included with additional ratios in the following section) is generally considered the best measure of a company's ability to pay all its obligations without problems. Acceptable measures vary by industry. Some industries are quite heavy on plant and equipment assets, and others, such as service businesses, have few long-term assets.

ADDITIONAL COMMON RATIOS

Additional Ratios	Year 1	Year 2	Year 3	
Assets to Sales	0.46	0.46	0.48	n.a
Current Debt/Total Assets	34%	31%	26%	n.a
Acid Test	0.57	0.52	0.59	n.a
Sales/Net Worth	4.03	3.64	3.07	n.a
Dividend Payout	0.00	0.00	0.00	n.a

These additional ratios are also quite common.

- **Assets to Sales:** assets divided by sales.

- **Debt/Assets:** total liabilities divided by total assets.

- **Current Debt/Total Assets:** divides short-term (current) liabilities by total assets.

- **Acid Test:** short-term assets (minus accounts receivable and inventory), divided by short-term liabilities.

- **Asset Turnover:** a repetition of the same ratio in activity ratios above (Total Assets Turnover).

- **Sales/Net Worth:** total sales divided by net worth.

- **Dividend Payout:** dividends divided by net profit.

Break-even Analysis

You prepared a preliminary break-even analysis in *Chapter 3: Initial Assessment*. Now it's time to go back to that and review the numbers. The next illustration shows (again) the standard break-even analysis included in a standard business plan.

BREAK-EVEN ASSUMPTIONS

Break Even Analysis	
Monthly Units Break-even	1,222
Monthly Sales Break-even	$397,262
Assumptions	
Average Per-unit Revenue	$343.04
Average Per-unit Variable Cost	$248.15
Estimated Monthly Fixed Costs	$97,778.00

This section of the model calculates technical break-even points, based on the assumptions for unit prices, variable costs, and fixed costs.

This is a monthly break-even analysis. It assumes monthly fixed costs, and per-unit sales price and variable costs. It uses the standard break-even formulas detailed below, but suggests some modified assumptions. Where standard fixed costs are supposed to be costs that would be sustained even if the business stopped, we suggest you use operating expenses instead. I suggest this change in standard financial analysis because you are better off knowing break-even points on real operations, rather than on some theoretical calculation of fixed expenses.

The units break-even point is:

Fixed Cost ÷ Unit Price - Unit Variable Costs

The sales break-even point is:

Fixed Cost ÷ (1-(Unit variable Costs/Unit Price))

The Break-even Chart

The break-even analysis depends on assumptions for fixed costs, unit price, and unit variable costs. These are rarely exact assumptions. This is not a true picture of fixed costs by any means, but is quite useful for determining a break-even point.

The analysis included in the chart in the illustration below shows a general break-even analysis for assumed fixed costs of $97,778, average per-unit revenue of $343, and average per-unit variable cost of $248.

The line on the chart shows profits increasing and crossing the break-even line at approximately 1,220 units.

BREAK-EVEN CHART

This illustration shows the break-even analysis that compares unit sales to profits. It uses data from the table shown earlier in this section.

Summary

Your financial tables are interrelated. The sales and personnel forecasts and assumptions affect the profit and loss, the profit and loss affects cash, and the cash and balance sheet work together.

Financial analysis is rarely a true step-by-step process. You will probably have to go back through your tables to review the assumptions for realism and accuracy. As you revise assumptions, make sure you constantly check back to keep your cash balance positive.

This page intentionally blank.

CHAPTER 18:

STRATEGY IS FOCUS

With most of the financials now done, it's time to turn to strategy and tactics. You've been developing strategy throughout the planning process, I know, because you can't do the numbers without thinking about the strategy. However, now you want to explain your strategy and develop the implementation. If you refer back to the text outline we discussed in Chapter 2: Pick Your Plan, *you probably have several topics still blank in your plan document. But not in your mind. It's time to write your thoughts on strategy and tactics into your text outline.*

Define Overall Strategy

Strategy is focus. Across the entire business, over the whole range of possibilities involving different products and services, different target customers, different kinds of financing, different levels of growth, what are your choices? What are your priorities?

General Principles of Real-World Strategy

In 30 years of working with businesses of all sizes, I've come across several of what I would call general principles of strategy. These don't necessarily apply in the academic world, or for larger corporate enterprises, but they do apply to small and medium businesses everywhere:

- **Strategy is Focus.** The more priorities in a plan, the less chance of successful implementation.

- **Strategy Needs to be Consistently Applied Over a Long Term to Work.** Better to have a mediocre long-term strategy consistently applied for years than a series of brilliant but contradictory strategies that never last long enough to matter.

- **Strategy Needs to be Tailored.** There are no standard strategies. Every company is different. A given strategy must always be tailored for a specific company.

- **Strategy Needs to be Realistic.** You have to deal with your company as it is at this point in time, understanding what choices you really have, what knobs you can actually turn.

- **The Best Strategies are Market Driven.** When possible, it's not "how to sell what we have," but rather, "how to make what people want or need what we offer."

- **Good Strategies Understand Displacement.** Displacement in business refers to the undeniable fact that everything you try to do rules out many other things that you therefore can't do. You have to choose carefully, because one project displaces many others.

The Strategy Pyramid

Imagine a pyramid made of three levels. The top of the pyramid is a single box, which contains a strategy. Strategy is an area of resource focus. In the middle level, you have three or so boxes which contain tactics. In the third level, you have four to six boxes that stand for programs. It would look something like this next illustration.

Don't get lost in defining strategy and tactics. Make the strategic view work logically.

Strategy is a main focus, which might be on a specific target market, product opportunity, positioning statement, or some other important or fundamental element.

Tactics are there to implement a strategy. For example, if a computer store's strategy is to build long-term relationships with business customers, its tactics might include increasing networking offerings, training, and support.

Programs are specific business activities which support the tactics. Each program has concrete dates and responsibilities, and probably a budget. In the computer store example, programs for the strategy might include upgrade mailings, seminars, installation services and network training.

You don't necessarily do a complete business strategy in a single pyramid. Each fundamental business strategy might be a different pyramid.

One important benefit of the pyramid method is integration and alignment. If your strategy is to focus on one thing, you should be able to trace that strategy into its tactics and, most important, into your actual spending and activity priorities. Flip back and forth between your strategy pyramid and your specific programs, and ask yourself: do your programs match the emphasis you put on strategy?

The discussion on Value-based Marketing on page 18.4 shows a completed strategy pyramid.

Your Marketing Strategy

Your marketing strategy normally involves target market focus, emphasis on certain services or media, or ways to position your company and your service uniquely.

Your marketing strategy depends a great deal on which market segments you've chosen as target market groups. You covered this in detail in *Chapter 10: Know Your Market* and *Chapter 12: Your Target Market*. You may also have developed strategy using the pyramid or value proposition. Obviously, you want to make sure to preserve the same basic focus and themes.

Aside from the target market strategy, your marketing strategy might also include the positioning statement, pricing, promotion, and whatever else you want to add. You might also want to look at media strategy, business development, or other factors. Strategy is creative, and hard to predict. Some of the material below will give you more ideas.

Positioning Tactics

Positioning statements can be a good way to define your marketing strategy. The positioning statements should focus on the most important target market, that market's most important market need, how your product meets that need, what the main competition is, and how your product is better than the competition.

Consider this simple template:

For [target market description] who [target market need], [this product] [how it meets the need]. Unlike [key competition], it [most important distinguishing feature].

For example, the positioning statement for the original Business Plan Pro®, was: "For the businessperson who is starting a new company, launching new products or seeking funding or partners, Business Plan Pro® is software that produces professional business plans quickly and easily. Unlike [name omitted], Business Plan Pro® does a real business plan, with real insights, not just cookie-cutter fill-in-the-blanks templates."

Pricing Tactics

You ought to provide detail on product pricing, and relate pricing to strategy. Pricing is also supposed to be intimately related to the positioning statement in the previous topic, since pricing is probably the most important factor in product positioning. Your value proposition, for example, will normally include implications about relative pricing, and therefore, you should check whether your detailed product-by-product pricing matches the implied pricing in the value proposition.

Promotion Tactics

Think of promotion in a broader sense than simply sales promotion, including the whole range of advertising, public relations, events, direct mail, seminars, and sales literature.

How will you spread the word about your business to your future customers?

- Do you look for expensive ads in mass media, or targeted marketing in specialized publications, or even more targeted, with direct mail?

- Do you have a way to leverage the news media, or reviewers?

- Do you advertise more effectively through public relations events, trade shows, newspaper, or radio?

- What about telemarketing, the World Wide Web, or even multilevel marketing?

Are you satisfied with how this is working for you now, or is it a problem area that needs to be addressed? Are you meeting your needs, and in line with your opportunities?

How does your promotion strategy fit with the rest of your strategy? Check for alignment between what you say here and what you say in your strategy pyramid, and your value proposition. As you described market trends and target market segments, did you see ways to improve your promotion strategy?

Value-Based Marketing

Value-based marketing is another conceptual framework. Like the strategy pyramid described in the previous topic, it doesn't have to be in your business plan at all, but we add it here because some people find that the framework helps them develop their strategy. Obviously, this has to be a quick treatment. There are textbooks written about value-based marketing, and the business literature on this topic is rich and varied.

This framework begins with defining your business offering as a value proposition. The value proposition is benefit offered minus price charged, in relative terms. The definition encourages you to think in broad conceptual terms, with emphasis on the real benefit offered, rather than the specific tangible. For example, a national fast food chain probably offers the value of convenience and reliability, probably at a slight price premium (at least when compared to the weaker chains). A prestigious local restaurant, on the other hand, is offering a completely different set of benefits (luxury, elegance, prestige, for example) at a marked price premium. A graphic designer is probably selling benefits related to communication and advertising, not just drawings.

Once you have a value proposition defined, then look at your business — and your business plan — in terms of how well you:

1. communicate the business proposition; and

2. fulfill your promise.

For example, if a computer store's business proposition has to do with reliable service for small businesses, peace of mind, and long-term relationships, then it probably shouldn't be taking out full-page newspaper advertisements promising the lowest prices in town on brand-name hardware. It probably should communicate its proposition with sales literature that emphasizes how the computer store will become a strategic ally of its clients. It might also think twice about how it handles overdue bills from customers, who might really be holding out for more service or better support.

Using the strategy pyramid, the framework helps you integrate your tactics and planned programs into a logical whole plan. This next illustration shows how the store might lay out its value-based marketing framework pyramid.

SAMPLE VALUE-BASED MARKETING FRAMEWORK

The computer store strategy is to emphasize service and support for its customers.

Define Sales Strategy

Describe sales strategy as different from marketing strategy. To help differentiate between marketing strategy and sales strategy, think of marketing as the broader effort of generating sales leads on a large scale, and sales as the efforts to bring those sales leads into the system as individual sales transactions. Marketing might affect image and awareness and propensity to buy, while sales should close the deals and get the order that marketing opens.

Sales tactics deal with how and when to close sales prospects, how to compensate sales people, how to optimize order processing and database management, how to maneuver price, delivery, and conditions.

As with your marketing strategy, your sales strategy depends a great deal on which market segments you've chosen as target market groups. Obviously, you don't sell major deals to large companies the same way you sell cereal boxes off grocery store shelves. Think about how you sell in your business. What is your strategy for optimizing your way of selling?

Summary

Is your strategy a reflection of your company's strengths and weaknesses? Make it consistent and realistic.

A mediocre strategy implemented well and with consistency will always beat a brilliant strategy that is never implemented.

Check your plan for consistency throughout. Does your spending reflect your strategy? Do your numbers, including your sales forecast, expense forecast, and personnel plan, reflect your strategy?

This page intentionally blank.

CHAPTER 19:

MAKE IT REAL

At this point, you've been through the main thinking and analysis. It is time to put some bite into your plan and management by listing specific actions to be taken. The best way to make a plan real is to fill it with specific concrete details. A good plan is full of dates, deadlines, specific business activities, and specific responsibility assignments. The value of a plan is measured in its implementation.

Implementation Milestones

Each action is called a milestone. This is where a business plan becomes a real plan, with specific and measurable activities, instead of just a document. Give it as many milestones as you can think of to make it more concrete. Give each milestone a name, a person responsible, a milestone date, and a budget. Then make sure that all your people know that you will be following the plan and tracking plan vs. actual results. If you don't follow up, your plan will not be implemented.

MILESTONES TABLE

Milestones

Milestone	Start Date	End Date	Budget	Manager	Department
Corporate Identity	28-Nov	14-Dec	$10,000	Tamzin J	Marketing
Seminar Implementation	29-Dec	7-Jan	$1,000	Irminsul R	Sales
Business Plan Review	30-Dec	8-Jan	$0	Reggie J	GM
Upgrade Mailer	30-Dec	14-Jan	$5,000	Irminsul R	Sales
New Corporate Brochure	30-Dec	14-Jan	$5,000	Tamzin J	Marketing
Delivery Vans	29-Dec	22-Jan	$12,500	Sepp D	Service
Direct Mail	30-Jan	14-Feb	$3,500	Isuldur R	Marketing
Advertising	30-Jan	14-Feb	$115,000	Reggie J	GM
X4 Prototype	29-Jan	22-Feb	$2,500	Geoffrey S	Product
Service Revamp	29-Jan	22-Feb	$2,500	Soren D	Product
6 Presentations	30-Jan	23-Feb	$0	Irminsul R	Sales
X4 Testing	27-Feb	4-Mar	$1,000	Geoffrey S	Product
3 Accounts	27-Feb	15-Mar	$0	SorenD	Sales
L30 Prototype	30-Mar	24-Mar	$2,500	Pamyla R	Product
Techo-Expo	30-Mar	10-Apr	$15,000	Todd B	Marketing
VP Sales & Marketing Hired	30-May	9-Jun	$1,000	Jemma K	Sales
Mailing System	29-Jun	23-Jul	$5,000	Sepp D	Service
Totals			**$181,500**		

Milestones are the heart and core of the business plan.

The Milestones table should be the most important section of the entire business plan. Each marketing and sales-related program you plan should be listed in the table and explained in the related text, along with relevant details. You want to cement your sales strategy with programs that make it real. How is this strategy to be implemented? Do you have concrete and specific plans? How will implementation be measured?

Manage Your Summaries

Each of your business plan chapters should begin with a summary paragraph that describes all the high points of the chapter. As you develop these summaries, keep in mind that many business plan readers will read only the summaries that begin each chapter, so make sure to include all the important points that you need to make, even for browsers who don't read every word.

One of the best tactics in preparing a business plan is to write your chapter summaries well enough to use them by themselves as the core of a Summary Memo document. In seeking investment, for example, you will need to have a Summary Memo that describes the complete plan in just a few pages. You should be able to pick out your summary paragraphs and use them to create the Summary Memo.

The Executive Summary is the most important of your chapter summaries. It is the doorway to the rest of the plan. Get it right or your target readers will go no further. The best length is a single page. Emphasize the main points of your plan and keep it brief.

Long-term Plan

While you're involved with summaries, consider adding a discussion of long-term plans. How do you expect your company to change over the next five, 10, or 20 years? What are the important drivers of change? What is your company doing to position itself to manage and even thrive on future growth?

I don't recommend including financial details beyond three years in a business plan. At the most, a brief summary of a five-year plan in text is sufficient. However, this is not because I don't believe in long-term planning. Far from it. Businesses should indeed plan for longer than three years, but the long-term plans running five years, 10 years, or more are much less dependent on specific information, and specific business numbers.

CHAPTER 20:

PLANNING FOR IMPLEMENTATION

◇◈◇

Some plans are more likely to be implemented than others. Successful implementation starts with a good plan, one that is full of specific information on milestones, managers, responsibilities, dates and budgets. Beyond the plan itself, however, there are other factors also critical to implementation. Are you going to track results, comparing the planned results to the actual results? Are you going to follow up with your management team, making revisions and checking on performance?

Start With a Good Plan

The illustration below shows a view of what it takes to develop and implement a business plan. I call this planning for implementation.

IMPLEMENTATION ISN'T AUTOMATIC

Results

Simple

Specific

Realistic

Complete

Plan

Actions

Follow Up

A business plan will be hard to implement unless it is simple, specific, realistic and complete. Even if it is all these things, a good plan will need someone to follow up and check on it.

There are some important factors beyond the plan that are also critical:

1. Is the plan simple? Is it easy to understand and to act on? Does it communicate its contents easily and practically?

2. Is the plan specific? Are its objectives concrete and measurable? Does it include specific actions and activities, each with specific dates of completion, specific persons responsible and specific budgets?

3. Is the plan realistic? Are the sales goals, expense budgets, and milestone dates realistic? Nothing stifles implementation like unrealistic goals.

4. Is the plan complete? Does it include all the necessary elements? Requirements of a business plan vary, depending on the context, but there is no guarantee that the plan will work if it doesn't cover the main bases.

Track and Follow-Up

Ironically, a good plan alone isn't enough. As the illustration on the previous page indicates, other elements are also critical. Even a good plan means virtually nothing if somebody doesn't follow-up on its concrete and specific milestones or results. A plan won't be implemented unless responsibilities are assigned to specific people, milestones are established and agreed upon, and the people responsible know that somebody will follow up to check on results.

A useful business plan is a live document. As you review implementation results with the people responsible, you will often find the need to set new goals and make course corrections. Keep track of the original plan and manage changes carefully. Although changes should be made only with good reason, don't be afraid to update your plan and keep it alive. We recommend using a computer for your financials so you can easily make changes, as described below.

Prescription for Live Planning

One of the main advantages of creating a plan on a computer is how easily you can change it. Month by month, as you record your actual results, you can make changes to your plan in the future months of the actual tables, preserve the plan tables, and be able to see the plan vs. actual variance.

1. After your plan starts, type actual results into the sales forecast, balance sheet, profit and loss, and cash plan. Watch what the plan vs. actual worksheets tell you.

2. Note when actual results indicate you need to make changes.

3. Stay in the Actual mode and make adjustments to future months of your Actual cash plan. After all, it is already more accurate than the original plan because it has actual results for the months already completed.

4. As each month closes, type actual results over your revised plan numbers into the Actual area, then repeat steps 2 and 3, above.

A Case Example of Plan vs. Actual

The illustrations on the following pages show an example of a planned sales forecast, the actual results achieved, and variance analysis of the difference between plan and actual.

The Starting Sales Plan

The example begins with the sales forecast portion of a finished business plan.

BEGINNING SALES PLAN

Unit Sales	Jan	Feb	Mar
Systems	85	115	145
Service	200	200	200
Software	150	200	250
Training	145	155	165
Other	160	176	192
Total Unit Sales	740	846	952

Unit Prices	Jan	Feb	Mar
Systems	$2,000	$2,000	$2,000
Service	$75	$69	$58
Software	$200	$200	$200
Training	$37	$35	$39
Other	$300	$300	$300

Sales	Jan	Feb	Mar
Systems	$170,000	$230,000	$290,000
Service	$15,000	$13,800	$11,600
Software	$30,000	$40,000	$50,000
Training	$5,365	$5,425	$6,435
Other	$48,000	$52,800	$57,600
Total Sales	$268,365	$342,025	$415,635
1st Year Planned	1st Year Actual		1st Year Variance

To set the scene, this illustration shows the sales forecast as the business plan is finished.

Actual Results for Sales

Here we see the actual results for the same company for the first three months of the plan.

ACTUAL SALES RESULTS

Unit Sales	Jan	Feb	Mar
Systems	63	74	108
Service	168	171	174
Software	174	235	289
Training	156	171	183
Other	162	151	220
Total Unit Sales	723	802	974

Unit Prices	Jan	Feb	Mar
Systems	$1,783	$1,801	$1,791
Service	$103	$106	$88
Software	$224	$185	$277
Training	$48	$39	$46
Other	$291	$371	$222

Sales	Jan	Feb	Mar
Systems	$112,329	$133,274	$193,428
Service	$17,304	$18,126	$15,312
Software	$38,976	$43,475	$80,053
Training	$7,488	$6,669	$8,418
Other	$47,142	$56,021	$48,840
Total Sales	$223,239	$257,565	$346,051
1st Year Planned	1st Year Actual		1st Year Variance

The numbers at the end of March show actual sales numbers plus adjustments and course corrections.

Plan vs. Actual Sales (Variance)

The illustration below shows the plan vs. actual results (or variance) for our hypothetical company.

SALES VARIANCE

Unit Sales	Jan	Feb	Mar
Systems	(22)	(41)	(37)
Service	(32)	(29)	(26)
Software	24	35	39
Training	11	16	18
Other	2	(25)	28
Total Unit Sales	(17)	(44)	22

Unit Prices	Jan	Feb	Mar
Systems	($217.00)	($199.00)	($209.00)
Service	$28.00	$37.00	$30.00
Software	$24.00	($15.00)	$77.00
Training	$11.00	$4.00	$7.00
Other	($9.00)	$71.00	($78.00)

Sales	Jan	Feb	Mar
Systems	($57,671)	($96,726)	($96,572)
Service	$2,304	$4,326	$3,712
Software	$8,976	$3,475	$30,053
Training	$2,123	$1,244	$1,983
Other	($858)	$3,221	($8,760)
Total Sales	($45,126)	($84,460)	($69,584)
1st Year Planned	1st Year Actual		1st Year Variance

The Variance setting automatically shows plan vs. actual results for the different tables in the menu.

In the sales variance, numbers in parentheses are negative, meaning the actual sales were lower than planned. Positive numbers here mean actual sales were higher than planned.

As you look at the variance for the sales forecast for the first three months, you should see several important trends:

1. Unit sales of systems are disappointing, well below expectations.

2. The average revenue for systems sales is also disappointing.

3. Unit sales for service are disappointing, but dollar sales are way up.

4. Sales are well above expectations for software and training.

Adjusting the Sales Plan

The Adjusted Sales Plan in Actual Table illustration shows how the company from the previous page makes its course corrections. Compare the difference in the February and March columns in the Beginning Sales Plan illustration, the original plan, page 20.3, and the Adjusted Sales Plan in Actual Table shown below.

ADJUSTED SALES PLAN IN ACTUAL TABLE

	Jan	Feb	Mar	Apr	May
Unit Sales					
Systems	63	74	108	150	200
Service	168	171	174	175	255
Software	174	235	289	375	450
Training	156	171	183	200	250
Other	162	151	220	240	200
Total Unit Sales	723	802	974	1,140	1,355
Unit Prices	Jan	Feb	Mar	Apr	May
Systems	$1,783	$1,801	$1,791	$1,775	$1,775
Service	$103	$106	$88	$90	$90
Software	$224	$185	$277	$275	$275
Training	$48	$39	$46	$50	$50
Other	$291	$371	$222	$300	$150
Sales					
Systems	$112,329	$133,274	$193,428	$266,250	$355,000
Service	$17,304	$18,126	$15,312	$15,750	$22,950
Software	$38,976	$43,475	$80,053	$103,125	$123,750
Training	$7,488	$6,669	$8,418	$10,000	$12,500
Other	$47,142	$56,021	$48,840	$72,000	$30,000
Total Sales	$223,239	$257,565	$346,051	$467,125	$544,200
1st Year Planned	1st Year Actual		1st Year Variance		

The illustration shows revisions in the April and May columns, even before they happen, to reflect the changes shown in the January-March period.

In this example, if the company knows by March that real sales will be different from planned goals in April, they should estimate the revised forecast, as a correction to future results. When the actual results are available, they can replace revised plan numbers with actual results. The actual results area can then become a plan area for course corrections.

In the Adjusted Sales Plan in Actual Table illustration above, notice how the forecast has been revised for April and May. Since the company knew systems sales would be down, they planned on it and made a revised forecast in the actuals area. The same revision affects projected profits, balance sheet, and — most important — cash.

The Starting Plan for Profit and Loss

Following the sales example in this chapter, the Planned Profit and Loss illustration, at right, shows a portion of the profit and loss for the sample company, as it stood in the original plan.

PLANNED PROFIT AND LOSS

	Jan	Feb	Mar
Sales	$268,365	$342,025	$415,635
Direct Costs of Goods	$184,510	$243,061	$301,612
Fulfillment Payroll	$9,500	$9,500	$9,500
Other	$500	$500	$500
Cost of Goods Sold	$194,510	$253,061	$311,612
Gross Margin	$73,856	$88,965	$104,024
Gross Margin %	27.52%	26.01%	25.03%
Operating Expenses			
Sales and Marketing Expenses			
Sales and Marketing Payroll	$24,000	$24,000	$24,000
Ads	$5,000	$5,000	$7,000
Catalog	$2,000	$3,000	$2,000
Mailing	$3,000	$11,800	$5,500
Promo	$0	$0	$0
Shows	$0	$0	$0
Literature	$0	$7,000	$0
PR	$0	$0	$0
Seminar	$1,000	$0	$0
Service	$2,000	$1,000	$1,000
Training	$450	$450	$450
Total Sales and Marketing Expenses	$37,450	$52,250	$39,950
Sales and Marketing %	13.95%	15.28%	9.61%

1st Year Planned	1st Year Actual	1st Year Variance	

This table shows the gross margin and sales and marketing expense area of the original plan. This is a portion of the full table.

Actual Results for Profit and Loss

The next illustration, at right, shows the actual results recorded in that portion of profit and loss, after the end of March. The actual results mean little without comparison to the original budget illustration, above.

Unfortunately, many businesses also forget to compare the original plan to the actual results. Especially if business is going well — the operation shows a profit, and cash flow is satisfactory — comparisons with the original budget are made poorly or not at all.

ACTUAL PROFIT AND LOSS RESULTS

	Jan	Feb	Mar
Sales	$223,239	$257,565	$346,051
Direct Costs of Goods	$141,394	$176,275	$240,051
Fulfillment Payroll	$9,308	$9,224	$9,759
Other	$33	$782	$436
Cost of Goods Sold	$150,735	$186,281	$250,246
Gross Margin	$72,504	$71,284	$95,805
Gross Margin %	32.48%	27.68%	27.69%
Operating Expenses			
Sales and Marketing Expenses			
Sales and Marketing Payroll	$23,456	$24,529	$23,871
Ads	$0	$22,674	$7,896
Catalog	$2,200	$3,100	$2,095
Mailing	$1,873	$12,075	$6,621
Promo	$0	$0	$0
Shows	$0	$0	$0
Literature	$0	$0	$6,401
PR	$0	$0	$0
Seminar	$1,000	$0	$0
Service	$0	$3,023	$1,023
Training	$0	$1,000	$500
Total Sales and Marketing Expenses	$28,529	$66,401	$48,407
Sales and Marketing %	12.78%	25.78%	13.99%

1st Year Planned	1st Year Actual	1st Year Variance	

The illustration shows actual results on the actual worksheet. Note how actual sales, costs, and expenses are different from planned results. This is a portion of the full table.

Plan vs. Actual Profit and Loss

The following illustration, Plan vs. Actual Profit and Loss, shows the variance in expenses. The actual results are subtracted from the budget numbers, leaving negative numbers when the actual spending was more than budget or when the sales or profits were less than budget. Variances are calculated differently in different portions of the plan.

- In expense rows, variance becomes the **planned amount** minus the *actual amount*. Lower expenses are a positive variance.

- In the profits and sales areas, variance becomes *actual amount* minus **planned amount**. In these cases, higher sales are a positive variance.

PLAN VS. ACTUAL PROFIT AND LOSS

	Jan	Feb	Mar
Sales	($45,126)	($84,460)	($69,584)
Direct Costs of Goods	$43,116	$66,786	$61,561
Fulfillment Payroll	$192	$276	($259)
Other	$467	($282)	$64
Cost of Goods Sold	$43,775	$66,780	$61,366
Gross Margin	($1,352)	($17,681)	($8,219)
Gross Margin %	4.96%	1.67%	2.66%
Operating Expenses			
Sales and Marketing Expenses			
Sales and Marketing Payroll	$544	($529)	$129
Ads	$5,000	($17,674)	($896)
Catalog	($200)	($100)	($95)
Mailing	$1,127	($275)	($1,121)
Promo	$0	$0	$0
Shows	$0	$0	$0
Literature	$0	$7,000	($6,401)
PR	$0	$0	$0
Seminar	$0	$0	$0
Service	$2,000	($2,023)	($23)
Training	$450	($550)	($50)
Total Sales and Marketing Expenses	$8,921	($14,151)	($8,457)
Sales and Marketing %	1.18%	-10.50%	-4.38%
1st Year Planned	1st Year Actual	1st Year Variance	

The illustration shows a portion of the Profit and Loss Variance. March results showed sales below plan and costs also below plan, for a negative variance in Sales and a positive variance in Cost of Goods Sold. The result is a smaller negative variance in Gross Margin. This is a portion of the table.

Understanding Variance Analysis

Many businesses, especially the small, entrepreneurial kind, ignore or forget the other half of the budgeting. Budgets are too often proposed, discussed, accepted, and forgotten. Variance analysis looks after-the-fact at what caused a difference between plan vs. actual. Good management looks at what that difference means to the business.

Variance analysis ranges from simple and straightforward to sophisticated and complex. Some cost-accounting systems separate variances into many types and categories. Sometimes a single result can be broken down into many different variances, both positive and negative.

The most sophisticated systems separate unit and price factors on materials, hours worked, cost-per-hour on direct labor, and fixed and variable overhead variances. Though difficult, this kind of analysis can be invaluable in a complex business.

Look for Specifics

This presentation of variances shows how important good analysis is. In theory, the positive variances are good news because they mean spending less than budgeted. The negative variance means spending more than the budget.

Variance Analysis for Sample Company

Continuing our example, the $5,000 positive variance in advertising in January means $5,000 less than planned was spent, and the $7,000 positive variance for literature in February means $7,000 less than planned was spent. The negative variance for advertising in February and March, and the negative variance for literature in March, show that more was spent than was planned for those items.

Evaluating these variances takes thought. Positive variances aren't always good news. For example:

- The positive variance of $5,000 in advertising means that money wasn't spent, but it also means that advertising wasn't placed. Systems sales are way below expectations for this same period — could the advertising missed in January be a possible cause?

- For literature, the positive $7,000 in February may be evidence of a missed deadline for literature that wasn't actually completed until March. If so, at least it appears that the costs on completion were $6,401, a bit less than the $7,000 planned.

Among the larger single variances for an expense item in a month shown in the illustration was the positive $7,000 variance for the new literature expenses in February. Is this good news or bad news?

Every variance should stimulate questions.

- Why did one project cost more or less than planned?
- Were objectives met?
- Is a positive variance a cost saving or a failure to implement?
- Is a negative variance a change in plans, a management failure, or an unrealistic budget?

A variance table can provide management with significant information. Without this data, some of these important questions might go unasked.

More on Variance

Variance analysis on sales can be very complex. There can be significant differences between higher or lower sales because of different unit volumes, or because of different average prices. In the sales variance example in this chapter, the units variance shows that the sales of systems were disappointing. In the expenses variance, however, we can see that advertising and mailing costs were below plan. Could there be a correlation between the saved expenses in mailing, and the lower-than-planned sales? Yes, of course there could.

The mailing cost was much less than planned, but as a result the planned sales never came. The positive expense variance is thus not good for the company. Sales and Marketing expenses were also above plan in March, causing another negative variance.

The Sales Forecast Variance (see page 20.3) in Systems comparison between units variance and sales variance yields no surprises. The lower-than-expected unit sales also had lower-than-expected sales values. Compare that to Service, in which lower units yielded higher sales (indicating much higher prices than planned). Is this an indication of a new profit opportunity, or a new trend? This clearly depends on the specifics of your business.

It is often hard to tell what caused differences in costs. If spending schedules aren't met, variance might be caused simply by lower unit volume. Management probably wants to know the results per unit, and the actual price, and the detailed feedback on the marketing programs.

Summary

The quality of a business plan is measured not by the quality of its ideas, analysis, or presentation, but only by the implementation it causes. It is true, of course, that some business plans are developed only as selling documents to generate financial resources. For these plans, their worth is measured by their effectiveness in selling a business opportunity to a prospective investor. For plans created to help run a business, their worth is measured by how much they help run a business — in other words, their implementation.

Variance analysis is vital to good management. You have to track and follow up on budgets, mainly through variance analysis, or the budgets are useless.

Although variance analysis can be very complex, the main guide is common sense. In general, going under budget is a positive variance, and over budget is a negative variance. But the real test of management should be whether or not the result was good for business.

CHAPTER 21:

PRINT AND PUBLISH

So you're about ready to print your plan. Assemble your topics as indicated in the outline in Chapter 2: Pick Your Plan. *Browse through the sample plans at the end of this book to get a better sense of the topic sequence. Throughout this book, we have discussed portions of the plan in the order that you work on it, not in the final order it will print.*

Please make sure to run it through a final critical edit. Then make sure to publish it so that commitments made by managers are clearly known and acknowledged. Also make it clear that you will be tracking results, comparing your actual results to the planned results, and discussing the difference.

Publishing = Management

Don't forget the process of publishing within your own company. In this case, publishing means distributing the plan where all the managers can see it. People who make commitments as part of the plan need to see those commitments on record. They need to know that the plan will be tracked and that the difference between planned and actual results will be calculated and discussed.

Final Edit

Always run a business plan through a final edit. Have you run your spell check software? Have you read it over again? Do you have some friends who can read it for you? Sometimes you don't see the errors that others would see because you are too close to it.

Check the numbers in your charts and tables. Make sure they match each other, and go back and check the references to numbers in the text. People often change numbers after writing objectives, which results in conflicting information. For example, your objectives text might set sales objectives of $500,000, but your plan tables show sales projections of $400,000.

Presentation

Presentation is always important because it helps to communicate content. Good charts are dynamite when they make numbers easier to read quickly, and they can be essential when numbers are complex.

Good text formatting should make the text easy to read. Use a legible font and a good mix of section headings and subheadings to make the organization visible. Bullet points are generally easier to read than long paragraphs. Color is good for charts, when it makes numbers easier to understand, but gets in the way when used for text.

Fancy paper, expensive bindings, and excessive presentation are not really needed. Make the paper whatever quality it takes to make the plan easy to read, avoiding some of the more fibrous papers that end up interfering with the printed content. Make the binding a good coil, or some other binding that will hold up to use, but keep it practical so you impress with content, not expense.

Related Documents

In the process of finding investment financing for a new business or a small business, people normally use a two-to-ten-page Summary Document (sometimes called a Summary Memo).

The Summary Document should have the key points, such as competitive edge, market needs, defensibility, and of course track records and résumés of main team members. Sell your plan, but keep it short and rich. Focus on real content, not hype, and organize it so that potential investors can understand the main points quickly, then decide whether or not they want to know more.

When looking for loans for your business, you will probably want to prepare a slightly different two-to-six-page document, called a Loan Application Summary. It should include the Executive Summary and company ownership detail as well as financials, especially the Profit and Loss, Balance Sheet and Cash Flow tables.

Summary

As you finish your plan, review it from the point of view of the business purpose. Does it cover what you need it to cover? Is it going to achieve the purpose you planned for it? Are there topics that the plan's audience will ask about that you haven't covered? Think of the three most important questions you would expect to get from your intended reader. Have you answered them?

CHAPTER 22:

GETTING FINANCED

Contrary to popular belief, business plans do not generate business financing. True, there are many kinds of financing options that require a business plan, but nobody invests in a business plan. Investors need a business plan as a document that communicates ideas and information, but they invest in a company, in a product, and in people.

Small Business Financing Realities

Venture capital financing is very rare. I'll explain more later in this chapter, but start with the assumption that only a very few high-growth plans with high-power management teams are venture opportunities.

- Banks don't finance business start-ups. I'll have more on that later, too. Banks aren't supposed to invest depositors' money in new businesses.

- Business plans don't sell investors.

In *Chapter 2: Pick Your Plan*, I said the plan matches the needs of the company. So does the process of looking for money. Where you look for money, and how you look for money, depends on your company and the kind of money you need. There is an enormous difference, for example, between a high-growth Internet-related company looking for second-round venture funding and a local retail store looking to finance a branch store. In some of the following sections of this chapter, I want to talk more specifically about the types of investment and lending available.

- Venture Capital

- "Sort-of" Venture Capital: Angels and Others

- Commercial Banks

- The Small Business Administration

- Other Lenders

Venture Capital

The business of venture capital is frequently misunderstood. Many start-up companies resent venture capital companies for failing to invest in new ventures or risky ventures. People talk about venture capitalists as sharks — because of their supposedly predatory business practices — or sheep — because they supposedly think like a flock, all wanting the same kinds of deals.

This is not the case. The venture capital business is a business, and the people we call venture capitalists are business people who are charged with investing other people's money. They have a professional responsibility to reduce risk as much as possible. They should not take more risk than is absolutely necessary to produce the risk/return ratios that the sources of their capital ask of them.

Venture capital shouldn't be thought of as a source of funding for any but a very few exceptional start-up businesses. Venture capital can't afford to invest in start-ups unless there is a rare combination of product opportunity, market opportunity, and proven management. A venture capital investment has to have a reasonable chance of producing a tenfold increase in business value within three years. It needs to focus on newer products and markets that can reasonably project increasing sales by huge multiples over a short period of time. It needs to work with proven managers who have dealt with successful start-ups in the past.

If you are a potential venture capital investment, you probably know it already. You have management team members who have been through that already. You can convince yourself and a room full of intelligent people that your company can grow ten times over in three years.

If you have to ask whether your new company is a possible venture capital opportunity, it probably isn't. People in new growth industries, multimedia communications, biotechnology, or the far reaches of high-technology products generally know about venture capital and venture capital opportunities.

A business plan for venture capital is a more sophisticated business plan. It should always include discussions of valuation, exit strategy, investment offering, dilution, and returns for investors. There are examples later in this chapter. If you are looking for names and addresses of venture capitalists, there's no way around the dominance of the Internet search for detailed information. You should probably start with listings of venture capital firms using the search engines at Yahoo! and Google. There is also a very good listing of financing resources at www.Bplans.com in the Financing Your Business area, and additional resources at www.PaloAlto.com.

In addition, on the Internet, some of the better links for venture capital information include:

- The U.S. National Venture Capital Association. This site has an easy-to-use listing of hundreds of VC firms, including Web links. www.nvca.org

- U.S. Western Association of Venture Capitalists. More than 100 of the better-known mainstream VCs. www.wavc.net

- Venture One, which collects industry data. www.ventureone.com

- VCfodder.com has some venture capital information. www.vcfodder.com

- British Venture Capitalist Association. www.bvca.co.uk

- Canadian Venture Capitalist Association. www.cvca.ca

- Yahoo! listing of venture capital firms. http://dir.yahoo.com/Business_and_Economy/Finance_and_Investment/Financing/Corporate_Financing/

"Sort-of" Venture Capital: Angels and Others

Venture capital is not the only source of investment for start-up businesses or small businesses. Many companies are financed by smaller investors in what is called "private placement." For example, in some areas there are groups of potential investors who meet occasionally to hear proposals. There are also wealthy individuals who occasionally invest in new companies. In the lore of business start-ups, groups of investors are often referred to as "doctors and dentists," and individual investors are often called "angels." Many entrepreneurs turn to friends and family for investment.

Your next question of course is how to find the "doctors, dentists, and angels" that might want to invest in your business. The discussion in *Chapter 9: The Business You're In* includes some government agencies, business development centers, business incubators, and similar organizations that will be tied into the investment communities in your area. Turn first to the local Small Business Development Center (SBDC), which is most likely associated with your local community college, or the Small Business Administration (SBA) offices in your area. Names and website addresses are available at www.sba.gov for the SBA, www.score.org for SCORE, and www.bplans.com/sb/ for a list of SBDC addresses.

You may want to try some secondary listing services and online sourcing businesses, although I haven't had specific dealings with any of them and can't actually recommend any from experience. I don't know the owners and operators of the American Venture Capital Exchange, www.avce.com, but I do know that they've been operating that site for many years. However, I haven't actually used the service. Use these services carefully, and understand that there may be some risk. Another well-known offering is the Business Funding Directory at www.businessfinance.com.

And of course it's always good to look first at the main search engine sites. You could try the search for "angel investors" at www.yahoo.com and www.google.com.

Important: Be careful in dealing with anybody who offers to help you find financing as a service for money. These are shark-infested waters. I am aware of some legitimate providers of business plan consulting and related assistance, but the legitimate providers are harder to find than the sharks.

Commercial Banks

Banks are even less likely than venture capitalists to invest in or loan money to start-up businesses. They are, however, the most likely source of financing for most small businesses.

Start-up entrepreneurs and small business owners are too quick to criticize banks for failing to finance new businesses. Banks are not supposed to invest in businesses, and are strictly limited in this respect by Federal banking laws. The government prevents banks from investment in businesses because society, in general, doesn't want banks taking savings from depositors and investing in risky business ventures; obviously when (and if) those business ventures fail, bank depositors' money is at risk. Would you want your bank to invest in new businesses (other than your own, of course)?

Furthermore, banks should not be loaning money to start-up companies either, for many of the same reasons. Federal regulators want banks to keep money safe, in very conservative loans backed by solid collateral. Start-up businesses are not safe enough for bank regulators and they don't have enough collateral.

Why, then, do we say that banks are the most likely source of small business financing? Because small business owners borrow from banks. A great deal of small business financing is accomplished through bank loans based on the business owner's personal collateral, such as home ownership. Some would say that home equity is the greatest source of small business financing.

A business that has been around for a few years generates enough stability and assets to serve as collateral. Banks commonly make loans to well-established small businesses backed by the company's inventory or accounts receivable. Normally there are formulas that determine how much can be loaned, depending on how much is in inventory and in accounts receivable.

The Small Business Administration (SBA)

The SBA makes loans to small businesses and even to start-up businesses. SBA loans are almost always applied for and administered by local banks. You normally deal with a local bank throughout the process.

For start-up loans, the SBA will normally require that at least one third of the required capital be supplied by the new business owner. Furthermore, the rest of the amount must be guaranteed by reasonable business or personal assets.

The SBA works with "certified lenders," which are banks. It takes a certified lender as little as one week to get approval from the SBA. If your own bank isn't a certified lender, you should ask your banker to recommend a local bank that is. You can always contact the SBA directly using the contact information posted on its website, at www.sba.gov.

Other Lenders

Aside from standard bank loans, an established small business can also turn to accounts receivable specialists to borrow against its accounts receivable.

The most common accounts receivable financing is used to support cash flow when working capital is hung up in accounts receivable. For example, if your business sells to distributors that take 60 days to pay, and the outstanding invoices waiting for payment (but not late) come to $100,000, your company can probably borrow more than $50,000. Interest rates and fees may be relatively high, but this is still often a good source of small business financing. In most cases, the lender doesn't take the risk of payment — if your customer doesn't pay you, you have to pay the money back anyhow. These lenders will often review your debtors, and choose to finance some or all of the invoices outstanding.

Another related business practice is called factoring. So-called factors actually purchase obligations, so if a customer owes you $100,000 you can sell the related paperwork to the factor for some percentage of the total amount. In this case, the factor takes the risk of payment, so discounts are obviously quite steep. Ask your banker for additional information about factoring.

Important Words of Warning

Don't take private placement, angels, and friends and family as good sources of investment capital just because they are described here or taken seriously in some other source of information. Some investors are a good source of capital, and some aren't. These less established sources of investment may be necessary, but they should be handled with **extreme caution**.

Never, NEVER spend somebody else's money without first doing the legal work properly. Have the papers done by professionals, and make sure they're signed.

Never, NEVER spend money that has been promised but not delivered. It is amazing how often companies get investment commitments, contract for expenses, and then when the investment falls through, find themselves left in the lurch.

Submitting a Plan to a Bank

As we point out in the discussions in this chapter, the process of taking out a bank loan is quite different from raising venture capital or angel investment. Banks are not allowed to invest in a business plan in an entrepreneurial way because they are using depositors' money and they must by law have real collateral to back up any loans. Therefore, the plan you submit to a bank is different from what you submit to a potential investor.

For a bank loan, your plan needs to have the same critical information as for any other use. However, it should also have more financial detail, more past history, and more information on the personal financial position of the members of the management team, the balance sheet of the business, and financial history of the business. Owners should expect to submit a personal financial statement, and for most smaller businesses and newer businesses the owners will frequently have to place personal assets at risk, and offer personal guarantees.

What Banks Want to See

Along with your plan, commercial banks will also want to see a loan application, copies of past tax reports for company and principals, good documentation of past financial results, and personal financial statements of principals.

Most banks will use commercial scoring methods to evaluate a loan based on indicators including the worth of assets and ratios measuring debt and liquidity. Business ratios, which we discussed in *Chapter 17: Finish the Financials,* can be very important.

The Physical Document

For banks, submit a document a bank loan manager can pass around. It should be clean, bound, clearly marked with cover page and legal page, easy to read, and well illustrated. Wire coil binding is better than plastic and velobinding. Invest in strong covers, and make sure the vital information is clearly visible from the cover, or through a window on the cover page.

Legibility is important. Don't save paper with small fonts, and do use graphics and color where you can. Try to illustrate all key numbers with business charts.

Don't go overboard with your plan. Bankers are not going to be impressed by exaggeration of graphics, too many illustrations, or too much effort to make a plan flashy. They want to see that the business plan is developed by people who understand business. It should be easy to read, practical, complete, and concise.

Submitting a Plan to Investors

Mind the Law

Be aware that securities law covers investment offers. It is illegal to sell shares in your company to people not qualified as investors. This is not the format for a long legal discussion, but at least you should know the basics. Securities law regulates investment offerings carefully. You can do some good research at www.sec.gov/answers/accred.htm for example, but make sure you consult a qualified attorney before making an investment offer.

Avoid turning to friends and family for investment. The worst possible time to not have the support of friends and family is when your business is in trouble. When the business is financed by friends and family, you risk losing friends, family, and your business at the same time. I know an entrepreneur who stuck with a losing business for six years longer than he should have, because he started it with money from friends and family.

Form should follow function, of course, but there are some expectations you should meet. How you submit a plan, and the form you use, should depend a great deal on the underlying objective. What you do for a mainstream venture capitalist should be tailored for that use, and different from what you'd do for a bank loan application.

What Investors Want to See

- Show how much money you seek and how much ownership you offer. How much do you think your company is worth?

- List current shareholders and outstanding blocks of stock, existing options, and potential dilution.

- A strong management team, with a good track record.

- A believable business model.

- Good credible evidence of interesting potential growth.

Investors Expect a Summary Memo

Mainstream venture capitalists and most angel investors expect to see a 2-10 page Summary Memo first, before they see a complete business plan. The Summary Memo gives its readers a quick but practical view of the business concept, the market, the management team, strategy, and basic financials. Professional investors use this document to decide whether they want to see the full plan.

The Summary Memo is sometimes called an Executive Summary, but it is not the same thing as the first chapter of a normal business plan, also called Executive Summary. Its business objective is to interest investors in talking to the management team and looking at the complete plan. It needs to highlight and present the most important information that helps in that process.

Don't prepare just a Summary Memo instead of a plan. The purpose of the Summary Memo is to get an investor to ask for the whole plan, so of course you have to have the plan ready to go before you show the Summary Memo.

Most Investors Want a Presentation

If you are looking for venture capital or angel investment, you should prepare a slide presentation covering the same critical content as the Summary Memo. Most investors consider the face-to-face presentation a natural part of the process, most frequently coming after they've read the Summary Memo but before they analyze the complete business plan. They want to see the management team in person, listen to a summary explanation, and ask questions.

Important: A presentation is not a plan. It's a different medium, so you need to use different communications. Use PowerPoint or similar presentation software.

- No more than 10 words per slide. Use pictures. Use charts.

- Don't read bullet points. Show pictures and talk. Don't copy texts from your business plan into your presentation. Texts kill presentations.

- Keep it short. A standard presentation takes 20 minutes. Expect to be interrupted. If you don't get 40 minutes of discussion with a 20-minute presentation, they're not really interested.

- Highlight investors' return on investment.

You Probably Also Need an "Elevator Speech"

Many professional investors refer to the entrepreneur's "elevator speech" as a quick explanation of the key concepts and main points. The phrase comes from the idea that an entrepreneur should be able to explain the business plan in the very short time of a ride up or down the elevator. The underlying thought is that if it doesn't come out clearly in 30-60 seconds, it may not be that good.

If you are looking for investment, be aware of that phrase and know what it means. And prepare your elevator speech. Keep it in mind as you develop your plan, summary memo, and presentation.

Target Your Investors Carefully

Do not ever submit your plan to potential investors who have no reason to be interested. Information on mainstream venture capitalists is readily available, so you should always limit your submission to firms that have interest in the industry, geographic area, and deal stage you're in. Information on venture capital firms is readily available on the Web, so there is no excuse for submitting a plan to a firm whose interests don't match. Look at the discussion earlier in this chapter for more resources on where to get lists of venture capitalists and how to find angel investors.

We have mixed reports on the growing number of investment sites that offer variations on posting a plan where investors will look at it. Several of these sites offer services such as posting summaries of your plan, or matching your plan to potential investors. This sounds attractive, and we don't know for a fact that it doesn't work, but our experience is that the deals chase the money, the money doesn't chase the deals. Go slowly and carefully, and look for indications of successful previous deals.

You don't want your plan to be put off as "shopped." Among mainstream venture capitalists, they don't generally want a deal that has been turned down by others. Be very selective.

Use a Business Plan Website

You could make use of technology by putting your business plan onto a website. That doesn't mean it has to be public; it can easily be a private, password-protected website. Business Plan Pro®, www.paloalto.com/ps/bp/, for example, includes the facility to post a plan onto a secure website with a customizable cover page, password protection, and complete financial tables and charts. But don't depend on a website as your main medium. Have hard-copy physical plan and electronic (Adobe PDF or similar file format) copies readily available. You never want to depend on a Web connection for an important meeting.

Joe Tanous, mainstream venture capitalist and partner in eFund Group, www.efundllc.com, told us recently that his company, "won't accept a business plan submitted in paper." He explained that the website option was more practical and easier to deal with than tracking physical plans on paper.

For investors, bankers, potential partners, and management team members, a plan posted on a secure website can be an ideal vehicle for delivering the plan information. The website is always up to date, easily modified, and available to read whenever and wherever a reader has Internet access.

Investors Expect Additional Calculations

You Should Estimate Investor's Net Present Value (NPV)

The Net Present Value (NPV) is a measure of the present value of future cash. To calculate NPV you discount future money at some assumed discount rate. In the following illustration you can see two sample investments, both with the same NPV, although very different cash flows. Both are discounted at 10% for calculating NPV.

CALCULATING NET PRESENT VALUE (NPV)

	Start	Year 1	Year 2	Year 3	Year 4	Year 5
Case 1	($2,000)	$750	$750	$750	$750	$750
Net Present Value (NPV)	$766					
Internal Rate of Return (IRR)	25%					
Case 2	($2,000)	$0	$0	$0	$0	$4,578
Net Present Value (NPV)	$766					
Internal Rate of Return (IRR)	18%					
Discount Rate	10.00%					

You can calculate NPV in a spreadsheet. Most spreadsheets have an NPV function (this one from Business Plan Pro®).

In the illustration, the selected cell has an automatic function for calculating NPV based on defined discount rate and cash flows. Both of the investments have NPV of $766, even though one pays regular annual payments of $750, and the other pays nothing until a large payment at the end. Notice how the time value of money changes. The total payout of the first investment is less than that of the second, but because the first one's payout starts sooner, they both have equal NPV.

For more background on how the discounting calculation can be done manually, you should consult a finance textbook or search the Web for the term "net present value." The best option is to build an NPV analysis into an Investment Analysis prepared especially for the investors.

Calculate Investors' Internal Rate of Return (IRR)

The Internal Rate of Return (IRR) is based on the NPV calculation. It is the discount rate at which the NPV is zero. Most spreadsheets have functions that help you calculate IRR from a cash flow.

AN INTERNAL RATE OF RETURN (IRR) CALCULATION

	Start	Year 1	Year 2	Year 3	Year 4	Year 5
Case 1	($2,000)	$750	$750	$750	$750	$750
Net Present Value (NPV)	$766					
Internal Rate of Return (IRR)	25%					
Case 2	($2,000)	$0	$0	$0	$0	$4,578
Net Present Value (NPV)	$766					
Internal Rate of Return (IRR)	18%					
Discount Rate	10.00%					

You can see how the investment that pays sooner has a higher IRR, even though the second investment pays more.

One important point with IRR, as the two investments show, is that although they have equal NPV, they have very different IRRs. That's because the better one generates cash flow sooner.

Another important IRR point is that venture capitalists expect very high IRR on new investments. In recent years venture capital funds have generated overall Rates of Return of 50-100% or better, meaning that the winning deals have to generate IRRs of 200% or better. That's a very high return.

Use an Investment Analysis to Show Investor Returns

Although NPV and IRR calculations may be enough, it's generally better to use a complete investment analysis table to set the basic expectations of investment amount, percent of company acquired, and proposed return. The following table offers an example.

PROPOSED INVESTOR RETURNS

Investment Analysis	Start	Year 1	Year 2	Year 3	Year 4	Year 5
Investment	$1,000	$0	$0	$0	$0	$0
Dividends	$0	$0	$0	$0	$0	$0
Ending Valuation	$0	$0	$0	$0	$0	$88,000
Combination as Income Stream	($1,000)	$0	$0	$0	$0	$88,000
Percent Equity Acquired	55%					
Net Present Value (NPV)	$54,641					
Internal Rate of Return (IRR)	145%					
Assumptions						
Discount Rate	10.00%					
Valuation Earnings Multiple		10	10	10	10	10
Valuation Sales Multiple		2	2	2	2	2
Investment (calculated)	$1,000	$0	$0	$0	$0	$0
Dividends		$0	$0	$0	$0	$0
Calculated Earnings-based Valuation		$0	$0	$10,000	$30,000	$80,000
Calculated Sales-based Valuation		$0	$10,000	$20,000	$50,000	$160,000
Calculated Average Valuation		$0	$5,000	$15,000	$40,000	$120,000

The Investment Analysis Table lays the groundwork for the investor. (Note: for display purposes dollar values are displayed in thousands.)

You can see here that the investment proposal is that an initial investment of $1 million at start-up buys 55% of the company. That share will be worth $88 million in Year 5, which is a Net Present Value of $54.6 million, and an Internal Rate of Return (IRR) of 145%

In the real world, all of these values are the subject of negotiation. Investors rarely, if ever, accept the entrepreneurs' assumptions for future sales, valuation, investment amount, or percent of ownership. They do, however, expect the entrepreneurs seeking investment to calculate return on investment and to show their assumptions clearly as they suggest possible returns.

The sample shown here is just one example. The world of investing and start-up businesses doesn't have a set format for presenting this type of information. What's most important is to make sure that the information is available to investors as part of the plan.

The Investment Offering Table

Investors also want to know how you plan to distribute stock ownership and handle dilution. This is especially important when a start-up needs multiple rounds of financing, but even with a more simple investment plan, the investors want to know what you plan to do with shares. How many shares of stock are there, how many do the founders already own, how many are pledged to employees, and how many will be offered to future investors?

INVESTMENT OFFERING TABLE

Investment Offering Proposed Year:	Seed 1	Round 1 2	Round 2 3	Exit 6
Valuation, Investment, Shares				
Investment Amount	$1,000	$2,500	$5,000	
Equity Share Offering Percentage	55.00%	30.00%	15.00%	
Valuation	$1,818	$8,333	$33,333	$160,000
Investor Exit Payout	$50,617	$40,034	$23,793	
Investor Years Until Exit	5	4	3	
Investor IRR	119.21%	100.04%	68.20%	
Share Ownership	Year 1	Year 2	Year 3	Year 6
Founders' Shares	1,000	2,000	4,000	4,000
Stock Split Multiple		2	2	0
Stock Options Issued	500	100	200	200
Investor Shares Issued	1,833	2,900	3,447	
Price per share	$0.55	$0.86	$1.45	$6.90
Options Holders' Shares	500	1,100	2,400	2,600
Year 1 Investors' Shares	1,833	3,667	7,333	7,333
Year 2 Investors' Shares		2,900	5,800	5,800
Year 3 Investors' Shares			3,447	3,447
Total Shares Outstanding	3,333	9,667	22,980	23,180

The Investment Offering Table lays the groundwork for the investor. It shows the investors the plan for stock ownership and dilution through three rounds of investment. (Note: dollar values are displayed in thousands.)

The most important reason for the investment offering table is to show the impact of dilution as a growth company absorbs several rounds of investment. Perhaps the easiest way to explain this is to focus on the seed investors and the change in their return after dilution by comparing the table above to what it would be without any additional dilution, as shown in the table below.

THE OFFERING WITHOUT DILUTION

Investment Amount	$1,000	$0	$0	
Equity Share Offering Percentage	55.00%	0.00%	0.00%	
Valuation	$1,818	$0	$0	$160,000
Investor Exit Payout	$88,000	$0	$0	
Investor Years Until Exit	5	4	3	
Investor IRR	144.85%	0.00%	0.00%	

Without dilution, the projected IRR for the seed investors is still 145%. Compare this to the previous illustration, with dilution. Note: dollar values are displayed in thousands.

How and Why of Stock Shares and Dilution

Dilution is quite common in sophisticated growth companies because they need to bring in additional investors to finance high growth. The underlying reason goes back to what we discussed earlier in *Chapter 16: Cash is King*; growth takes cash, meaning more capital, meaning more investment. The next illustration, taken from the lower half of the Investment Offering table, shows details of dilution.

DETAILS OF DILUTION

Share Ownership	Year 1	Year 2	Year 3	Year 6
Founders' Shares	1,000	2,000	4,000	4,000
Stock Split Multiple		2	2	0
Stock Options Issued	500	100	200	200
Investor Shares Issued	1,833	2,900	3,447	
Price per Share	$1	$1	$1	$7
Options Holders' Shares	500	1,100	2,400	2,600
Year 1 Investors' Shares	1,833	3,667	7,333	7,333
Year 2 Investors' Shares		2,900	5,800	5,800
Year 3 Investors' Shares			3,447	3,447
Total Shares Outstanding	3,333	9,667	22,980	23,180

Equity Ownership Percent	Year 1	Year 2	Year 3	Year 6
Founders' Equity	30.00%	20.69%	17.41%	17.26%
Option Holders' Equity	15.00%	11.38%	10.44%	11.22%
Year 1 Investors' Equity	55.00%	37.93%	31.91%	31.64%
Year 2 Investors' Equity		30.00%	25.24%	25.02%
Year 3 Investors' Equity			15.00%	14.87%
Total Equity	100.00%	100.00%	100.00%	100.00%
Investors' Equity	55.00%	67.93%	72.15%	71.53%
Founders' & Employees' Equity	45.00%	32.07%	27.85%	28.47%

Dilution is a matter of simple mathematics as stock ownership spreads. The ownership associated with each share decreases as the numbers of shares increase. (Note: dollar values are displayed in thousands.)

Stock Ownership is Simple Math

You can study the Investment Offering table to see that sophisticated-sounding concepts like stock ownership, shares, value per share, and valuation are based on relatively simple math. You can calculate valuation by multiplying the price of a single share of stock by the number of shares. You calculate percent of ownership by dividing the number of shares owned by the total number of shares. You can easily decrease the price of a share by increasing the number of shares available.

Therefore, if you tell an investor you're offering 10% of the company for $1 million, for example, you are saying your company is worth $10 million.

Summary

Most businesses are financed by home equity or savings as they start. Only a few can attract outside investment. Venture capital deals are extremely rare. Borrowing will always depend on collateral and guarantees, not on business plans or ideas. And yes, it seems obvious, but still, with emphasis: investors need to make money.

SAMPLE PLAN:

ACME CONSULTING

This sample business plan has been made available to users of Business Plan Pro®, business planning software published by Palo Alto Software. Names, locations and numbers may have been changed, and substantial portions of the original plan text may have been omitted to preserve confidentiality and protect proprietary information.

You are welcome to use this plan as a starting point to create your own, but you do not have permission to reproduce, publish, distribute or even copy this plan as it exists here.

Requests for reprints, academic use, and other dissemination of this sample plan should be emailed to the marketing department of Palo Alto Software at marketing@paloalto.com. For product information visit our Website: www.paloalto.com or call: 1-800-229-7526.

Acme Consulting
Table of Contents

1.0 Executive Summary

Acme Consulting will be formed as a consulting company specializing in marketing of high-technology products in international markets. Its founders are former marketers of consulting services, personal computers, and market research, all in international markets. They are founding Acme to formalize the consulting services they offer.

Business Plan Highlights

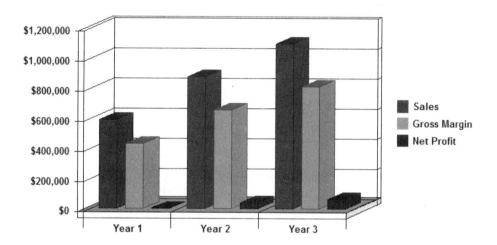

1.1 Objectives

1. Sales of over $1 million by Year 3.

2. Gross margin higher than 80%.

3. Net income more than 10% of sales by Year 3.

1.2 Mission

Acme Consulting offers high-tech manufacturers a reliable, high-quality alternative to in-house resources for business development, market development, and channel development on an international scale. A true alternative to in-house resources offers a very high level of practical experience, know-how, contacts, and confidentiality. Clients must know that working with Acme is a more professional, less risky way to develop new areas even than working completely in-house with their own people. Acme must also be able to maintain financial balance, charging a high value for its services, and delivering an even higher value to its clients. Initial focus will be development in the European and Latin American markets, or for European clients in the United States market.

1.3 Keys to Success

1. Excellence in fulfilling the promise—completely confidential, reliable, trustworthy expertise and information.

2. Developing visibility to generate new business leads.

3. Leveraging from a single pool of expertise into multiple revenue generation opportunities: retainer consulting, project consulting, market research, and market research published reports.

2.0 Company Summary

Acme Consulting is a new company providing high-level expertise in international high-tech business development, channel development, distribution strategies, and marketing of high-tech products. It will focus initially on providing two kinds of international triangles:

- Providing United States clients with development for European and Latin American markets.

- Providing European clients with development for the United States and Latin American markets.

As it grows it will take on people and consulting work in related markets, such as the rest of Latin America, the Far East, and similar markets. It will also look for additional leverage by taking brokerage positions and representation positions to create percentage holdings in product results.

2.1 Company Ownership

Acme Consulting will be created as a California C corporation based in Santa Clara County, owned by its principal investors and principal operators. As of this writing, it has not been chartered yet and is still considering alternatives of legal formation.

2.2 Start-up Summary

Total start-up expense (including legal costs, logo design, stationery and related expenses) come to $18,350. Start-up assets required include $3,000 in short-term assets (office furniture, etc.) and $50,000 in initial cash to handle the first few months of consulting operations as sales and accounts receivable play through the cash flow. The details are included in the following table:

Start-up Plan	
Start-up Expenses	
Legal	$1,000
Stationery etc.	$3,000
Brochures	$5,000
Consultants	$5,000
Insurance	$350
Expensed equipment	$3,000
Other	$1,000
Total Start-up Expense	$18,350
Start-up Assets Needed	
Cash Requirements	$25,000
Other Short-term Assets	$7,000
Total Short-term Assets	$32,000
Long-term Assets	$0
Total Assets	$32,000
Total Start-up Requirements:	$50,350
Left to finance:	$0
Start-up Funding Plan	
Investment	
Investor 1	$20,000
Investor 2	$20,000
Other	$10,000
Total investment	$50,000
Short-term Liabilities	
Unpaid Expenses	$350
Short-term Loans	$0
Interest-free Short-term Loans	$0
Subtotal Short-term Liabilities	$350
Long-term Liabilities	$0
Total Liabilities	$350
Loss at Start-up	($18,350)
Total Capital	$31,650
Total Capital and Liabilities	$32,000
Checkline	$0

Start-up Financing

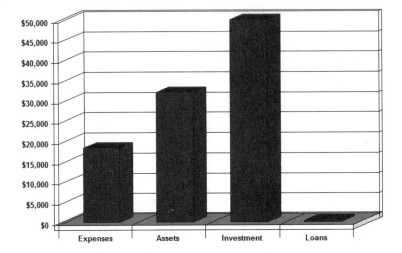

2.3 Company Services

Acme offers expertise in channel distribution/development, and market development, sold and packaged in various ways that allow clients to choose their preferred relationship: these include retainer consulting relationships, project-based consulting, relationship and alliance brokering, sales representation and market representation, project-based market research, published market research, and information forums.

2.4 Company Locations and Facilities

The initial office will be established in a standard or better quality office space in the Santa Clara County "Silicon Valley" area of California, the heart of the U.S. high-tech industry.

3.0 Services

Acme offers the expertise a high-technology company needs to develop new product distribution and new market segments in new markets. This can be taken as high-level retainer consulting, market research reports, or project-based consulting.

3.1 Service Description

1. Retainer consulting: We represent a client company as an extension of its business development and market development functions. This begins with complete understanding of the client company's situation, objectives, and constraints. We then represent the client company quietly and confidentially, sifting through new market developments and new opportunities as is appropriate to the client, representing the client in initial talks with possible allies, vendors, and channels.

2. Project consulting: Proposed and billed on a per-project and per-milestone basis, project consulting offers a client company a way to harness our specific qualities and use our expertise to solve specific problems, develop and/or implement plans, and develop specific information.

3. Market research: Group studies available to selected clients at $5,000 per unit. A group study is a packaged and published complete study of a specific market, channel, or topic. Examples might be studies of developing consumer channels in Japan or Mexico, or implications of changing margins in software.

3.2 Competitive Comparison

The competition comes in several forms:

1. The most significant competition is no consulting at all, companies choosing to do business development, channel development and market research in-house. Their own managers do this on their own, as part of their regular business functions. Our key advantage in competition with in-house development is that managers are already overloaded with responsibilities, they don't have time for additional responsibilities in new market development or new channel development. Also, Acme can approach alliances, vendors, and channels on a confidential basis, gathering information and making initial contacts in ways that the corporate managers can't.

2. The high-level prestige management consulting: McKinsey, Bain, Arthur Anderson, Boston Consulting Group, etc. These are essentially generalists who take their name-brand management consulting into specialty areas. Their other very important weakness is the management structure that has the partners selling new jobs, and inexperienced associates delivering the work. We compete against them as experts in our specific fields, and with the guarantee that our clients will have the top-level people doing the actual work.

3. The third general kind of competitor is the international market research company: International Data Corporation (IDC), Dataquest, Stanford Research Institute, etc. These companies are formidable competitors for published market research and market forums, but cannot provide the kind of high-level consulting that Acme will provide.

4. The fourth kind of competition is the market-specific smaller house. For example: Nomura Research in Japan, Select S.A. de C.V. in Mexico (now affiliated with IDC).

5. Sales representation, brokering, and deal catalysts are an ad-hoc business form that will be defined in detail by the specific nature of each individual case.

3.3 Sales Literature

The business will begin with a general corporate brochure establishing the positioning. This brochure will be developed as part of the start-up expenses. Literature and mailings for the initial market forums will be very important.

3.4 Fulfillment

1. The key fulfillment and delivery will be provided by the principals of the business. The real core value is professional expertise, provided by a combination of experience, hard work, and education (in that order).

2. We will turn to qualified professionals for freelance backup in market research and presentation and report development, which are areas that we can afford to subcontract without risking the core values provided to the clients.

3.5 Technology

Acme Consulting will maintain the latest Windows and Macintosh capabilities including:

1. Complete email facilities on the Internet, CompuServe, America-Online, and Applelink, for working with clients directly through email delivery of drafts and information.

2. Complete presentation facilities for preparation and delivery of multimedia presentations on Macintosh or Windows machines, in formats including on-disk presentation, live presentation, or video presentation.

3. Complete desktop publishing facilities for delivery of regular retainer reports, project output reports, marketing materials, and market research reports.

3.6 Future Services

In the future, Acme will broaden the coverage by expanding into coverage of additional markets (e.g., all of Latin America, Far East, Western Europe) and additional product areas (e.g., telecommunications and technology integration).

We are also studying the possibility of newsletter or electronic newsletter services, or perhaps special on-topic reports.

4.0 Market Analysis Summary

Acme will be focusing on high-technology manufacturers of computer hardware and software, services, and networking, who want to sell into markets in the United States, Europe, and Latin America. These are mostly larger companies, and occasionally medium-sized companies.

Our most important group of potential customers are executives in larger corporations. These are marketing managers, general managers, sales managers, sometimes charged with international focus and sometimes charged with market or even specific channel focus. They do not want to waste their time or risk their money looking for bargain information or questionable expertise. As they go into markets looking at new opportunities, they are very sensitive to risking their company's name and reputation.

4.1 Market Segmentation

Large manufacturer corporations: Our most important market segment is the large manufacturer of high-technology products, such as Apple, Hewlett-Packard, IBM, Microsoft, Siemens, or Olivetti. These companies will be calling on Acme for development functions that are better spun off than managed in-house, for market research, and for market forums.

Medium-sized growth companies: particularly in software, multimedia, and some related high-growth fields, Acme will offer an attractive development alternative to the company that is management constrained and unable to address opportunities in new markets and new market segments.

Market Analysis Potential Customers	Growth	Year 1	Year 2	Year 3	Year 4	Year 5	CAGR
U.S. High Tech	10%	5,000	5,500	6,050	6,655	7,321	10.00%
European High Tech	15%	1,000	1,150	1,323	1,521	1,749	15.00%
Latin America	35%	250	338	456	616	832	35.07%
Other	2%	10,000	10,200	10,404	10,612	10,824	2.00%
Total	6.27%	16,250	17,188	18,233	19,404	20,726	6.27%

Potential Market by Segment

- U.S. High Tech
- European High Tech
- Latin America
- Other

4.2 Target Market Segment Strategy

As indicated by the previous table and illustration, we must focus on a few thousand well-chosen potential customers in the United States, Europe, and Latin America. These few thousand high-tech manufacturing companies are the key customers for Acme.

4.3 Service Business Analysis

The consulting "industry" is pulverized and disorganized, with thousands of smaller consulting organizations and individual consultants for every one of the few dozen well-known companies.

Consulting participants range from major international name-brand consultants to tens of thousands of individuals. One of Acme's challenges will be establishing itself as a real consulting company, positioned as a relatively risk-free corporate purchase.

4.3.1 Business Participants

At the highest level are the few well-established major names in management consulting. Most of these are organized as partnerships established in major markets around the world, linked together by interconnecting directors and sharing the name and corporate wisdom. Some evolved from accounting companies (e.g. Arthur Andersen, Touche Ross) and some from management consulting (McKinsey, Bain). These companies charge very high rates for consulting, and maintain relatively high overhead structures and fulfillment structures based on partners selling and junior associates fulfilling.

At the intermediate level are some function-specific or market-specific consultants, such as the market research firms (IDC, Dataquest) or channel development firms (ChannelCorp, Channel Strategies, ChannelMark).

Some kinds of consulting are little more than contract expertise provided by somebody who, while temporarily out of work, offers consulting services.

4.3.2 Distributing a Service

Consulting is sold and purchased mainly on a word-of-mouth basis, with relationships and previous experience being, by far, the most important factor.

The major name-brand houses have locations in major cities and major markets, and executive-level managers or partners develop new business through industry associations, business associations, chambers of commerce and industry, etc., and in some cases social associations such as country clubs.

The medium-level houses are generally area specific or function specific, and are not easily able to leverage their business through distribution.

4.3.3 Competition and Buying Patterns

The key element in purchase decisions made at the Acme client level is trust in the professional reputation and reliability of the consulting firm.

4.3.4 Main Competitors

1. The high-level prestige management consulting:

    Strengths: International locations managed by owner-partners with a high level of presentation and understanding of general business. Enviable reputations which make purchase of consulting an easy decision for a manager, despite the very high prices.

    Weaknesses: General business knowledge doesn't substitute for the specific market, channel, and distribution expertise of Acme, focusing on high-technology markets and products only. Also, fees are extremely expensive, and work is generally done by very junior-level consultants, even though sold by high-level partners.

2. The international market research company:

    Strengths: International offices, specific market knowledge, permanent staff developing market research information on permanent basis, good relationships with potential client companies.

    Weaknesses: Market numbers are not marketing, not channel development nor market development. Although these companies compete for some of the business Acme is after, they cannot really offer the same level of business understanding at a high level.

3. Market specific or function specific experts:

    Strengths: Expertise in market or functional areas. Acme should not try to compete with Nomura or Select in their markets with market research, or with ChannelCorp in channel management.

    Weaknesses: The inability to spread beyond a specific focus, or to rise above a specific focus, to provide actual management expertise, experience, and wisdom beyond the specifics.

4. The most significant competition is no consulting at all, companies choosing to do business development, channel development, and market research in-house.

    Strengths: No incremental cost except travel; also, the general work is done by the people who are entirely responsible, the planning is done by those who will implement it.

    Weaknesses: Most managers are terribly overburdened already, unable to find incremental resources in time and people to apply to incremental opportunities. Also, there is a lot of additional risk in market and channel development done in-house from the ground up. Finally, retainer-based antenna consultants can greatly enhance a company's reach and extend its position into conversations that might otherwise never have taken place.

5.0 Strategy and Implementation Summary

Acme will focus on three geographical markets, the United States, Europe, and Latin America, and in limited product segments: personal computers, software, networks, telecommunications, personal organizers, and technology integration products.

The target customer is usually a manager in a larger corporation, and occasionally an owner or president of a medium-sized corporation in a high-growth period.

5.1 Pricing Strategy

Acme Consulting will be priced at the upper edge of what the market will bear, competing with the name-brand consultants. The pricing fits with the general positioning of Acme as providing high-level expertise.

Consulting should be based on $5,000 per day for project consulting, $2,000 per day for market research, and $10,000 per month and up for retainer consulting. Market research reports should be priced at $5,000 per report, which will, of course, require that reports be very well planned, focused on very important topics, and very well presented.

5.2 Sales Forecast

The sales forecast monthly summary is included in the appendix. The annual sales projections are included here.

Sales Forecast

Sales	Year 1	Year 2	Year 3
Retainer Consulting	$200,000	$350,000	$425,000
Project Consulting	$270,000	$325,000	$350,000
Market Research	$122,000	$150,000	$200,000
Strategic Reports	$0	$50,000	$125,000
Other	$0	$0	$0
Total Sales	$592,000	$875,000	$1,100,000
Direct Cost of sales	Year 1	Year 2	Year 3
Retainer Consulting	$30,000	$38,000	$48,000
Project Consulting	$45,000	$56,000	$70,000
Market Research	$84,000	$105,000	$131,000
Strategic Reports	$0	$20,000	$40,000
Other	$0	$0	$0
Subtotal Cost of Sales	$159,000	$219,000	$289,000

5.3 Strategic Alliances

At this writing, strategic alliances with Smith and Jones are possibilities, given the content of existing discussions. Given the background of prospective partners, we might also be talking to European companies including Siemens, Olivetti, and others, and to United States companies related to Apple Computer. In Latin America we would be looking at the key local high-technology vendors, beginning with Printaform.

6.0 Management Summary

The initial management team depends on the founders themselves, with little backup. As we grow, we will take on additional consulting help, plus graphic/editorial, sales, and marketing.

6.1 Organizational Structure

Acme should be managed by working partners, in a structure taken mainly from Smith Partners. In the beginning we assume 3-5 partners:

- Ralph Sampson.

- At least one, probably two, partners from Smith and Jones.

- One strong European partner, based in Paris.

  The organization has to be very flat in the beginning, with each of the founders responsible for his or her own work and management.

- One other strong partner.

6.2 Management Team

The Acme business requires a very high level of international experience and expertise, which means that it will not be easily leveragable in the common consulting company mode in which partners run the business and make sales, while associates fulfill. Partners will necessarily be involved in the fulfillment of the core business proposition, providing the expertise to the clients. The initial personnel plan is still tentative. It should involve 3-5 partners, 1-3 consultants, one strong editorial/graphic person with good staff support, one strong marketing person, an office manager, and a secretary. Later, we add more partners, consultants, and sales staff. Founders' resumes are included as an attachment to this plan.

6.3 Personnel Plan

The detailed monthly personnel plan for the first year is included in the appendix. The annual personnel estimates are included here.

Personnel Plan

	Year 1	Year 2	Year 3
Partners	$144,000	$175,000	$200,000
Consultants	$0	$50,000	$63,000
Editorial/graphic	$18,000	$22,000	$26,000
VP Marketing	$20,000	$50,000	$55,000
Sales people	$0	$30,000	$33,000
Office Manager	$7,500	$30,000	$33,000
Secretarial	$5,250	$20,000	$22,000
Other	$0	$0	$0
Other	$0	$0	$0
Total Payroll	$194,750	$377,000	$432,000
Total Headcount	7	10	11
Payroll Burden	$27,265	$52,780	$60,480
Total Payroll Expenditures	$222,015	$429,780	$492,480

7.0 Financial Plan

7.1 Important Assumptions

The following table summarizes key financial assumptions, including 45-day average collection days, sales entirely on invoice basis, expenses mainly on net 30 basis, 35 days on average for payment of invoices, and present-day interest rates.

General Assumptions

	Year 1	Year 2	Year 3
Short-term Interest Rate %	8.00%	8.00%	8.00%
Long-term Interest Rate %	10.00%	10.00%	10.00%
Payment Days Estimator	35	35	35
Collection Days Estimator	45	45	45
Tax Rate %	25.00%	25.00%	25.00%
Expenses in Cash %	25.00%	25.00%	25.00%
Sales on Credit %	100.00%	100.00%	100.00%
Personnel Burden %	14.00%	14.00%	14.00%

7.2 Key Financial Indicators

The following benchmark chart indicates our key financial indicators for the first three years. We foresee major growth in sales and operating expenses, and a bump in our collection days as we spread the business during expansion.

Benchmark Comparison

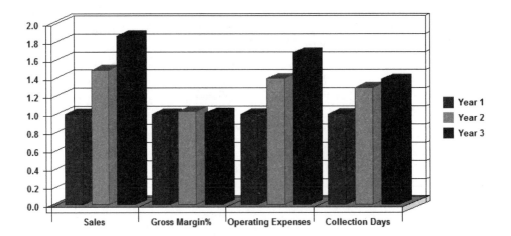

7.3 Break-even Analysis

This table and chart summarizes the break-even analysis, including monthly units and sales break-even points.

Break-even Analysis:
Monthly Units Break-even	12,500
Monthly Sales Break-even	$12,500

Assumptions:
Average Per-Unit Revenue	$1.00
Average Per-Unit Variable Cost	$0.20
Estimated Monthly Fixed Cost	$10,000

Break-even Analysis

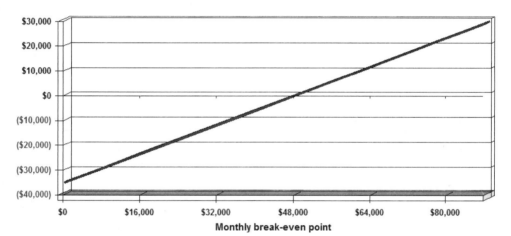

7.4 Projected Profit and Loss

The detailed monthly pro forma income statement for the first year is included in the appendix. The annual estimates are included here.

Profit and Loss (Income Statement)

	Year 1	Year 2	Year 3
Sales	$592,000	$875,000	$1,100,000
Direct Cost of Sales	$159,000	$219,000	$289,000
Other	$0	$0	$0
Total Cost of Sales	$159,000	$219,000	$289,000
Gross Margin	$433,000	$656,000	$811,000
Gross Margin %	73.14%	74.97%	73.73%
Operating expenses:			
Advertising/Promotion	$36,000	$40,000	$44,000
Public Relations	$30,000	$30,000	$33,000
Travel	$90,000	$60,000	$110,000
Miscellaneous	$6,000	$7,000	$8,000
Travel	$0	$0	$0
Miscellaneous	$0	$0	$0
Payroll Expense	$194,750	$377,000	$432,000
Payroll Burden	$27,265	$52,780	$60,480
Depreciation	$0	$0	$0
Leased Equipment	$6,000	$7,000	$7,000
Utilities	$12,000	$12,000	$12,000
Insurance	$3,600	$2,000	$2,000
Rent	$18,000	$0	$0
Other	$0	$0	$0
Contract/Consultants	$0	$0	$0
Total Operating Expenses	$423,615	$587,780	$708,480
Profit Before Interest and Taxes	$9,385	$68,220	$102,520
Interest Expense Short-term	$3,600	$8,800	$12,800
Interest Expense Long-term	$5,000	$5,000	$5,000
Taxes Incurred	$196	$13,605	$21,180
Net Profit	$589	$40,815	$63,540
Net Profit/Sales	0.10%	4.66%	5.78%

7.5 Projected Cash Flow

Cash flow projections are critical to our success. The monthly cash flow is shown in the illustration, with one bar representing the cash flow per month and the other representing the monthly balance. The annual cash flow figures are included here. Detailed monthly numbers are included in the appendix.

Pro-Forma Cash Flow

	Year 1	Year 2	Year 3
Net Profit	$589	$40,815	$63,540
Plus:			
Depreciation	$0	$0	$0
Change in Accounts Payable	$25,896	$1,405	$10,967
Current Borrowing (repayment)	$60,000	$100,000	$0
Increase (decrease) Other Liabilities	$0	$0	$0
Long-term Borrowing (repayment)	$50,000	$0	$0
Capital Input	$0	$0	$0
Subtotal	$136,485	$142,220	$74,507
Less:			
Change in Accounts Receivable	$100,000	$47,804	$38,007
Change in Other ST Assets	$0	$0	$0
Capital Expenditure	$0	$0	$0
Dividends	$0	$0	$0
Subtotal	$100,000	$47,804	$38,007
Net Cash Flow	$36,485	$94,416	$36,500
Cash Balance	$61,485	$155,901	$192,401

Cash Analysis

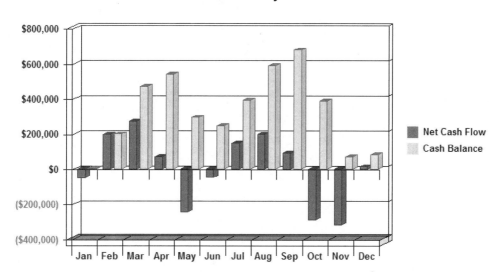

7.6 Projected Balance Sheet

The balance sheet shows healthy growth of net worth, and strong financial position. The monthly estimates are included in the appendix.

Pro forma Balance Sheet

Assets

	Starting Balances	Year 1	Year 2	Year 3
Short-term Assets				
Cash	$25,000	$61,485	$155,901	$192,401
Accounts Receivable	$0	$100,000	$147,804	$185,811
Other Short-term Assets	$7,000	$7,000	$7,000	$7,000
Total Short-term Assets	$32,000	$168,485	$310,705	$385,212
Long-term Assets				
Capital Assets	$0	$0	$0	$0
Accumulated Depreciation	$0	$0	$0	$0
Total Long-term Assets	$0	$0	$0	$0
Total Assets	$32,000	$168,485	$310,705	$385,212

Liabilities and Capital

	Starting Balances	Year 1	Year 2	Year 3
Accounts Payable	$5,000	$30,896	$32,301	$43,268
Short-term Notes	$0	$60,000	$160,000	$160,000
Other Short-term Liabilities	$0	$0	$0	$0
Subtotal Short-term Liabilities	$5,000	$90,896	$192,301	$203,268
Long-term Liabilities	$0	$50,000	$50,000	$50,000
Total Liabilities	$5,000	$140,896	$242,301	$253,268
Paid in Capital	$50,000	$50,000	$50,000	$50,000
Retained Earnings	($23,000)	($23,000)	($22,411)	$18,404
Earnings	$0	$589	$40,815	$63,540
Total Capital	$27,000	$27,589	$68,404	$131,944
Total Liabilities and Capital	$32,000	$168,485	$310,705	$385,212
Net Worth	$27,000	$27,589	$68,404	$131,944

7.7 Business Ratios

The following table shows the projected business ratios. We expect to maintain healthy ratios for profitability, risk, and return.

Ratio Analysis

Profitability Ratios:	Year 1	Year 2	Year 3
Gross Margin	73.14%	74.97%	73.73%
Net Profit Margin	0.10%	4.66%	5.78%
Return on Assets	0.35%	13.14%	16.49%
Return on Equity	2.13%	59.67%	48.16%

Activity Ratios	Year 1	Year 2	Year 3
AR Turnover	5.92	5.92	5.92
Collection Days	31	52	55
Inventory Turnover	0.00	0.00	0.00
Accts Payable Turnover	8.75	8.75	8.75
Total Asset Turnover	3.51	2.82	2.86

Debt Ratios	Year 1	Year 2	Year 3
Debt to Net Worth	5.11	3.54	1.92
Short-term Liab. to Liab.	0.65	0.79	0.80

Liquidity Ratios	Year 1	Year 2	Year 3
Current Ratio	1.85	1.62	1.90
Quick Ratio	1.85	1.62	1.90
Net Working Capital	$77,589	$118,404	$181,944
Interest Coverage	1.09	4.94	5.76

Additional Ratios	Year 1	Year 2	Year 3
Assets to Sales	0.28	0.36	0.35
Debt/Assets	84%	78%	66%
Current Debt/Total Assets	54%	62%	53%
Acid Test	0.75	0.85	0.98
Asset Turnover	3.51	2.82	2.86
Sales/Net Worth	21.46	12.79	8.34

ACME CONSULTING — APPENDIX TABLES

Sales Forecast

Sales	Jan	Feb	Mar	Apr	May	Jun	Jul	Aug	Sep	Oct	Nov	Dec
Retainer Consulting	$10,000	$10,000	$10,000	$10,000	$20,000	$20,000	$20,000	$20,000	$20,000	$20,000	$20,000	$20,000
Project Consulting	$0	$0	$10,000	$20,000	$30,000	$40,000	$20,000	$10,000	$30,000	$45,000	$50,000	$15,000
Market Research	$0	$0	$0	$4,000	$8,000	$15,000	$10,000	$5,000	$20,000	$20,000	$20,000	$20,000
Strategic Reports	$0	$0	$0	$0	$0	$0	$0	$0	$0	$0	$0	$0
Other	$0	$0	$0	$0	$0	$0	$0	$0	$0	$0	$0	$0
Total Sales	$10,000	$10,000	$20,000	$34,000	$58,000	$75,000	$50,000	$35,000	$70,000	$85,000	$90,000	$55,000

Direct Cost of sales

	Jan	Feb	Mar	Apr	May	Jun	Jul	Aug	Sep	Oct	Nov	Dec
Retainer Consulting	$2,500	$2,500	$2,500	$2,500	$2,500	$2,500	$2,500	$2,500	$2,500	$2,500	$2,500	$2,500
Project Consulting	$0	$0	$1,500	$3,500	$5,000	$6,500	$3,500	$1,500	$5,000	$7,500	$8,500	$2,500
Market Research	$0	$0	$0	$2,000	$6,000	$10,000	$6,000	$4,000	$14,000	$14,000	$14,000	$14,000
Strategic Reports	$0	$0	$0	$0	$0	$0	$0	$0	$0	$0	$0	$0
Other	$0	$0	$0	$0	$0	$0	$0	$0	$0	$0	$0	$0
Subtotal Cost of Sales	$2,500	$2,500	$4,000	$8,000	$13,500	$19,000	$12,000	$8,000	$21,500	$24,000	$25,000	$19,000

Personnel Plan

	Jan	Feb	Mar	Apr	May	Jun	Jul	Aug	Sep	Oct	Nov	Dec
Partners	$12,000	$12,000	$12,000	$12,000	$12,000	$12,000	$12,000	$12,000	$12,000	$12,000	$12,000	$12,000
Consultants	$0	$0	$0	$0	$0	$0	$0	$0	$0	$0	$0	$0
Editorial/graphic	$0	$0	$0	$0	$0	$0	$0	$0	$0	$6,000	$6,000	$6,000
VP Marketing	$0	$0	$0	$0	$0	$0	$0	$0	$5,000	$5,000	$5,000	$5,000
Sales people	$0	$0	$0	$0	$0	$0	$0	$0	$0	$0	$0	$0
Office Manager	$0	$0	$0	$0	$0	$0	$0	$0	$0	$2,500	$2,500	$2,500
Secretarial	$0	$0	$0	$0	$0	$0	$0	$0	$0	$1,750	$1,750	$1,750
Other	$0	$0	$0	$0	$0	$0	$0	$0	$0	$0	$0	$0
Other	$0	$0	$0	$0	$0	$0	$0	$0	$0	$0	$0	$0
Total Payroll	$12,000	$12,000	$12,000	$12,000	$12,000	$12,000	$12,000	$12,000	$17,000	$27,250	$27,250	$27,250
Total Headcount	3	3	3	3	3	3	3	3	4	7	7	7
Payroll Burden	$1,680	$1,680	$1,680	$1,680	$1,680	$1,680	$1,680	$1,680	$2,380	$3,815	$3,815	$3,815
Total Payroll Expenditures	$13,680	$13,680	$13,680	$13,680	$13,680	$13,680	$13,680	$13,680	$19,380	$31,065	$31,065	$31,065

General Assumptions

	Jan	Feb	Mar	Apr	May	Jun	Jul	Aug	Sep	Oct	Nov	Dec
Short-term Interest Rate %	8.00%	8.00%	8.00%	8.00%	8.00%	8.00%	8.00%	8.00%	8.00%	8.00%	8.00%	8.00%
Long-term Interest Rate %	10.00%	10.00%	10.00%	10.00%	10.00%	10.00%	10.00%	10.00%	10.00%	10.00%	10.00%	10.00%
Payment Days Estimator	35	35	35	35	35	35	35	35	35	35	35	35
Collection Days Estimator	45	45	45	45	45	45	45	45	45	45	45	45
Tax Rate %	25.00%	25.00%	25.00%	25.00%	25.00%	25.00%	25.00%	25.00%	25.00%	25.00%	25.00%	25.00%
Expenses in Cash %	25.00%	25.00%	25.00%	25.00%	25.00%	25.00%	25.00%	25.00%	25.00%	25.00%	25.00%	25.00%
Sales on Credit %	100.00%	100.00%	100.00%	100.00%	100.00%	100.00%	100.00%	100.00%	100.00%	100.00%	100.00%	100.00%
Personnel Burden %	14.00%	14.00%	14.00%	14.00%	14.00%	14.00%	14.00%	14.00%	14.00%	14.00%	14.00%	14.00%

Profit and Loss (Income Statement)

	Jan	Feb	Mar	Apr	May	Jun	Jul	Aug	Sep	Oct	Nov	Dec
Sales	$10,000	$10,000	$20,000	$34,000	$58,000	$75,000	$50,000	$35,000	$70,000	$85,000	$90,000	$55,000
Direct Cost of Sales	$2,500	$2,500	$4,000	$8,000	$13,500	$19,000	$12,000	$8,000	$21,500	$24,000	$25,000	$19,000
Other	$0	$0	$0	$0	$0	$0	$0	$0	$0	$0	$0	$0
Total Cost of Sales	$2,500	$2,500	$4,000	$8,000	$13,500	$19,000	$12,000	$8,000	$21,500	$24,000	$25,000	$19,000
Gross Margin	$7,500	$7,500	$16,000	$26,000	$44,500	$56,000	$38,000	$27,000	$48,500	$61,000	$65,000	$36,000
Gross Margin %	75.00%	75.00%	80.00%	76.47%	76.72%	74.67%	76.00%	77.14%	69.29%	71.76%	72.22%	65.45%
Operating expenses:												
Advertising/Promotion	$3,000	$3,000	$3,000	$3,000	$3,000	$3,000	$3,000	$3,000	$3,000	$3,000	$3,000	$3,000
Public Relations	$2,500	$2,500	$2,500	$2,500	$2,500	$2,500	$2,500	$2,500	$2,500	$2,500	$2,500	$2,500
Travel	$7,500	$7,500	$7,500	$7,500	$7,500	$7,500	$7,500	$7,500	$7,500	$7,500	$7,500	$7,500
Miscellaneous	$500	$500	$500	$500	$500	$500	$500	$500	$500	$500	$500	$500
Travel	$0	$0	$0	$0	$0	$0	$0	$0	$0	$0	$0	$0
Miscellaneous	$0	$0	$0	$0	$0	$0	$0	$0	$0	$0	$0	$0
Payroll Expense	$12,000	$12,000	$12,000	$12,000	$12,000	$12,000	$12,000	$12,000	$17,000	$27,250	$27,250	$27,250
Payroll Burden	$1,680	$1,680	$1,680	$1,680	$1,680	$1,680	$1,680	$1,680	$2,380	$3,815	$3,815	$3,815
Depreciation	$0	$0	$0	$0	$0	$0	$0	$0	$0	$0	$0	$0
Leased Equipment	$500	$500	$500	$500	$500	$500	$500	$500	$500	$500	$500	$500
Utilities	$1,000	$1,000	$1,000	$1,000	$1,000	$1,000	$1,000	$1,000	$1,000	$1,000	$1,000	$1,000
Insurance	$300	$300	$300	$300	$300	$300	$300	$300	$300	$300	$300	$300
Rent	$1,500	$1,500	$1,500	$1,500	$1,500	$1,500	$1,500	$1,500	$1,500	$1,500	$1,500	$1,500
Other	$0	$0	$0	$0	$0	$0	$0	$0	$0	$0	$0	$0
Contract/Consultants	$0	$0	$0	$0	$0	$0	$0	$0	$0	$0	$0	$0
Total Operating Expenses	$30,480	$30,480	$30,480	$30,480	$30,480	$30,480	$30,480	$30,480	$36,180	$47,865	$47,865	$47,865
Profit Before Int. & Taxes	($22,980)	($22,980)	($14,480)	($4,480)	$14,020	$25,520	$7,520	($3,480)	$12,320	$13,135	$17,135	($11,865)
Interest Expense ST	$0	$0	$133	$267	$400	$400	$400	$400	$400	$400	$400	$400
Interest Expense LT	$417	$417	$417	$417	$417	$417	$417	$417	$417	$417	$417	$417
Taxes Incurred	($5,849)	($5,849)	($3,758)	($1,291)	$3,301	$6,176	$1,676	($1,074)	$2,876	$3,080	$4,080	($3,170)
Net Profit	($17,548)	($17,548)	($11,273)	($3,873)	$9,903	$18,528	$5,028	($3,223)	$8,628	$9,239	$12,239	($9,511)
Net Profit/Sales	-175.48%	-175.48%	-56.36%	-11.39%	17.07%	24.70%	10.06%	-9.21%	12.33%	10.87%	13.60%	-17.29%

Pro Forma Cash Flow

	Jan	Feb	Mar	Apr	May	Jun	Jul	Aug	Sep	Oct	Nov	Dec
Net Profit	($17,548)	($17,548)	($11,273)	($3,873)	$9,903	$18,528	$5,028	($3,223)	$8,628	$9,239	$12,239	($9,511)
Plus:												
Depreciation	$0	$0	$0	$0	$0	$0	$0	$0	$0	$0	$0	$0
Change in Accounts Payable	$9,475	$2,181	$1,295	$3,452	$4,747	$4,747	($6,041)	($3,452)	$11,651	$2,158	$863	($5,178)
Current Borrowing (repayment)	$0	$0	$20,000	$20,000	$20,000	$0	$0	$0	$0	$0	$0	$0
Increase (decrease) Other Liab.	$0	$0	$0	$0	$0	$0	$0	$0	$0	$0	$0	$0
LT Borrowing (repayment)	$50,000	$0	$0	$0	$0	$0	$0	$0	$0	$0	$0	$0
Capital Input	$0	$0	$0	$0	$0	$0	$0	$0	$0	$0	$0	$0
Subtotal	$41,928	($15,366)	$10,022	$19,580	$34,649	$23,274	($1,014)	($6,675)	$20,278	$11,396	$13,102	($14,689)
Less:												
Change in Accounts Receivable	$10,000	$4,795	$14,795	$14,411	$31,000	$29,000	($16,500)	($27,500)	$27,500	$32,500	$12,500	($32,500)
Change in Other ST Assets	$0	$0	$0	$0	$0	$0	$0	$0	$0	$0	$0	$0
Capital Expenditure	$0	$0	$0	$0	$0	$0	$0	$0	$0	$0	$0	$0
Dividends	$0	$0	$0	$0	$0	$0	$0	$0	$0	$0	$0	$0
Subtotal	$10,000	$4,795	$14,795	$14,411	$31,000	$29,000	($16,500)	($27,500)	$27,500	$32,500	$12,500	($32,500)
Net Cash Flow	$31,928	($20,161)	($4,773)	$5,169	$3,649	($5,726)	$15,486	$20,825	($7,222)	($21,104)	$602	$17,811
Cash Balance	$56,928	$36,767	$31,994	$37,163	$40,812	$35,086	$50,572	$71,398	$64,176	$43,072	$43,674	$61,485

Pro Forma Balance Sheet

Assets

	Starting Balances	Jan	Feb	Mar	Apr	May	Jun	Jul	Aug	Sep	Oct	Nov	Dec
Short-term Assets													
Cash	$25,000	$56,928	$36,767	$31,994	$37,163	$40,812	$35,086	$50,572	$71,398	$64,176	$43,072	$43,674	$61,485
Accounts Receivable	$0	$10,000	$14,795	$29,589	$44,000	$75,000	$104,000	$87,500	$60,000	$87,500	$120,000	$132,500	$100,000
Other ST Assets	$7,000	$7,000	$7,000	$7,000	$7,000	$7,000	$7,000	$7,000	$7,000	$7,000	$7,000	$7,000	$7,000
Total ST Assets	$32,000	$73,928	$58,561	$68,583	$88,163	$122,812	$146,086	$145,072	$138,398	$158,676	$170,072	$183,174	$168,485
Long-term Assets													
Capital Assets	$0	$0	$0	$0	$0	$0	$0	$0	$0	$0	$0	$0	$0
Accum. Depreciation	$0	$0	$0	$0	$0	$0	$0	$0	$0	$0	$0	$0	$0
Total LT Assets	$0	$0	$0	$0	$0	$0	$0	$0	$0	$0	$0	$0	$0
Total Assets	$32,000	$73,928	$58,561	$68,583	$88,163	$122,812	$146,086	$145,072	$138,398	$158,676	$170,072	$183,174	$168,485

Liabilities and Capital

	Starting Balances	Jan	Feb	Mar	Apr	May	Jun	Jul	Aug	Sep	Oct	Nov	Dec
Accounts Payable	$5,000	$14,475	$16,656	$17,951	$21,403	$26,149	$30,896	$24,855	$21,403	$33,053	$35,211	$36,074	$30,896
ST Notes	$0	$0	$0	$20,000	$40,000	$60,000	$60,000	$60,000	$60,000	$60,000	$60,000	$60,000	$60,000
Other ST Liabilities	$0	$0	$0	$0	$0	$0	$0	$0	$0	$0	$0	$0	$0
Subtotal ST Liabilities	$5,000	$16,656	$16,656	$37,951	$61,403	$86,149	$90,896	$84,855	$81,403	$93,053	$95,211	$96,074	$90,896
LT Liabilities	$0	$50,000	$50,000	$50,000	$50,000	$50,000	$50,000	$50,000	$50,000	$50,000	$50,000	$50,000	$50,000
Total Liabilities	$5,000	$64,475	$66,656	$87,951	$111,403	$136,149	$140,896	$134,855	$131,403	$143,053	$145,211	$146,074	$140,896
Paid in Capital	$50,000	$50,000	$50,000	$50,000	$50,000	$50,000	$50,000	$50,000	$50,000	$50,000	$50,000	$50,000	$50,000
Retained Earnings	($23,000)	($23,000)	($23,000)	($23,000)	($23,000)	($23,000)	($23,000)	($23,000)	($23,000)	($23,000)	($23,000)	($23,000)	($23,000)
Earnings	$0	($17,548)	($35,095)	($46,368)	($50,240)	($40,338)	($21,810)	($16,783)	($20,005)	($11,378)	($2,139)	$10,100	$589
Total Capital	$27,000	$9,453	($8,095)	($19,368)	($23,240)	($13,338)	$5,190	$10,218	$6,995	$15,623	$24,861	$37,100	$27,589
Total Liab. & Capital	$32,000	$73,928	$58,561	$68,583	$88,163	$122,812	$146,086	$145,072	$138,398	$158,676	$170,072	$183,174	$168,485
Net Worth	$27,000	$9,453	($8,095)	($19,368)	($23,240)	($13,338)	$5,190	$10,218	$6,995	$15,623	$24,861	$37,100	$27,589

American Management Technologies (AMT), Inc.
Table of Contents

1.0 Executive Summary

By focusing on its strengths, its key customers, and the underlying values they need, American Management Technologies, Inc. (AMT, Inc.) will increase sales to approximately $9 million in three years, while also improving the gross margin on sales and cash management and working capital.

This business plan leads the way. It renews our vision and strategic focus: adding value to our target market segments, the small business and high-end home office users, in our local market. It also provides the step-by-step plan for improving our sales, gross margin, and profitability.

This plan includes this summary, and chapters on the company, products and services, market focus, action plans and forecasts, management team, and financial plan.

HIGHLIGHTS CHART

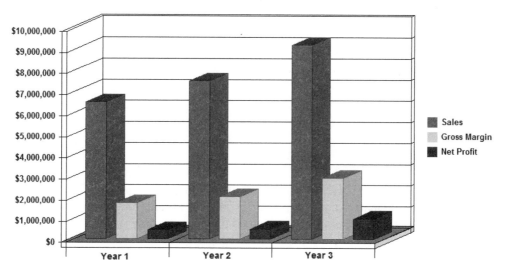

1.1 Objectives

1. Sales increasing to approximately $9 million by the third year.

2. Bring gross margin back up to above 30%, and maintain that level.

3. Sell $2 million of service, support, and training by Year 3.

4. Improve inventory turnover to 6 turns next year, 7 in Year 2, and 8 in Year 3.

1.2 Mission

AMT is built on the assumption that the management of information technology for business is like legal advice, accounting, graphic arts, and other bodies of knowledge, in that it is not inherently a do-it-yourself prospect. Smart business people who aren't computer hobbyists need to find quality vendors of reliable hardware, software, service, and support. They need to use these quality vendors as they use their other professional service suppliers, as trusted allies. AMT is such a vendor. It serves its clients as a trusted ally, providing them with the loyalty of a business partner and the economics of an outside vendor. We make sure that our clients have what they need to run their businesses as well as possible, with maximum efficiency and reliability. Many of our information applications are mission critical, so we give our clients the assurance that we will be there when they need us.

1.3 Keys to Success

1. Differentiate from box-pushing, price-oriented businesses by offering and delivering service and support — and charging for it.

2. Increase gross margin to more than 25%.

3. Increase our non-hardware sales to 20% of the total sales by the third year.

2.0 Company Summary

AMT is a computer reseller based in the Uptown area. It was founded as a consulting-oriented VAR, became a reseller to fill the market need for personal computers, and is emphasizing service and support to differentiate itself from more price-oriented national chains.

2.1 Company Ownership

AMT is a privately-held C corporation owned in majority by its founder and president, Ralph Jones. There are six part owners, including four investors and two past employees. The largest of these (in percent of ownership) are Frank Dudley, our attorney, and Paul Karots, our public relations consultant. Neither owns more than 15%, but both are active participants in management decisions.

2.2 Company History

AMT has been caught in the vise grip of margin squeezes that have affected computer resellers worldwide. Although the chart titled Past Performance shows that we have had healthy growth in sales, it also shows declining gross margin and declining profits. The more detailed numbers in the following table include other indicators of some concern:

The gross margin % has been declining steadily, as we see in the chart. Inventory turnover is getting steadily worse. All of these concerns are part of the general trend affecting computer resellers. The margin squeeze is happening throughout the computer industry worldwide.

Past Performance

	Prior Year	Previous Year	Last Year
Sales	$3,773,889	$4,661,902	$5,301,059
Gross Margin	$1,189,495	$1,269,261	$1,127,568
Gross % (calculated)	31.52%	27.23%	21.27%
Operating Expenses	$752,083	$902,500	$1,052,917
Collection period (days)	48	52	65
Inventory turnover	7	6	5

Balance Sheet

	Last Year
Short-term Assets	
Cash	$55,432
Accounts receivable	$395,107
Inventory	$251,012
Other Short-term Assets	$25,000
Total Short-term Assets	$726,551
Long-term Assets	
Capital Assets	$350,000
Accumulated Depreciation	$50,000
Total Long-term Assets	$300,000
Total Assets	$1,026,551

Capital and Liabilities

	Last Year
Accounts Payable	$223,897
Short-term Notes	$90,000
Other ST Liabilities	$15,000
Subtotal Short-term Liabilities	$328,897
Long-term Liabilities	$284,862
Total Liabilities	$613,759
Paid in Capital	$500,000
Retained Earnings	($161,860)
Earnings	$74,652
Total Capital	$412,792
Total Capital and Liabilities	$1,026,551

Other Inputs	Last Year
Payment days	30
Sales on credit	$3,445,688
Receivables turnover	8.72

PAST PERFORMANCE CHART

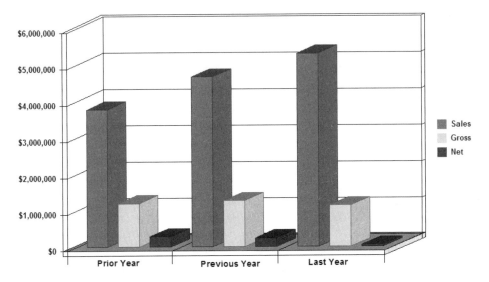

2.3 Company Locations and Facilities

We have one location – a 7,000 square foot store in a suburban shopping center located conveniently close to the downtown area. It includes a training area, service department, offices, and showroom area.

3.0 Products and Services

AMT provides both computer products and services to make them useful to small business. We are especially focused on providing network systems and services to small and medium business. The systems include both PC-based LAN systems and minicomputer server-based systems. Our services include design and installation of network systems, training, and support.

3.1 Product and Service Description

In personal computers, we support three main lines:

1. The Super Home is our smallest and least expensive line, initially positioned by its manufacturer as a home computer. We use it mainly as a cheap workstation for small business installations. Its specifications include ...[additional specifics omitted].

2. The Power User is our main upscale line. It is our most important system for high-end home and small business main workstations, because of .... Its key strengths are .... Its specifications include ....[additional specifics omitted].

3. The Business Special is an intermediate system, used to fill the gap in the positioning. Its specifications include ... [additional specifics omitted].

In peripherals, accessories and other hardware, we carry a complete line of necessary items from cables to forms to mousepads ... [additional specifics omitted].

In service and support, we offer a range of walk-in or depot service, maintenance contracts and on-site guarantees. We have not had much success selling service contracts. Our networking capabilities ...[additional specifics omitted].

In software, we sell a complete line of ... [additional specifics omitted].

In training, we offer ... [additional specifics omitted].

3.2 Competitive Comparison

The only way we can hope to differentiate well is to define the vision of the company to be an information technology ally to our clients. We will not be able to compete in any effective way with the chains using boxes or products as appliances. We need to offer a real alliance.

The benefits we sell include many intangibles: confidence, reliability, knowing that somebody will be there to answer questions and help at the important times.

These are complex products, products that require serious knowledge and experience to use, and our competitors sell only the products themselves.

Unfortunately, we cannot sell the products at a higher price just because we offer services; the market has shown that it will not support that concept. We have to also sell the service and charge for it separately.

3.3 Sales Literature

Copies of our brochure and advertisements are attached as appendices. Of course, one of our first tasks will be to change the message of our literature to make sure we are selling the company, rather than the product.

3.4 Sourcing

Our costs are part of the margin squeeze. As competition on price increases, the squeeze between manufacturers' price into channels and end-users' ultimate buying price continues.

With the hardware lines, our margins are declining steadily. We generally buy at ... Our margins are thus being squeezed from the 25% of five years ago to more like 13-15% at present. In the mainline peripherals a similar trend shows, with prices for printers and monitors declining steadily. We are also starting to see that same trend with software ....

In order to hold costs down as much as possible, we concentrate our purchasing with Hauser, which offers 30-day net terms and overnight shipping from the warehouse in Dayton. We need to concentrate on making sure our volume gives us negotiating strength.

In accessories and add-ons we can still get decent margins, 25% to 40%.

For software, margins are ... [additional specifics omitted].

3.5 Technology

We have for years supported both Windows and Macintosh technology for CPUs, although we've switched vendors many times for the Windows (and previously DOS) lines. We are also supporting Novell, Banyon, and Microsoft networking, Xbase database software, and Claris application products.

3.6 Service and Support

Our strategy hinges on providing excellent service and support. This is critical. We need to differentiate on service and support, and to therefore deliver as well.

1. Training: details would be essential in a real business plan, but not in this sample plan.

2. Upgrade offers: details would be essential in a real business plan, but not in this sample plan.

3. Our own internal training: details would be essential in a real business plan, but not in this sample plan.

4. Installation services: details would be essential in a real business plan, but not in this sample plan.

5. Custom software services: details would be essential in a real business plan, but not in this sample plan.

6. Network configuration services: details would be essential in a real business plan, but not in this sample plan.

3.7 Future Products and Services

We must remain on top of the new technologies, because this is our bread and butter. For networking, we need to provide better knowledge of cross platform technologies. Also, we are under pressure to improve our understanding of direct-connect Internet and related communications. Finally, although we have a good command of desktop publishing, we are concerned about getting better at the integration of technologies that creates fax, copier, printer, and voice mail as part of the computer system.

4.0 Market Analysis Summary

AMT focuses on local markets, small business and home office, with special focus on the high-end home office and the 5-20 unit small business office.

4.1 Market Segmentation

The segmentation allows some room for estimates and nonspecific definitions. We focus on a small-medium level of small business, and it is hard to find information to make an exact classification. Our target companies are large enough to need the high-quality information technology management we offer, but too small to have a separate computer management staff such as an IT department. We say that our target market has 10-50 employees, and needs 5-20 workstations tied together in a local area network; the definition is flexible.

Defining the high-end home office is even more difficult. We generally know the characteristics of our target market, but we can't find easy classifications that fit into available demographics. The high-end home office business is a business, not a hobby. It generates enough money to merit the owner's paying real attention to the quality of information technology management, meaning that there is both budget and concerns that warrant working with our level of quality service and support. We can assume that we aren't talking about home offices used only part-time by people who work elsewhere during the day, and that our target market home office wants to have powerful technology and a lot of links between computing, telecommunications, and video.

Market Analysis

Potential Customers	Growth	Year 1	Year 2	Year 3	Year 4	Year 5	CAGR
Consumer	2%	12,000	12,240	12,485	12,735	12,990	2.00%
Small Business	5%	15,000	15,750	16,538	17,365	18,233	5.00%
Large Business	8%	33,000	35,640	38,491	41,570	44,896	8.00%
Government	-2%	36,000	35,280	34,574	33,883	33,205	-2.00%
Other	0%	19,000	19,000	19,000	19,000	19,000	0.00%
Total	2.78%	115,000	117,910	121,088	124,553	128,324	2.78%

POTENTIAL MARKET BY SEGMENT

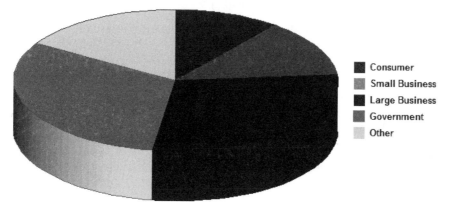

- Consumer
- Small Business
- Large Business
- Government
- Other

4.2 Target Market Segment Strategy

We are part of the computer reselling business, which includes several kinds of businesses:

1.   Computer dealers: storefront computer resellers, usually less than 5,000 square feet, often focused on a few main brands of hardware, usually offering only a minimum of software, and variable amounts of service and support. These are usually old-fashioned computer stores and they usually offer relatively few reasons for buyers to shop with them. Their service and support is not usually very good and their prices are usually higher than the larger stores.

2.   Chain stores and computer superstores: these include major chains such as Costco, Circuit City, BestBuy, etc. They are almost always more than 10,000 square feet of space, usually offer decent walk-in service, and are often warehouse-like locations where people go to find products in boxes with very aggressive pricing, and little support.

3.   Online/Catalog: the market is served increasingly by businesses such as Tiger Direct, Tech Depot, etc., that offer aggressive pricing of boxed product. For the purely price-driven buyer, who buys boxes and expects no service, these are very good options.

4.   Others: there are many other channels through which people buy their computers, usually variations of the main three types above.

4.2.1 Market Needs

Since our target market is the service seeker, the most important market needs are support, service, training, and installation, in that order. One of the key points of our strategy is the focus on target segments that know and understand these needs and are willing to pay to have them filled.

All personal computer users need support and service. The self reliant ones, however, supply those needs themselves. In home offices, these are the knowledgeable computer users who like to do it themselves. Among the businesses, these are businesses that have people on staff.

4.2.2 Market Trends

The most obvious and important trend in the market is declining prices. This has been true for years, but the trend seems to be accelerating. We see the major brand-name manufacturers putting systems together with amazing specs—more power, more speed, more memory, more disk storage—at amazing prices. The major chain shops are selling brand-name powerful computers for less than $1,000.

This may be related to a second trend, which is the computer as throw-away appliance. By the time a system needs upgrading, it is cheaper to buy completely new. The increasing power and storage of a sub-$1000 system means buyers are asking for less service.

A third trend is ever greater connectivity. Everybody wants onto the Internet, and every small office wants a LAN. A lot of small offices want their LAN connected to the Internet.

4.2.3 Market Growth

As prices fall, unit sales increase. The published market research on sales of personal computers is astounding, as the United States market alone is absorbing more than 30 million units per year, and sales are growing at more than 20 percent per year. We could quote Dataquest, Infocorp, IDC, or others; it doesn't matter, they all agree on high growth of CPU sales.

Where growth is not as obvious is the retail market. A report in CRW says Dell is now selling $5 million monthly over the Web, and we assume Gateway and Micron are both close to that. Direct mail has given way to the Web, but catalogs are still powerful, and the non-retail sale is more accepted every day. The last study we saw published has retail sales growing at 5% per year, while Web sales and direct sales are growing at 25% or 30%.

4.3 Industry Analysis

We are part of the computer reselling business, which includes several kinds of businesses:

1. Computer dealers: storefront computer resellers, usually less than 5,000 square feet, often focused on a few main brands of hardware, usually offering only a minimum of software, and variable amounts of service and support. These are usually old-fashioned computer stores and they usually offer relatively few reasons for buyers to shop with them. Their service and support is not usually very good and their prices are usually higher than the larger stores.

2. Chain stores and computer superstores: these include major chains such as Costco, CircuitCity, BestBuy, etc. They are almost always more than 10,000 square feet of space, usually offer decent walk-in service, and are often warehouse-like locations where people go to find products in boxes with very aggressive pricing, and little support.

3. Online/Catalog: the market is served increasingly by businesses such as TechDepot, TigerDirect, etc., that offer aggressive pricing of boxed product. For the purely price-driven buyer, who buys boxes and expects no service, these are very good options.

4. Others: there are many other channels through which people buy their computers, usually variations of the main three types above.

4.3.1 Industry Participants

1. The national chains are a growing presence. CompUSA, Computer City, Incredible Universe, Babbages, Egghead, and others. They benefit from national advertising, economies of scale, volume buying, and a general trend toward name-brand loyalty for buying in the channels as well as for products.

2. Local computer stores are threatened. These tend to be small businesses, owned by people who started them because they liked computers. They are undercapitalized and under-managed. Margins are squeezed as they compete against the chains, in a competition based on price more than on service and support.

4.3.2 Distribution Patterns

Small Business target buyers are accustomed to buying from vendors who visit their offices. They expect the copy machine vendors, office products vendors, and office furniture vendors, as well as the local graphic artists, freelance writers, or whomever, to visit their office to make their sales.

There is usually a lot of leakage in ad-hoc purchasing through local chain stores and mail order. Often the administrators try to discourage this, but are only partially successful.

Unfortunately our Home Office target buyers may not expect to buy from us. Many of them turn immediately to the superstores (office equipment, office supplies, and electronics) and mail order to look for the best price, without realizing that there is a better option for them at only a little bit more.

4.3.3 Competition and Buying Patterns

The Small Business buyers understand the concept of service and support, and are much more likely to pay for it when the offering is clearly stated.

There is no doubt that we compete much more against all the box pushers than against other service providers. We need to effectively compete against the idea that businesses should buy computers as plug-in appliances that don't need ongoing service, support, and training.

Our focus group sessions indicated that our target Home Offices think about price but would buy based on quality service if the offering were properly presented. They think about price because that's all they ever see. We have very good indications that many would rather pay 10-20% more for a relationship with a long-term vendor providing backup and quality service and support; they end up in the box-pusher channels because they aren't aware of the alternatives.

Availability is also very important. The Home Office buyers tend to want immediate, local solutions to problems.

4.3.4 Main Competitors

Chain stores:

We have Store 1 and Store 2 already within the valley, and Store 3 is expected by the end of next year. If our strategy works, we will have differentiated ourselves sufficiently to not have to compete against these stores.

Strengths: national image, high volume, aggressive pricing, economies of scale.

Weaknesses: lack of product, service and support knowledge, lack of personal attention.

Other local computer stores:

Store 4 and Store 5 are both in the downtown area. They are both competing against the chains in an attempt to match prices. When asked, the owners will complain that margins are squeezed by the chains and customers buy on price only. They say they tried offering services and that buyers didn't care, instead preferring lower prices. We think the problem is also that they didn't really offer good service, and also that they didn't differentiate from the chains.

5.0 Strategy and Implementation Summary

The home offices in Tintown are an important growing market segment. Nationally, there are approximately 30 million home offices, and the number is growing at 10% per year. Our estimate in this plan for the home offices in our market service area is based on an analysis published four months ago in the local newspaper.

Home offices include several types. The most important, for our plan's focus, are the home offices that are the only offices of real businesses, from which people make their primary living. These are likely to be professional services such as graphic artists, writers, and consultants, some accountants and the occasional lawyer, doctor, or dentist. There are also part-time home offices with people who are employed during the day but work at home at night, people who work at home to provide themselves with a part-time income, or people who maintain home offices relating to their hobbies; we will not be focusing on this segment.

Small business within our market includes virtually any business with a retail, office, professional, or industrial location outside of someone's home, and fewer than 30 employees. We estimate 45,000 such businesses in our market area.

The 30-employee cutoff is arbitrary. We find that the larger companies turn to other vendors, but we can sell to departments of larger companies, and we shouldn't be giving up leads when we get them.

5.1 Strategy Pyramids

For placing emphasis on service and support, our main tactics are networking expertise, excellent training, and developing our own proprietary software/network administrative system. Our specific programs for networking include mailers and internal training. Specific programs for training include direct mail promotion, and train-the-trainers programs. For developing our own proprietary systems, our programs are company direct mail marketing, and working with VARs.

Our second strategy is emphasizing relationships. The tactics are marketing the company (instead of the products), more regular contacts with the customer, and increasing sales per customer. Programs for marketing the company include new sales literature, revised ad strategy, and direct mail. Programs for more regular contacts include callbacks after installation, direct mail, and sales management. Programs for increasing sales per customer include upgrade mailings and sales training.

5.2 Value Proposition

Our value proposition has to be different from the standard box-oriented retail chain. We offer our target customer, who is service seeking and not self reliant, a vendor who acts as a strategic ally, at a premium price that reflects the value of reassurance that systems will work.

5.3 Competitive Edge

Our competitive edge is our positioning as a strategic ally with our clients, who are clients more than customers. By building a business based on long-standing relationships with satisfied clients, we simultaneously build defenses against competition. The longer the relationship stands, the more we help our clients understand what we offer them and why they need it.

5.4 Marketing Strategy

The marketing strategy is the core of the main strategy:

1. Emphasize service and support.

2. Build a relationship business.

3. Focus on small business and high-end home office as key target markets.

5.4.1 Positioning Statements

For businesspeople who want to be sure their computer systems are always working reliably, AMT is a vendor and trusted strategic ally who makes sure their systems work, their people are trained, and their down time is minimal. Unlike the chain retail stores, it knows the customer and goes to his or her site when needed, and offers proactive support, service, training, and installation.

5.4.2 Pricing Strategy

We must charge appropriately for the high-end, high-quality service and support we offer. Our revenue structure has to match our cost structure, so the salaries we pay to assure good service and support must be balanced by the revenue we charge.

We cannot build the service and support revenue into the price of products. The market can't bear the higher prices and the buyer feels ill-used when they see the same product priced lower at the chains. Despite the logic behind this, the market doesn't support this concept.

Therefore, we must make sure that we deliver and charge for service and support. Training, service, installation, networking support—all of this must be readily available and priced to sell and deliver revenue.

5.4.3 Promotion Strategy

We depend on newspaper advertising as our main way to reach new buyers. As we change strategies, however, we need to change the way we promote ourselves:

1. Advertising

    We'll be developing our core positioning message: "24 Hour On-Site Service - 365 Days a Year With No Extra Charges" to differentiate our service from the competition. We will be using local newspaper advertising, radio, and cable TV to launch the initial campaign.

2. Sales Brochure

    Our collaterals have to sell the store, and visiting the store, not the specific book or discount pricing.

3. Direct Mail

    We must radically improve our direct mail efforts, reaching our established customers with training, support services, upgrades, and seminars.

4. Local Media

    It's time to work more closely with the local media. We could offer the local radio a regular talk show on technology for small business, as one example.

5.4.4 Distribution Strategy

Our most important marketing program is [specifics omitted]. [Name] will be responsible, with budget of $XX,XXX and milestone date of [date]. This program is intended to [objectives omitted]. Achievement should be measured by [specific concrete measurement].

Another key marketing program is [specifics omitted]. [Name] will be responsible, with budget of $XX,XXX and milestone date of [date]. This program is intended to [objectives omitted]. Achievement should be measured by [specific concrete measurement].

5.5 Sales Strategy

1. We need to sell the company, not the product. We sell AMT, not Apple, IBM, Hewlett-Packard, or Compaq, or any of our software brand names.

2. We have to sell our service and support. The hardware is like the razor, and the support, service, software services, training, and seminars are the razor blades. We need to serve our customers with what they really need.

3. The Yearly Total Sales chart summarizes our ambitious sales forecast. We expect sales to increase from $5.3 million last year to more than $7 million next year and $9 million in the last year of this plan.

SALES BY YEAR

5.5.1 Sales Forecast

The important elements of the sales forecast are shown in the Total Sales by Month in Year 1 table. The non-hardware sales increase to about $2 million total in the third year.

Sales Forecast Unit Sales	Year 1	Year 2	Year 3
Systems	2,255	2,500	2,800
Service	3,128	6,000	7,500
Software	3,980	5,000	6,500
Training	2,230	4,000	8,000
Other	2,122	2,500	3,000
Total Unit Sales	13,715	20,000	27,800

Unit Prices	Year 1	Year 2	Year 3
Systems	$1,980.80	$1,984.50	$1,980.80
Service	$68.47	$84	$87
Software	$212.86	$195	$180
Training	$46.58	$72	$79
Other	$394.21	$300	$394

Sales	Year 1	Year 2	Year 3
Systems	$4,466,708	$4,961,240	$5,546,245
Service	$214,159	$504,000	$652,500
Software	$847,183	$975,000	$1,170,000
Training	$103,865	$288,000	$632,000
Other	$836,520	$750,000	$1,182,639
Total Sales	$6,468,434	$7,478,240	$9,183,384

Direct Unit Costs	Year 1	Year 2	Year 3
Systems	$1,700.00	$1,686.82	$1,683.68
Service	$58.08	$33.60	$34.80
Software	$120.00	$117.00	$108.00
Training	$11.10	$21.60	$23.70
Other	$90.00	$90.00	$118.26

Direct Cost of Sales	Year 1	Year 2	Year 3
Systems	$3,833,500	$4,217,054	$4,714,308
Service	$181,680	$201,600	$261,000
Software	$477,600	$585,000	$702,000
Training	$24,753	$86,400	$189,600
Other	$190,980	$225,000	$354,792
Subtotal Direct Cost of Sales	$4,708,513	$5,315,054	$6,221,700

YEAR 1 SALES BY MONTH

5.5.2 Sales Programs

1. Direct mail: Use great detail to describe your company's programs here.

2. Seminars: Use great detail to describe your company's programs here.

5.6 Milestones

Our important milestones are shown in the following table. Row by row, they track the need to follow up on strategy with specific activities. Most of the activities on the list can be easily tied to our strategic goals of selling more service and enhancing the relationship with the customer.

Business Plan Milestones

Milestone	Manager	Planned Date	Department	Budget	Actual Date	Actual Budget	Date Variance	Budget Variance
Corporate identity	TJ	Dec 17	Marketing	$10,000	Jan 15	$12,004	(29)	($2,004)
Seminar implementation	IR	Jan 10	Sales	$1,000	Dec 27	$5,000	14	($4,000)
Business plan review	RJ	Jan 10	GM	$0	Jan 23	$500	(13)	($500)
Upgrade mailer	IR	Jan 16	Sales	$5,000	Feb 12	$12,500	(27)	($7,500)
New corporate brochure	TJ	Jan 16	Marketing	$5,000	Jan 15	$5,000	1	$0
Delivery vans	SD	Jan 25	Service	$12,500	Feb 26	$3,500	(32)	$9,000
Direct mail	IR	Feb 16	Marketing	$3,500	Feb 25	$2,500	(9)	$1,000
Advertising	RJ	Feb 16	GM	$115,000	Mar 6	$100,000	(19)	$15,000
X4 prototype	SG	Feb 25	Product	$2,500	Feb 25	$181,500	0	($179,000)
Service revamp	SD	Feb 25	Product	$2,500	Feb 25	$2,500	0	$0
6 Presentations	IR	Feb 25	Sales	$0	Jan 10	$0	46	$0
X4 Testing	SG	Mar 6	Product	$1,000	Jan 16	$0	50	$1,000
3 Accounts	SD	Mar 17	Sales	$0	Mar 17	$0	0	$0
L30 prototype	PR	Mar 26	Product	$2,500	Apr 11	$0	(16)	$2,500
Tech Expo	TB	Apr 12	Marketing	$15,000	Jan 25	$0	78	$15,000
VP S&M hired	JK	Jun 11	Sales	$1,000	Jul /25	$181,500	(44)	($180,500)
Mailing system	SD	Jul 25	Service	$5,000	Jul 14	$7,654	11	($2,654)

6.0 Management Summary

Our management philosophy is based on responsibility and mutual respect. People who work at AMT want to work at AMT because we have an environment that encourages creativity and achievement.

6.1 Organizational Structure

1.   The team includes 22 employees, under a president and four managers.

2.   Our main management divisions are sales, marketing, service, and administration. Service handles service, support, training, and development.

6.2 Management Team

Ralph Jones, President: 46 years old, founded AMT to focus on reselling high-powered personal computers to small business. Degree in computer science, 15 years with Large Computer Company, Inc. in positions ending with project manager. Ralph has been attending courses at the local Small Business Development Center for more than six years now, steadily adding business skills and business training to his technical background.

Sabrina Benson, VP Marketing: 36 years old, joined us last year following a very successful career with Continental Computers. Her hiring was the culmination of a long recruiting search. With Continental she managed the VAR marketing division. She is committed to re-engineering AMT to be a service and support business that sells computers, not vice-versa. MBA, undergraduate degree in history.

Gary Andrews, VP Service and Support: 48 years old, has been with AMT for seven years, and prior to that spent 18 years with Large Computers, Inc. in programming and service-related positions. MS in computer science and BS in electrical engineering.

Laura Dannis, VP Sales: 32 years old, joined AMT part-time and moved into a full-time position. A former teacher, she has very high people skills. BA in elementary education. She has also taken several sales management courses at the local SBDC.

John Peters, Director of Administration: 43 years old, started with AMT as a part-time bookkeeper, and has become the full-time administrative and financial backbone of the company.

6.3 Management Team Gaps

At present we believe we have a good team for covering the main points of the business plan. The addition of Sabrina Benson was important as a way to cement our fundamental repositioning and re-engineering.

At present, we are weakest in the area of technical capabilities to manage the database marketing programs and upgraded service and support, particularly with cross-platform networks. We also need to find a training manager.

6.4 Personnel Plan

The Personnel Plan reflects the need to bolster our capabilities to match our positioning. Our total headcount should increase to 22 this first year, and to 30 by the third year.

Personnel Plan

Production	Year 1	Year 2	Year 3
Manager	$36,000	$40,000	$40,000
Assistant	$12,000	$13,000	$14,000
Technical	$12,500	$35,000	$35,000
Technical	$12,500	$35,000	$35,000
Technical	$24,000	$27,500	$27,500
Fulfillment	$24,000	$30,000	$60,000
Fulfillment	$18,000	$22,000	$50,000
Other	$0	$0	$0
Subtotal	$139,000	$202,500	$261,500
Sales and Marketing Personnel			
Manager	$72,000	$76,000	$80,000
Technical sales	$60,000	$63,000	$85,000
Technical sales	$45,500	$46,000	$46,000
Salesperson	$40,500	$55,000	$64,000
Salesperson	$40,500	$50,000	$55,000
Salesperson	$33,500	$34,000	$45,000
Salesperson	$31,000	$38,000	$45,000
Salesperson	$21,000	$30,000	$33,000
Salesperson	$0	$30,000	$33,000
Other	$0	$0	$0
Subtotal	$344,000	$422,000	$486,000
General and Administrative Personnel			
President	$66,000	$69,000	$95,000
Finance	$28,000	$29,000	$30,000
Admin Assistant	$24,000	$26,000	$28,000
Bookkeeping	$18,000	$25,000	$30,000
Clerical	$12,000	$15,000	$18,000
Clerical	$7,000	$15,000	$18,000
Clerical	$0	$0	$15,000
Other	$0	$0	$0
Subtotal	$155,000	$179,000	$234,000
Other Personnel			
Programming	$36,000	$40,000	$44,000
Other technical	$0	$30,000	$33,000
Other	$0	$0	$0
Subtotal	$36,000	$70,000	$77,000

Total Payroll	$674,000	$873,500	$1,058,500
Payroll Burden	$107,840	$139,760	$169,360
Total Payroll Expenditures	$781,840	$1,013,260	$1,227,860

6.5 Other Management Considerations

Our attorney, Frank Dudley, is also a cofounder. He invested significantly in the company over a period of time. He remains a good friend of Ralph and has been a steady source of excellent legal and business advice.

Paul Karots, public relations consultant, is also a cofounder and co-owner. Like Dudley, he invested in the early stages and remains a trusted confidant and vendor of public relations and advertising services.

7.0 Financial Plan

The most important element in the financial plan is the critical need for improving several of the key factors that impact cash flow:

1. We must at any cost stop the slide in inventory turnover and develop better inventory management to bring the turnover back up to 8 turns by the third year. This should also be a function of the shift in focus towards service revenues to add to the hardware revenues.

2. We must also bring the gross margin back up to 25%. This too is related to improving the mix between hardware and service revenues, because the service revenues offer much better margins.

3. We plan to borrow another $150,000 long-term this year. The amount seems in line with the balance sheet capabilities.

7.1 Important Assumptions

The financial plan depends on important assumptions, most of which are shown in next table. The key underlying assumptions are:

1. We assume a slow-growth economy, without major recession.

2. We assume of course that there are no unforeseen changes in technology to make products immediately obsolete.

In our General Assumptions table, the most ambitious and also the most questionable assumption is our projected improvement in inventory turnover. This is critical to healthy cash flow, but will also be difficult.

General Assumptions

	Year 1	Year 2	Year 3
Short-term Interest Rate %	8.00%	8.00%	8.00%
Long-term Interest Rate %	8.50%	8.50%	8.50%
Payment Days Estimator	45	45	45
Collection Days Estimator	45	45	45
Inventory Turnover Estimator	7.00	7.00	7.00
Tax Rate %	20.00%	20.00%	20.00%
Expenses in Cash %	14.00%	14.00%	14.00%
Sales on Credit %	70.00%	70.00%	70.00%
Personnel Burden %	16.00%	16.00%	16.00%

7.2 Key Financial Indicators

The Benchmark Comparison chart highlights our ambitious plans to correct declining gross margin and inventory turnover. The chart illustrates why we think the ambitious sales increases we plan are reasonable. We have had similar increases in the recent past.

BENCHMARK COMPARISON

7.3 Break-even Analysis

For our break-even analysis, we assume running costs of approximately $96,000 per month, which includes our full payroll, rent, and utilities, and an estimation of other running costs. Payroll alone, at our present run rate, is only about $55,000.

Margins are harder to assume. Our overall average of $343/248 is based on past sales. We hope to attain a margin that high in the future.

The chart shows that we need to sell about $350,000 per month to break even, according to these assumptions. This is about half of our planned Year 1 sales level, and significantly below our last year's sales level, so we believe we can maintain it.

Break-even Analysis:

Monthly Units Break-even	824
Monthly Sales Break-even	$352,336

Assumptions:

Average Per-Unit Revenue	$427.69
Average Per-Unit Variable Cost	$311.41
Estimated Monthly Fixed Cost	$95,792

BREAK-EVEN ANALYSIS

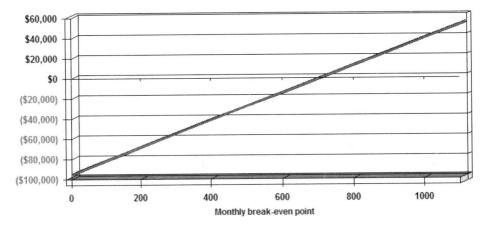

Monthly break-even point

7.4 Projected Profit and Loss

The most important assumption in the Projected Profit and Loss statement is the gross margin, which is supposed to increase. This is up from barely 21% in the last year. The increase in gross margin is based on changing our sales mix, and it is critical.

Month-by-month assumptions for profit and loss are included in the appendices.

Profit and Loss (Income Statement)

	Year 1	Year 2	Year 3
Sales	$6,468,434	$7,478,240	$9,183,384
Direct Cost of Sales	$4,708,513	$5,315,054	$6,221,700
Production payroll	$139,000	$202,500	$261,500
Other	$6,000	$6,600	$7,260
Total Cost of Sales	$4,853,513	$5,524,154	$6,490,460
Gross Margin	$1,614,921	$1,954,086	$2,692,924
Gross Margin %	24.97%	26.13%	29.32%
Operating expenses:			
Sales and Marketing Expenses			
Sales and Marketing Payroll	$344,000	$422,000	$486,000
Ads	$125,000	$140,000	$175,000
Catalog	$25,000	$19,039	$19,991
Mailing	$113,300	$120,000	$150,000
Promo	$16,000	$20,000	$25,000
Shows	$20,200	$25,000	$30,000
Literature	$7,000	$10,000	$12,500
PR	$1,000	$1,250	$1,500
Seminar	$31,000	$45,000	$60,000
Service	$10,250	$12,000	$15,000
Training	$5,400	$7,000	$15,000
Total Sales and Marketing Expenses	$698,150	$821,289	$989,991
Sales and Marketing %	10.79%	10.98%	10.78%
General and Administrative Expenses			
General and Administrative Payroll	$155,000	$179,000	$234,000
Payroll Burden	$107,840	$139,760	$169,360
Depreciation	$12,681	$13,315	$13,981
Leased Equipment	$30,000	$31,500	$33,075
Utilities	$9,000	$9,450	$9,923
Insurance	$6,000	$6,300	$6,615
Rent	$84,000	$88,200	$92,610
Other	$0	$0	$0
Other	$6,331	$6,648	$6,980
Total General and Administrative Expenses	$410,852	$474,173	$566,544
General and Administrative %	6.35%	6.34%	6.17%

Other Expenses			
Other Payroll	$36,000	$70,000	$77,000
Contract/Consultants	$1,500	$5,000	$30,000
Other			
Total Other Expenses	$37,500	$75,000	$107,000
Other %	0.58%	1.00%	1.17%
Total Operating Expenses	$1,149,502	$1,370,462	$1,663,535
Profit Before Interest and Taxes	$465,419	$583,624	$1,029,389
Interest Expense Short-term	$7,867	$8,000	$8,000
Interest Expense Long-term	$29,628	$26,833	$21,162
Taxes Incurred	$85,585	$109,758	$200,045
Net Profit	$342,339	$439,033	$800,182
Net Profit/Sales	5.29%	5.87%	8.71%

7.5 Projected Cash Flow

The cash flow depends on assumptions for inventory turnover, payment days, and accounts receivable management. Our projected 45-day collection days is critical, and it is also reasonable. We need $300,000 in new financing in March to get through a cash flow dip as we build up for midyear sales.

Pro-Forma Cash Flow

	Year 1	Year 2	Year 3
Net Profit	$342,339	$439,033	$800,182
Plus:			
Depreciation	$12,681	$13,315	$13,981
Change in Accounts Payable	$537,079	$96,220	$152,274
Current Borrowing (repayment)	$10,000	$0	$0
Increase (decrease) Other Liabilities	$0	$0	$0
Long-term Borrowing (repayment)	$63,292	($64,953)	($68,484)
Capital Input	$325,000	$0	$0
Subtotal	$1,290,391	$483,615	$897,953
Less:	Year 1	Year 2	Year 3
Change in Accounts Receivable	$449,771	$131,896	$222,718
Change in Inventory	$746,874	$137,884	$198,673
Change in Other ST Assets	$0	$0	$0
Capital Expenditure	$90,000	$200,000	$400,000
Dividends	$0	$0	$0
Subtotal	$1,286,645	$469,780	$821,391
Net Cash Flow	$3,746	$13,835	$76,562
Cash Balance	$59,178	$73,013	$149,575

CASH ANALYSIS

7.6 Projected Balance Sheet

The Projected Balance Sheet is quite solid. We do not project any real trouble meeting our debt obligations—as long as we can achieve our specific objectives.

Pro forma Balance Sheet
Assets

	Starting Balances	Year 1	Year 2	Year 3
Short-term Assets				
Cash	$55,432	$59,178	$73,013	$149,575
Accounts Receivable	$395,107	$844,878	$976,775	$1,199 ,493
Inventory	$251,012	$997,886	$1,135,770	$1,334,443
Other Short-term Assets	$25,000	$25,000	$25,000	$25,000
Total Short-term Assets	$726,551	$1,926,942	$2,210,558	$2,708,511
Long-term Assets				
Capital Assets	$350,000	$440,000	$640,000	$1,040,000
Accumulated Depreciation	$50,000	$62,681	$75,996	$89,977
Total Long-term Assets	$300,000	$377,319	$564,004	$950,023
Total Assets	$1,026,551	$2,304,261	$2,774,562	$3,658,534

Liabilities and Capital

		Year 1	Year 2	Year 3
Accounts Payable	$223,897	$760,976	$857,196	$1,009,471
Short-term Notes	$90,000	$100,000	$100,000	$100,000
Other Short-term Liabilities	$15,000	$15,000	$15,000	$15,000
Subtotal Short-term Liabilities	$328,897	$875,976	$972,196	$1,124,471
Long-term Liabilities	$284,862	$348,154	$283,201	$214,717
Total Liabilities	$613,759	$1,224,130	$1,255,397	$1,339,188
Paid in Capital	$500,000	$825,000	$825,000	$825,000
Retained Earnings	($161,860)	($87,208)	$255,131	$694,165
Earnings	$74,652	$342,339	$439,033	$800,182
Total Capital	$412,792	$1,080,131	$1,519,165	$2,319,347
Total Liabilities and Capital	$1,026,551	$2,304,261	$2,774,562	$3,658,534
Net Worth	$412,792	$1,080,131	$1,519,165	$2,319,347

7.7 Business Ratios

The table follows with our main business ratios. We do intend to improve gross margin, collection days, and inventory turnover.

Ratio Analysis

Profitability Ratios:	Year 1	Year 2	Year 3
Gross Margin	24.97%	26.13%	29.32%
Net Profit Margin	5.29%	5.84%	8.68%
Return on Assets	14.86%	15.74%	21.83%
Return on Equity	31.69%	28.78%	34.46%

Activity Ratios	Year 1	Year 2	Year 3
AR Turnover	5.36	5.36	5.36
Collection Days	50	64	62
Inventory Turnover	7.77	5.18	5.25
Accts Payable Turnover	5.90	5.90	5.90
Total Asset Turnover	2.81	2.70	2.51

Debt Ratios	Year 1	Year 2	Year 3
Debt to Net Worth	1.13	0.83	0.58
Short-term Liab. to Liab.	0.72	0.77	0.84

Liquidity Ratios	Year 1	Year 2	Year 3
Current Ratio	2.20	2.27	2.40
Quick Ratio	1.06	1.10	1.22
Net Working Capital	$1,050,966	$1,235,842	$1,578,874
Interest Coverage	12.41	16.66	35.19

Additional Ratios	Year 1	Year 2	Year 3
Assets to Sales	0.36	0.37	0.40
Debt/Assets	53%	45%	37%
Current Debt/Total Assets	38%	35%	31%
Acid Test	0.10	0.10	0.15
Asset Turnover	2.81	2.70	2.51
Sales/Net Worth	5.99	4.93	3.97

AMT, INC. — APPENDIX TABLES

Pro Forma Balance Sheet

Assets

	Starting Balances	Jan	Feb	Mar	Apr	May	Jun	Jul	Aug	Sep	Oct	Nov	Dec
Short-term Assets													
Cash	$55,432	$108,508	$141,078	$153,148	$5,027	$32,208	$73,174	$58,626	$23,036	$11,478	$21,518	$7,873	$59,178
Accounts Receivable	$395,107	$277,923	$354,332	$430,575	$636,674	$696,256	$565,392	$423,890	$341,268	$466,541	$707,840	$918,115	$844,878
Inventory	$251,012	$333,445	$444,104	$544,477	$699,578	$879,836	$648,051	$459,866	$401,460	$666,411	$994,975	$1,250,220	$997,886
Other ST Assets	$25,000	$25,000	$25,000	$25,000	$25,000	$175,000	$175,000	$475,000	$475,000	$325,000	$25,000	$25,000	$25,000
Total ST Assets	$726,551	$744,876	$964,514	$1,153,200	$1,366,278	$1,783,300	$1,461,618	$1,417,381	$1,240,763	$1,469,430	$1,749,332	$2,201,208	$1,926,942
Long-term Assets													
Capital Assets	$350,000	$375,000	$375,000	$390,000	$390,000	$440,000	$440,000	$440,000	$440,000	$440,000	$440,000	$440,000	$440,000
Accum. Depreciation	$50,000	$51,000	$52,010	$53,030	$54,060	$55,100	$56,150	$57,211	$58,283	$59,366	$60,460	$61,565	$62,681
Total LT Assets	$300,000	$324,000	$322,990	$336,970	$335,940	$384,900	$383,850	$382,789	$381,717	$380,634	$379,540	$378,435	$377,319
Total Assets	$1,026,551	$1,068,876	$1,287,504	$1,490,170	$1,702,218	$2,168,200	$1,845,468	$1,800,170	$1,622,480	$1,850,064	$2,128,872	$2,579,643	$2,304,261

Liabilities and Capital

	Starting Balances	Jan	Feb	Mar	Apr	May	Jun	Jul	Aug	Sep	Oct	Nov	Dec
Accounts Payable	$223,897	$268,569	$369,549	$428,414	$560,724	$702,163	$514,886	$378,036	$324,275	$555,293	$795,989	$984,178	$760,976
Short-term Notes	$90,000	$90,000	$190,000	$220,000	$140,000	$140,000	$0	$100,000	$0	$0	$0	$200,000	$100,000
Other ST Liabilities	$15,000	$15,000	$15,000	$15,000	$15,000	$15,000	$15,000	$15,000	$15,000	$15,000	$15,000	$15,000	$15,000
Subtotal ST Liabilities	$328,897	$373,569	$574,549	$663,414	$715,724	$857,163	$529,886	$493,036	$339,275	$570,293	$810,989	$1,199,178	$875,976
Long-term Liabilities	$284,862	$281,920	$278,958	$375,974	$372,970	$369,944	$366,897	$363,828	$360,737	$357,624	$354,490	$351,333	$348,154
Total Liabilities	$613,759	$655,489	$853,506	$1,039,388	$1,088,694	$1,227,107	$896,783	$856,863	$700,012	$927,917	$1,165,479	$1,550,511	$1,224,130
Paid in Capital	$500,000	$500,000	$525,000	$525,000	$525,000	$825,000	$825,000	$825,000	$825,000	$825,000	$825,000	$825,000	$825,000
Retained Earnings	($161,860)	($87,208)	($87,208)	($87,208)	($87,208)	($87,208)	($87,208)	($87,208)	($87,208)	($87,208)	($87,208)	($87,208)	($87,208)
Earnings	$74,652	$595	($3,795)	$12,990	$175,732	$203,300	$210,893	$205,515	$184,355	$184,676	$225,601	$291,340	$342,339
Total Capital	$412,792	$413,387	$433,997	$450,782	$613,524	$941,092	$948,685	$943,307	$922,468	$922,147	$963,393	$1,029,132	$1,080,131
Total Liab. & Capital	$1,026,551	$1,068,876	$1,287,504	$1,490,170	$1,702,218	$2,168,200	$1,845,468	$1,800,170	$1,622,480	$1,850,064	$2,128,872	$2,579,643	$2,304,261
Net Worth	$412,792	$413,387	$433,997	$450,782	$613,524	$941,092	$948,685	$943,307	$922,468	$922,147	$963,393	$1,029,132	$1,080,131

Pro Forma Cash Flow

	Jan	Feb	Mar	Apr	May	Jun	Jul	Aug	Sep	Oct	Nov	Dec
Net Profit	$595	($4,390)	$16,784	$162,743	$27,568	$7,593	($5,378)	($20,839)	($321)	$41,246	$65,739	$50,999
Plus:												
Depreciation	$1,000	$1,010	$1,020	$1,030	$1,040	$1,050	$1,061	$1,072	$1,083	$1,094	$1,105	$1,116
Change in Accounts Payable	$44,672	$100,980	$58,866	$132,310	$141,439	($187,277)	($136,850)	($53,761)	$231,018	$240,697	$188,189	($223,202)
Current Borrowing (repayment)	$0	$100,000	$30,000	($80,000)	$0	($140,000)	$100,000	($100,000)	$0	$0	$200,000	($100,000)
Increase (decrease) Other Liabilities	$0	$0	$0	$0	$0	$0	$0	$0	$0	$0	$0	$0
Long-term Borrowing (repayment)	($2,942)	($2,962)	$97,017	($3,005)	($3,026)	($3,047)	($3,069)	($3,091)	($3,113)	($3,135)	($3,157)	($3,179)
Capital Input	$0	$25,000	$0	$0	$300,000	$0	$0	$0	$0	$0	$0	$0
Subtotal	$43,325	$219,638	$203,686	$213,078	$467,021	($321,682)	($44,236)	($176,618)	$228,667	$279,902	$451,876	($274,266)
Less:												
Change in Accounts Receivable	($117,184)	$76,409	$76,243	$206,099	$59,582	($130,864)	($141,502)	($82,622)	$125,273	$241,299	$210,276	($73,237)
Change in Inventory	$82,433	$110,659	$100,373	$155,101	$180,258	($231,784)	($188,186)	($58,406)	$264,951	$328,563	$255,245	($252,334)
Change in Other ST Assets	$0	$0	$0	$0	$150,000	$0	$300,000	$0	($150,000)	($300,000)	$0	$0
Capital Expenditure	$25,000	$0	$15,000	$0	$50,000	$0	$0	$0	$0	$0	$0	$0
Dividends	$0	$0	$0	$0	$0	$0	$0	$0	$0	$0	$0	$0
Subtotal	($9,751)	$187,068	$191,616	$361,200	$439,840	($362,648)	($29,688)	($141,028)	$240,224	$269,862	$465,521	($325,571)
Net Cash Flow	$53,076	$32,570	$12,071	($148,122)	$27,181	$40,967	($14,549)	($35,590)	($11,557)	$10,040	($13,645)	$51,305
Cash Balance	$108,508	$141,078	$153,148	$5,027	$32,208	$73,174	$58,626	$23,036	$11,478	$21,518	$7,873	$59,178

General Assumptions

	Jan	Feb	Mar	Apr	May	Jun	Jul	Aug	Sep	Oct	Nov	Dec
Short-term Interest Rate %	8.00%	8.00%	8.00%	8.00%	8.00%	8.00%	8.00%	8.00%	8.00%	8.00%	8.00%	8.00%
Long-term Interest Rate %	8.50%	8.50%	8.50%	8.50%	8.50%	8.50%	8.50%	8.50%	8.50%	8.50%	8.50%	8.50%
Payment Days Estimator	45	45	45	45	45	45	45	45	45	45	45	45
Collection Days Estimator	45	45	45	45	45	45	45	45	45	45	45	45
Inventory Turnover Estimator	7.00	7.00	7.00	7.00	7.00	7.00	7.00	7.00	7.00	7.00	7.00	7.00
Tax Rate %	20.00%	20.00%	20.00%	20.00%	20.00%	20.00%	20.00%	20.00%	20.00%	20.00%	20.00%	20.00%
Expenses in Cash %	14.00%	14.00%	14.00%	14.00%	14.00%	14.00%	14.00%	14.00%	14.00%	14.00%	14.00%	14.00%
Sales on Credit %	70.00%	70.00%	70.00%	70.00%	70.00%	70.00%	70.00%	70.00%	70.00%	70.00%	70.00%	70.00%
Personnel Burden %	16.00%	16.00%	16.00%	16.00%	16.00%	16.00%	16.00%	16.00%	16.00%	16.00%	16.00%	16.00%

Personnel Plan

	Jan	Feb	Mar	Apr	May	Jun	Jul	Aug	Sep	Oct	Nov	Dec
Production												
Manager	$1,000	$1,000	$1,000	$1,000	$1,000	$1,000	$1,000	$1,000	$1,000	$1,000	$1,000	$1,000
Assistant	$3,000	$3,000	$3,000	$3,000	$3,000	$3,000	$3,000	$3,000	$3,000	$3,000	$3,000	$3,000
Technical								$2,500	$2,500	$2,500	$2,500	$2,500
Technical								$2,500	$2,500	$2,500	$2,500	$2,500
Technical	$2,000	$2,000	$2,000	$2,000	$2,000	$2,000	$2,000	$2,000	$2,000	$2,000	$2,000	$2,000
Fulfillment	$2,000	$2,000	$2,000	$2,000	$2,000	$2,000	$2,000	$2,000	$2,000	$2,000	$2,000	$2,000
Fulfillment	$1,500	$1,500	$1,500	$1,500	$1,500	$1,500	$1,500	$1,500	$1,500	$1,500	$1,500	$1,500
Other	$0	$0	$0	$0	$0	$0	$0	$0	$0	$0	$0	$0
Subtotal	$9,500	$9,500	$9,500	$9,500	$9,500	$9,500	$9,500	$14,500	$14,500	$14,500	$14,500	$14,500
Sales and Marketing												
Manager	$6,000	$6,000	$6,000	$6,000	$6,000	$6,000	$6,000	$6,000	$6,000	$6,000	$6,000	$6,000
Technical sales	$5,000	$5,000	$5,000	$5,000	$5,000	$5,000	$5,000	$5,000	$5,000	$5,000	$5,000	$5,000
Technical sales	$3,500	$3,500	$3,500	$3,500	$3,500	$4,000	$4,000	$4,000	$4,000	$4,000	$4,000	$4,000
Salesperson	$2,500	$2,500	$2,500	$2,500	$2,500	$4,000	$4,000	$4,000	$4,000	$4,000	$4,000	$4,000
Salesperson	$2,500	$2,500	$2,500	$2,500	$2,500	$4,000	$4,000	$4,000	$4,000	$4,000	$4,000	$4,000
Salesperson	$2,500	$2,500	$2,500	$2,500	$2,500	$3,000	$3,000	$3,000	$3,000	$3,000	$3,000	$3,000
Salesperson	$2,000	$2,000	$2,000	$2,000	$2,000	$3,000	$3,000	$3,000	$3,000	$3,000	$3,000	$3,000
Salesperson						$3,000	$3,000	$3,000	$3,000	$3,000	$3,000	$3,000
Salesperson												
Other	$0	$0	$0	$0	$0	$0	$0	$0	$0	$0	$0	$0
Subtotal	$24,000	$24,000	$24,000	$24,000	$24,000	$32,000	$32,000	$32,000	$32,000	$32,000	$32,000	$32,000
General and Administrative												
President	$5,500	$5,500	$5,500	$5,500	$5,500	$5,500	$5,500	$5,500	$5,500	$5,500	$5,500	$5,500
Finance						$4,000	$4,000	$4,000	$4,000	$4,000	$4,000	$4,000
Admin Assistant	$2,000	$2,000	$2,000	$2,000	$2,000	$2,000	$2,000	$2,000	$2,000	$2,000	$2,000	$2,000
Bookkeeping	$1,500	$1,500	$1,500	$1,500	$1,500	$1,500	$1,500	$1,500	$1,500	$1,500	$1,500	$1,500
Clerical	$1,000	$1,000	$1,000	$1,000	$1,000	$1,000	$1,000	$1,000	$1,000	$1,000	$1,000	$1,000
Clerical						$1,000	$1,000	$1,000	$1,000	$1,000	$1,000	$1,000
Clerical												
Other												
Subtotal	$10,000	$10,000	$10,000	$10,000	$10,000	$15,000	$15,000	$15,000	$15,000	$15,000	$15,000	$15,000
Other Personnel												
Programming	$3,000	$3,000	$3,000	$3,000	$3,000	$3,000	$3,000	$3,000	$3,000	$3,000	$3,000	$3,000
Other technical	$0	$0	$0	$0	$0	$0	$0	$0	$0	$0	$0	$0
Other	$0	$0	$0	$0	$0	$0	$0	$0	$0	$0	$0	$0
Subtotal	$3,000	$3,000	$3,000	$3,000	$3,000	$3,000	$3,000	$3,000	$3,000	$3,000	$3,000	$3,000
Total Headcount	0	0	0	0	0	0	0	0	0	0	0	0
Total Payroll	$46,500	$46,500	$46,500	$46,500	$46,500	$59,500	$59,500	$64,500	$64,500	$64,500	$64,500	$64,500
Payroll Burden	$7,440	$7,440	$7,440	$7,440	$7,440	$9,520	$9,520	$10,320	$10,320	$10,320	$10,320	$10,320
Total Payroll Expenditures	$53,940	$53,940	$53,940	$53,940	$53,940	$69,020	$69,020	$74,820	$74,820	$74,820	$74,820	$74,820

Profit and Loss (Income Statement)

	Jan	Feb	Mar	Apr	May	Jun	Jul	Aug	Sep	Oct	Nov	Dec
Sales	$268,365	$342,146	$415,767	$701,651	$643,826	$485,790	$362,662	$306,194	$513,389	$754,505	$934,341	$739,799
Direct Cost of Sales	$184,510	$249,061	$307,612	$398,087	$503,238	$368,030	$258,255	$219,185	$373,740	$565,402	$714,295	$567,100
Production payroll	$9,500	$9,500	$9,500	$9,500	$9,500	$9,500	$9,500	$14,500	$14,500	$14,500	$14,500	$14,500
Other	$500	$500	$500	$500	$500	$500	$500	$500	$500	$500	$500	$500
Total Cost of Sales	$194,510	$259,061	$317,612	$408,087	$513,238	$378,030	$268,255	$234,185	$388,740	$580,402	$729,295	$582,100
Gross Margin	$73,856	$83,086	$98,155	$293,564	$130,589	$107,760	$94,407	$72,009	$124,649	$174,103	$205,046	$157,699
Gross Margin %	27.52%	24.28%	23.61%	41.84%	20.28%	22.18%	26.03%	23.52%	24.28%	23.08%	21.95%	21.32%

Operating expenses:

Sales & Marketing Expenses

	Jan	Feb	Mar	Apr	May	Jun	Jul	Aug	Sep	Oct	Nov	Dec
Sales & Marketing Payroll	$24,000	$24,000	$24,000	$24,000	$24,000	$32,000	$32,000	$32,000	$32,000	$32,000	$32,000	$32,000
Ads	$5,000	$5,000	$7,000	$10,000	$15,000	$10,000	$4,000	$4,000	$20,000	$15,000	$20,000	$10,000
Catalog	$2,000	$3,000	$2,000	$2,000	$2,000	$2,000	$2,000	$2,000	$2,000	$2,000	$2,000	$2,000
Mailing	$3,000	$11,800	$5,500	$10,500	$10,500	$5,500	$10,500	$10,500	$10,500	$22,000	$8,000	$5,000
Promo	$0	$0	$0	$0	$0	$0	$0	$0	$1,000	$0	$15,000	$0
Shows	$0	$7,000	$0	$0	$0	$0	$3,200	$0	$10,000	$7,000	$0	$0
Literature	$0	$0	$0	$0	$0	$0	$0	$0	$0	$0	$0	$0
PR	$0	$0	$0	$1,000	$0	$0	$0	$0	$0	$0	$0	$0
Seminar	$1,000	$0	$0	$5,000	$5,000	$5,000	$5,000	$5,000	$5,000	$0	$0	$0
Service	$2,000	$1,000	$1,000	$500	$2,500	$500	$500	$500	$500	$500	$500	$250
Training	$450	$450	$450	$450	$450	$450	$450	$450	$450	$450	$450	$450
Total Sales & Mktg. Exp.	$37,450	$52,250	$39,950	$53,450	$59,450	$55,450	$57,650	$54,450	$81,450	$78,950	$77,950	$49,700
Sales and Marketing %	13.95%	15.27%	9.61%	7.62%	9.23%	11.41%	15.90%	17.78%	15.87%	10.46%	8.34%	6.72%

General & Administrative Expenses

	Jan	Feb	Mar	Apr	May	Jun	Jul	Aug	Sep	Oct	Nov	Dec
General & Admin. Payroll	$10,000	$10,000	$10,000	$10,000	$10,000	$15,000	$15,000	$15,000	$15,000	$15,000	$15,000	$15,000
Payroll Burden	$7,440	$7,440	$7,440	$7,440	$7,440	$9,520	$9,520	$10,320	$10,320	$10,320	$10,320	$10,320
Depreciation	$1,000	$1,010	$1,020	$1,030	$1,040	$1,050	$1,061	$1,072	$1,083	$1,094	$1,105	$1,116
Leased Equipment	$2,500	$2,500	$2,500	$2,500	$2,500	$2,500	$2,500	$2,500	$2,500	$2,500	$2,500	$2,500

Profit & Loss (cont'd.)

	Jan	Feb	Mar	Apr	May	Jun	Jul	Aug	Sep	Oct	Nov	Dec
Utilities	$750	$750	$750	$750	$750	$750	$750	$750	$750	$750	$750	$750
Insurance	$500	$500	$500	$500	$500	$500	$500	$500	$500	$500	$500	$500
Rent	$7,000	$7,000	$7,000	$7,000	$7,000	$7,000	$7,000	$7,000	$7,000	$7,000	$7,000	$7,000
Other	$0	$0	$0	$0	$0	$0	$0	$0	$0	$0	$0	$0
Other	$500	$505	$510	$515	$520	$525	$530	$535	$540	$545	$550	$556
Total Gen. & Admin. Exp.	$29,690	$29,705	$29,720	$29,735	$29,750	$36,845	$36,861	$37,677	$37,693	$37,709	$37,725	$37,742
General & Admin. %	11.06%	8.68%	7.15%	4.24%	4.62%	7.58%	10.16%	12.30%	7.34%	5.00%	4.04%	5.10%
Other Expenses												
Other Payroll	$3,000	$3,000	$3,000	$3,000	$3,000	$3,000	$3,000	$3,000	$3,000	$3,000	$3,000	$3,000
Contract/Consultants	$125	$125	$125	$125	$125	$125	$125	$125	$125	$125	$125	$125
Other	9/6/00	9/6/00	9/6/00	9/6/00	9/6/00	9/6/00	9/6/00	9/6/00	9/6/00	9/6/00	9/6/00	9/6/00
Total Other Expenses	$3,375	$3,375	$3,375	$3,375	$3,375	$3,375	$3,375	$3,375	$3,375	$3,375	$3,375	$3,375
Other %	1.26%	0.99%	0.81%	0.48%	0.52%	0.69%	0.93%	1.10%	0.66%	0.45%	0.36%	0.46%
Total Operating Exp.	$70,515	$85,330	$73,045	$86,560	$92,575	$95,670	$97,886	$95,502	$122,518	$120,034	$119,050	$90,817
Profit Before Int. & Taxes	$3,341	($2,244)	$25,110	$207,004	$38,014	$12,090	($3,479)	($23,493)	$2,131	$54,069	$85,996	$66,882
Interest Expense ST	$600	$1,267	$1,467	$933	$933	$0	$667	$0	$0	$0	$1,333	$667
Interest Expense LT	$1,997	$1,976	$2,663	$2,642	$2,620	$2,599	$2,577	$2,555	$2,533	$2,511	$2,489	$2,466
Taxes Incurred	$149	($1,097)	$4,196	$40,686	$6,892	$1,898	($1,345)	($5,210)	($80)	$10,312	$16,435	$12,750
Net Profit	$595	($4,390)	$16,784	$162,743	$27,568	$7,593	($5,378)	($20,839)	($321)	$41,246	$65,739	$50,999
Net Profit/Sales	0.22%	-1.28%	4.04%	23.19%	4.28%	1.56%	-1.48%	-6.81%	-0.06%	5.47%	7.04%	6.89%

Sales Forecast

Unit Sales

	Jan	Feb	Mar	Apr	May	Jun	Jul	Aug	Sep	Oct	Nov	Dec
Systems	85	115	145	190	245	175	120	100	180	275	350	275
Service	200	200	200	200	244	256	269	282	296	311	327	343
Software	150	200	250	330	430	310	210	180	320	490	620	490
Training	145	155	165	170	225	200	150	150	200	220	250	200
Other	160	176	192	240	200	175	125	100	104	200	250	200
Total Unit Sales	740	846	952	1,130	1,344	1,116	874	812	1,100	1,496	1,797	1,508

Unit Prices

	Jan	Feb	Mar	Apr	May	Jun	Jul	Aug	Sep	Oct	Nov	Dec
Systems	$2,000.00	$2,000.00	$2,000.00	$1,828.95	$1,890.63	$1,966.17	$2,131.58	$2,115.38	$2,083.33	$1,966.40	$1,980.29	$1,984.50
Service	$75	$69	$58	$46	$50	$47	$50	$50	$91	$124	$75	$67
Software	$200	$200	$200	$200	$223	$217	$242	$253	$220	$211	$204	$207
Training	$37	$35	$39	$41	$56	$50	$33	$33	$50	$55	$60	$50
Other	$300	$300	$300	$300	$300	$300	$300	$300	$300	$300	$300	$300

Sales

	Jan	Feb	Mar	Apr	May	Jun	Jul	Aug	Sep	Oct	Nov	Dec
Systems	$170,000	$230,000	$290,000	$347,500	$463,203	$344,079	$255,789	$211,538	$375,000	$540,761	$693,100	$545,736
Service	$15,000	$13,846	$11,667	$9,231	$12,200	$11,947	$13,450	$14,100	$26,909	$38,418	$24,525	$22,867
Software	$30,000	$40,000	$50,000	$66,000	$95,923	$67,264	$50,923	$45,556	$70,280	$103,326	$126,715	$101,196
Training	$5,365	$5,500	$6,500	$7,000	$12,500	$10,000	$5,000	$5,000	$10,000	$12,000	$15,000	$10,000
Other	$48,000	$52,800	$57,600	$271,920	$60,000	$52,500	$37,500	$30,000	$31,200	$60,000	$75,000	$60,000
Total Sales	$268,365	$342,146	$415,767	$701,651	$643,826	$485,790	$362,662	$306,194	$513,389	$754,505	$934,341	$739,799

Direct Unit Costs

		Jan	Feb	Mar	Apr	May	Jun	Jul	Aug	Sep	Oct	Nov	Dec
Systems	85.00%	$1,700.00	$1,700.00	$1,700.00	$1,700.00	$1,700.00	$1,700.00	$1,700.00	$1,700.00	$1,700.00	$1,700.00	$1,700.00	$1,700.00
Service	40.00%	$30.00	$60.00	$60.00	$60.00	$60.00	$60.00	$60.00	$60.00	$60.00	$60.00	$60.00	$60.00
Software	60.00%	$120.00	$120.00	$120.00	$120.00	$120.00	$120.00	$120.00	$120.00	$120.00	$120.00	$120.00	$120.00
Training	30.00%	$11.10	$11.10	$11.10	$11.10	$11.10	$11.10	$11.10	$11.10	$11.10	$11.10	$11.10	$11.10
Other	30.00%	$90.00	$90.00	$90.00	$90.00	$90.00	$90.00	$90.00	$90.00	$90.00	$90.00	$90.00	$90.00

Direct Cost of Sales

	Jan	Feb	Mar	Apr	May	Jun	Jul	Aug	Sep	Oct	Nov	Dec
Systems	$144,500	$195,500	$246,500	$323,000	$416,500	$297,500	$204,000	$170,000	$306,000	$467,500	$595,000	$467,500
Service	$6,000	$12,000	$12,000	$12,000	$14,640	$15,360	$16,140	$16,920	$17,760	$18,660	$19,620	$20,580
Software	$18,000	$24,000	$30,000	$39,600	$51,600	$37,200	$25,200	$21,600	$38,400	$58,800	$74,400	$58,800
Training	$1,610	$1,721	$1,832	$1,887	$2,498	$2,220	$1,665	$1,665	$2,220	$2,442	$2,775	$2,220
Other	$14,400	$15,840	$17,280	$21,600	$18,000	$15,750	$11,250	$9,000	$9,360	$18,000	$22,500	$18,000
Subtotal Direct Cost of Sales	$184,510	$249,061	$307,612	$398,087	$503,238	$368,030	$258,255	$219,185	$373,740	$565,402	$714,295	$567,100

GLOSSARY

A

Accounts payable | Bills to be paid as part of the normal course of business.

Accounts receivable | Debts owed to your company, usually from sales on credit.

Accumulated depreciation | Total accumulated depreciation reduces the formal accounting value (called book value) of assets. Each month's accumulated balance is the same as last month's balance plus this month's depreciation.

Acid test | Short-term assets minus accounts receivable and inventory, divided by short-term liabilities. This is a test of a company's ability to meet its immediate cash requirements.

Assets | Property that a business owns, including cash and receivables, inventory, etc. Assets are any possessions that have value in an exchange. The more formal definition is the entire property of a person, association, corporation, or estate applicable or subject to the payment of debts. What most people understand as business assets are cash and investments, accounts receivable, inventory, office equipment, plant and equipment, etc. Assets can be long-term or short-term, and the distinction between these two categories might be whether they last three years, five years, 10 years, or whatever; normally the accountants decide for each company and what's important is consistency. The government also has a say in defining assets, because it has to do with tax treatment; when you buy a piece of equipment, if you call that purchase an expense then you can deduct it from taxable income. If you call it an asset you can't deduct it, but you can list it on your financial statement among the assets. The tax code controls how businesses decide to categorize spending into assets or expenses.

Asset turnover | Sales divided by total assets. Important for comparison over time and to other companies of the same industry.

B

Break-even point | The unit sales volumes or actual sales amounts that a company needs to equal its running expense rate and not lose or make money in a given month. The formula for break-even point in units is:

=Regular running costs/(Unit Price-Unit Variable Cost)

The formula for break-even point in sales amount is:

=Regular running costs/(1-(Unit Variable Cost/Unit Price))

Burden rate | Refers to personnel burden, the sum of employer costs over and above salaries (including employer taxes, benefits, etc.).

C

Capital assets	Long-term assets, also known as Plant and Equipment.
Capital expenditure	Spending on capital assets (also called plant and equipment, or fixed assets).
Capital input	New money being invested in the business. New capital will increase your cash, and will also increase the total amount of paid-in capital.
Cash	The bank balance, or checking account balance, or real cash in bills and coins.
Collection days	See Collection period, below.
Collection period (days)	The average number of days that pass between delivering an invoice and receiving the money. The formula is:
	=(Accounts_receivable_balance*360)/(Sales_on_credit*12)
Commissions	Gross margin multiplied by the commissions percentage.
Commissions percent	An assumed percentage used to calculate commissions expense as the product of this percentage multiplied by gross margin.
Cost of sales	The costs associated with producing the sales. In a standard manufacturing or distribution company, this is about the same as the cost of the goods sold. In a services company, this is more likely to be personnel costs for people delivering the service, or subcontracting costs.
Current assets	The same as short-term assets.
Current debt	Short-term debt, on terms of less than five years, e.g. credit cards.
Current liabilities	Debts; money that must be paid. Usually debt on terms of less than five years.

D

Debt and equity	The sum of liabilities and capital. This should always be equal to total assets.
Depreciation	An accounting and tax concept used to estimate the loss of value of assets over time. For example, cars depreciate with use.
Directory	A computer term related to the operating system on IBM and compatible computers. Disk storage space is divided into directories.
Dividends	Money distributed to the owners of a business as profits.

E

Earnings	Also called income or profits, earnings are the famous "bottom line": sales less costs of sales and expenses.
EBIT	Earnings before interest and taxes.
Equity	Business ownership; capital. Equity can be calculated as the difference between assets and liabilities.
Expense	Webster's calls it "a spending or consuming; disbursement, expenditure." What's important about expenses for the purpose of business accounting is that expenses are deductible against taxable income. Common expenses are rent, salaries, advertising, travel, etc. Questions arise because some businesses have trouble distinguishing between expenses and purchase of assets, especially with development expenses. When your business purchases office equipment, if you call that an expense then you can deduct that amount from taxable income, so it reduces taxes.

F

Fiscal year	Standard accounting practice allows the accounting year to begin in any month. Fiscal years are numbered according to the year in which they end. For example, a fiscal year ending in February of 2007 is Fiscal 2007, even though most of the year takes place in 2006.
Fixed costs	Running costs that take time to wind down: usually rent, overhead, some salaries. Technically, fixed costs are those that the business would continue to pay even if it went bankrupt. In practice, fixed costs are usually considered the running costs.

G

Gross margin	Sales minus cost of sales.
Gross margin percent	Gross margin divided by sales, displayed as a percentage. Acceptable levels depend on the nature of the business.

I

Interest expense	Interest is paid on debts, and interest expense is deducted from profits as expenses. Interest expense is either long-term or short-term interest.
Inventory	Goods in stock, either finished goods or materials to be used to manufacture goods.

Inventory turnover	Total cost of sales divided by inventory. Usually calculated using the average inventory over an accounting period, not an ending-inventory value.
Inventory turns	Inventory turnover (above).

L

Labor	The labor costs associated with making goods to be sold. This labor is part of the cost of sales, part of the manufacturing and assembly. The row heading refers to fulfillment costs as well, for service companies.
Liabilities	Debts; money that must be paid. Usually debt on terms of less than five years is called short-term liabilities, and debt for longer than five years in long-term liabilities.
Long-term assets	Assets like plant and equipment that are depreciated over terms of more than five years, and are likely to last that long, too.
Long-term interest rate	The interest rate charged on long-term debt.
Long-term liabilities	This is the same as long-term loans. Most companies call a debt long-term when it is on terms of five years or more.

M

Materials	Included in the cost of sales. These are materials involved in the assembly or manufacture of goods for sale.

N

Net cash flow	This is the projected change in cash position, an increase or decrease in cash balance.
Net profit	The operating income less taxes and interest. The same as earnings, or net income.
Net worth	This is the same as assets minus liabilities, and the same as total equity.

O

Other short-term assets	These might be securities, business equipment, etc.
Other short-term liabilities	These are short-term debts that don't cause interest expenses. For example, they might be loans from founders or accrued taxes (taxes owed, already incurred, but not yet paid).

P

Paid-in capital

Real money paid into the company as investments. This is not to be confused with par value of stock, or market value of stock. This is actual money paid into the company as equity investments by owners.

Payment days

The average number of days that pass between receiving an invoice and paying it. It is not a simple estimate; it is calculated with a financial formula: =(Accounts_payable_balance*360)/(Total entries to accounts payable*12)

Payroll burden

Payroll burden includes payroll taxes and benefits. It is calculated using a percentage assumption that is applied to payroll. For example, if payroll is $1,000 and the burden rate is 10 percent, the burden is an extra $100. Acceptable payroll burden rates vary by market, by industry, and by company.

Personnel burden

Payroll burden. See above description.

Plant and equipment

This is the same as long-term, fixed, or capital assets.

Product development

Expenses incurred in development of new products (salaries, laboratory equipment, test equipment, prototypes, research and development, etc.).

Profit before interest / taxes

This is also called EBIT, for Earnings Before Interest and Taxes. It is gross margin minus operating expenses.

R

Receivables turnover

Sales on credit for an accounting period divided by the average accounts receivables balance.

Retained earnings

Earnings (or losses) that have been reinvested into the company, not paid out as dividends to the owners. When retained earnings are negative, the company has accumulated losses.

Return on assets

Net profits divided by total assets. A measure of profitability.

Return on investment

Net profits divided by net worth or total equity; yet another measure of profitability. Also called ROI.

Return on sales

Net profits divided by sales; another measure of profitability.

ROI

Return on investment; net profits divided by net worth or total equity, another measure of profitability.

S

Sales break-even

The sales volume at which costs are exactly equal to sales. The exact formula is:

=Fixed_costs/(1-(Unit_Variable_Cost/Unit_Price))

Sales on credit

Sales made on account; shipments against invoices to be paid later.

Short term

Normally used to distinguish between short-term and long-term, when referring to assets or liabilities. Definitions vary because different companies and accountants handle this in different ways. Accounts payable is always a short-term liability, and cash, accounts receivable and inventory are always short-term assets. Most companies call any debt of less than five-year terms short-term debt. Assets that depreciate over more than five years (e.g., plant and equipment) are usually long-term assets.

Short-term assets

Cash, securities, bank accounts, accounts receivable, inventory, business equipment, assets that last less than five years or are depreciated over terms of less than five years.

Short-term debt

Debt, on terms of less than five years, e.g. credit cards.

Short-term liabilities

Debts; money that must be paid. Usually debt on terms of less than five years.

Short-term notes

These are the same as short-term loans. These are debts with terms of five years or less.

Starting date

The starting date for the entire business plan.

T

Tax rate percent

An assumed percentage applied against pre-tax income to determine taxes.

Taxes incurred

Taxes owed but not yet paid.

U

Unit variable cost

The specific labor and materials associated with a single unit of goods sold. Does not include general overhead.

Units break-even

The unit sales volume at which the fixed and variable costs are exactly equal to sales. The formula is:

UBE=Fixed_costs/(Unit_Price-Unit_Variable_Cost)

INDEX